BUILDING COMPREHENSION
IN EVERY CLASSROOM

Building Comprehension in Every Classroom

Instruction with Literature, Informational Texts, and Basal Programs

Rachel Brown
Peter Dewitz

Foreword by Nell K. Duke

THE GUILFORD PRESS
New York   London

To the men in my life, Stuart and Evan,
my gratitude forever.
—R. B.

To David, Erica, and Rachel, who help to inspire my work,
and especially to Pam, who supported it.
—P. D.

© 2014 The Guilford Press
A Division of Guilford Publications, Inc.
72 Spring Street, New York, NY 10012
www.guilford.com

Printed in the United States of America

This book is printed on acid-free paper.

Last digit is print number: 9   8   7   6   5   4   3   2   1

Library of Congress Cataloging-in-Publication Data

Brown, Rachel.
   Building comprehension in every classroom : instruction with literature, informational texts, and basal programs / Rachel Brown, Peter Dewitz ; foreword by Nell K. Duke.
      pages cm
   Includes bibliographical references and index.
   ISBN 978-1-4625-1120-4 (pbk.: alk. paper) — ISBN 978-1-4625-1122-8 (hardcover: alk. paper)
   1. Reading comprehension.   2. Basal reading instruction.   I. Title.
   LB1050.45.B76 2014
   372.47—dc23

                                                            2013020951

About the Authors

Rachel Brown, PhD, is Associate Professor in the Reading and Language Arts Center at Syracuse University, where she teaches graduate courses in literacy education and is affiliated with the undergraduate and graduate elementary teacher education programs. Dr. Brown worked as a middle school learning specialist in the American School in London, where her responsibilities included teaching seventh-grade students with learning difficulties, acting as a student advocate, and providing instructional support in reading, learning, and study strategies. Her research focuses on elementary and middle school literacy instruction. Her specific areas of expertise include comprehension strategies instruction, self-regulated learning, teacher professional development, and technology and literacy. Dr. Brown has published articles in research and practitioner journals, including *The Reading Teacher, Reading Research and Instruction,* the *Journal of Educational Psychology,* and *The Elementary School Journal,* and has contributed chapters to edited volumes such as *Best Practices in Adolescent Literacy Instruction, Comprehension Instruction: Research-Based Best Practices,* and *Self-Regulation of Learning and Performance: Issues and Educational Applications.* She is a recipient of a Graduate Teaching Recognition Award from Syracuse University and an Elva Knight Research Grant from the International Reading Association.

Peter Dewitz, PhD, is Professor of Education at Mary Baldwin College. Formerly he taught at California State University, Los Angeles; the University of Toledo; and the University of Virginia. Dr. Dewitz is also a researcher and staff developer who has worked with many public schools to help them improve their reading comprehension instruction. His staff development work spans many states, school districts, and countries. Before becoming a professor, he taught fifth and sixth grade in Los Angeles, California. Dr. Dewitz has published over 40 articles on reading instruction and reading programs and three previous books on reading: *The Essential Guide to Selecting and Using Core Reading Programs* (with Susan B. Leahy, Jennifer Jones, and Pamela Maslin Sullivan), *Teaching Reading in the Twenty-First Century* (with Michael F. Graves, Connie Juel, and Bonnie B. Graves), and *Making the Most of Your Core Reading Program* (with Jonni Wolskee).

Foreword

What Kind of Comprehension Instruction
Will Address the Common Core State Standards?

There is no doubt that the Common Core State Standards (CCSS) demand sophisticated comprehension when they ask 7- and 8-year-old children to:

> Describe the connections between a series of historical events, scientific ideas or concepts, or steps in technical procedures in a text.
>
> Know and use various text features (e.g., captions, bold print, subheadings, glossaries, indexes, electronic menus, icons) to locate key facts or information in a text efficiently.
>
> Explain how specific images (e.g., a diagram showing how a machine works) contribute to and clarify a text.

Such standards will require more ambitious comprehension instruction than has typically been offered to students. What will it take to provide such instruction? In this book, Brown and Dewitz go a long way toward showing us. In the following sections, I discuss three crucial elements for meeting the demands of the CCSS that are elucidated in this book.

A TEACHER DEEPLY KNOWLEDGEABLE
ABOUT COMPREHENSION

> "Understanding models of reading comprehension will help you become a more insightful teacher whose instructional decisions are derived from sound principles, not the latest fad." (Chapter 1, p. 15)

Reading comprehension is extremely complex, involving processes from matching sequences of sounds with sequences of symbols, to constructing a mental model of the text, to rendering an emotional response, and much more. Just as a cardiologist with a strong understanding of the circulatory system is better positioned to diagnose and treat his or her patients, a teacher with a deep understanding of reading comprehension is better able to recognize and respond to children's reading comprehension growth and challenges.

Brown and Dewitz take the time and space in this book to help readers understand how comprehension works; how it is affected by the reader, the text, and the context; and what attributes characterize the most successful comprehenders. They do this in a way that is accessible and readily linked to our everyday practice. For example, in Chapter 3 they write, "Good readers, however, do not plod along using one strategy at a time" (p. 53). We can easily grasp their point and immediately think of some of its potential implications for practice.

A MORE MULTIFACETED APPROACH TO INSTRUCTION

". . . comprehension instruction must change with the context, materials, and abilities of the readers." (Chapter 2, p. 28)

All too common in U.S. classrooms is a version of comprehension instruction that goes something like this: Across the course of the year, the teacher teaches six comprehension strategies, which are presented one at a time and generically, as though they apply equally to any type of reading for any type of purpose. For each of the six strategies, the teacher carries out a series of whole-class lessons, closing each by encouraging students to use this helpful strategy when they read. To see whether students seem to be using the strategies, the teacher asks students a series of comprehension questions about some of the texts they read.

The problems with this approach are myriad. Good readers use more than six strategies to comprehend, and these strategies vary in both type and application, depending on the reader's purpose, the type of text, and the context of reading. Good readers also coordinate multiple strategies simultaneously, and aggressively integrate what they are reading with their existing knowledge base. The challenges and successes that students encounter in this process are highly varied, so whole-class lessons, without considerable small-group and individual assessment and coaching, are likely to be largely ineffective. Merely asking students a series of comprehension questions is unlikely to be adequate to understand their comprehension processes to guide them to the next steps in instruction.

Brown and Dewitz, however, help us to see what a more multifaceted approach to instruction looks like. They show us how we might help students engage in application of a wide range of strategies tailored to the specific text and purpose for which they are reading. They show us how three students—Miguel, Brody, and Tanisha—experience somewhat different comprehension challenges and successes, and how teachers can respond to these differences in their instruction. They offer tools, such as a sheet for tracking students' comprehension moves during discussion, that can really inform our understanding of a student's comprehension and where instruction might go next.

RETHINKING THE MATERIALS AND FRAMEWORKS USED TO GUIDE INSTRUCTION

"We wrote this book because we believe that the current approach to teaching and developing reading comprehension has gone off track. . . . Also lost in the embrace of comprehension skills and strategies were motivation and metacognition." (Preface, p. xi)

I can certainly understand the tendency to trust basal reading programs. After all, basal reading programs are often developed by teams of experts, thoughtfully designed, and very well polished. Unfortunately, as earlier research by Dewitz, Jones, and Leahy (2009) makes clear, basal reading programs alone have not been providing students with what research suggests is most likely to yield strong comprehenders.

Many professional books respond to this situation by simply ignoring the basal reading program as an instructional tool. Recognizing that many teachers are required to use a basal reading program, however, Brown and Dewitz take a different and welcome tack. They help teachers to understand how to supplement and recast basal reading programs in a way that is more supportive of comprehension development. They also consider two other instructional frameworks: literature-based instruction and inquiry learning with informational texts. Again they help show how teachers can incorporate ambitious comprehension into these frameworks.

I especially appreciate Brown and Dewitz's concern with motivation and engagement in each of the three frameworks they present. John Guthrie recently argued that the demands of the CCSS will require unprecedented attention to motivation and engagement (Guthrie, 2013). CCSS aside, as Brown and Dewitz make clear early in the book, comprehension is such substantial cognitive work that comprehenders must be motivated to engage in it, and they offer many strategies for providing that motivation.

I hope that you are motivated to engage with this book. I believe it will help you to provide the kind of ambitious comprehension instruction the present era requires.

NELL K. DUKE, EdD
University of Michigan

REFERENCES

Dewitz, P., Jones, J., & Leahy, S. (2009). Comprehension strategy instruction in core reading programs. *Reading Research Quarterly, 44*(2), 102–126.

Guthrie, J. (2013, April 15). Attaining the CCSS is impossible without engagement. Retrieved from *www.reading.org/general/Publications/blog/BlogSinglePost. aspx/literacy-research-panel/2013/04/12/attaining-the-ccss-is-impossible-without-engagement*

Preface

The ability of schoolchildren in the United States to understand what they read has remained remarkably stable over the past two decades, a period of time that witnessed an intense national focus on literacy and an expenditure of billions of federal dollars. Through No Child Left Behind and Reading First, the federal government and the individual states defined reading standards and exerted control over methods and materials of reading instruction. In 1992, the National Assessment of Educational Progress (NAEP, 2011) found that 62% of fourth graders and 69% of eighth graders were reading at a basic level, meaning the students were able "to locate relevant information, make simple inferences, and use their understanding of the text to identify details that support a given interpretation or conclusion." At that time, only 34% of fourth- and eighth-grade students were reading at a proficient level. That meant that a majority of students were unable to "integrate and interpret texts and apply their understanding of the text to draw conclusions and make evaluations." Especially troubling is the fact that while 43% of white students were reading at a proficient level, only 15% of African Americans were able to do the same (NAEP, 2011).

When we look internationally, fourth graders in the United States score somewhat better than average among the 44 nations that participated in the most recent international study. Our students scored significantly better than those in France, Norway, and New Zealand; significantly worse than students in Canada, Italy, and Singapore; and on par with Germany, England, and Denmark (Baer, Baldi, Ayotte, & Green, 2007). We all believe that education and literacy are key to a productive economy and pave the way to social advancement (Labaree, 2010). Raising the literacy levels of our children becomes paramount, especially for those trying to enter the middle class or for those in danger of slipping out of it. That many children can read at a basic level, but not at a proficient level, has spurred us to write this book. It is not that our students can't read the words on the page. Rather, they have difficulty integrating, interpreting, critiquing, and evaluating what they read—the thinking necessary to succeed in our information age. The students in our country demonstrated only modest improvement in literacy during the very time we made a significant national push.

We wrote this book because we believe that the current approach to teaching and developing reading comprehension has gone off track. From the mid-1980s to the mid-1990s, researchers spent their time and energy exploring the cognitive strategies of good readers and developing instructional techniques for helping children and adolescents acquire this brand of thinking. Through this research we learned that children could become strategic readers and their comprehension would improve (Duke & Pearson, 2002). Many books, articles, and workshops followed this research, guiding teachers to implement a strategies approach to comprehension instruction. However, in the process we ignored an even older understanding—that good comprehension is built on and enabled by knowledge (R. C. Anderson & Pearson, 1984). Schema theory, an attempt to explain how knowledge is stored and built in the mind, provided a strong foundation for understanding reading comprehension, but after an early embrace of these ideas 30 years ago, literacy education quickly moved past schema theory to focus on strategies. Knowledge of the concepts, experiences, text structures, and words is essential to good comprehension. Many approaches to comprehension instruction have become too narrow, teaching skills and strategies for their own sake and ignoring that these cognitive activities are a means for building understanding and critical thinking.

Also lost in the embrace of comprehension skills and strategies were motivation and metacognition. We sometimes forgot that reading a complex text requires purpose, planning, and effort. From research, we learned that effective readers set their own purposes for reading and monitor whether those purposes have been met. They know when reading goes off the rails. These metacognitive insights can happen only when the purpose of reading is learning or enjoyment, not skill attainment. Thus, our book is built on the premise that the good comprehender is knowledgeable, motivated, strategic, and metacognitive, and, accordingly, that instruction must constantly focus on these four attributes.

The development of reading comprehension is most effective when learning and teaching are set within a rich, meaningful context. That context might be a unit of instruction on marine life, the civil rights movement, or the day-to-day difficulties of Maniac Magee or Harry Potter. Context

matters because the knowledge base, the types of text, and even the strategies used by students to decipher those texts may vary.

In addition, we believe there are three important contexts or frameworks, as we call them, in which comprehension instruction occurs: literature, inquiry, and basal reading programs. A framework describes a set of
beliefs or philosophy about reading instruction. It establishes specific goals;
it defines the materials that students read, the instructional practices and
learning activities chosen by teachers, and the way time is allocated in the
classroom. The reading of literature and informational texts (a key feature
in inquiry instruction) is found in all classrooms. At times students work
with one type of text, at other times with both. We have also chosen to focus
on basal reading because 74% of teachers in the United States use a published reading series in some respect, either following it faithfully or choosing among its many elements (Education Market Research, 2010). As is the
case in any instructional framework, a basal program has goals, materials,
instructional activities, and a recommended pacing structure. As a framework it organizes how teachers think and teach. Even so, a basal framework
can coexist with a literature-based framework or an information–inquiry
frame.

As we wrote this book, the Common Core State Standards (CCSS;
National Governors Association & Council of Chief State School Officers
[NGA & CCSSO], 2010) were dominating the conversation about reading
instruction. At the beginning of Chapters 5, 7, and 9 we restate the anchor
standards for literature and informational text. Throughout this book we
regularly indicate how the instructional principles and activities we advocate will help you and your students meet the CCSS. We have placed side-
bars in chapters in the second half of the book to signal how our text can
help you think more about key standards and help you to plan specific lessons and activities to meet them. We also pay particular attention to the
notion of *close reading* that is a key objective of the CCSS.

In one important way our book takes a different focus than do the new
standards. The CCSS describe what students must accomplish to meet the
standards but purposefully avoid specifying how students might achieve
these goals. Also, the CCSS do not list instructional practices that can help
students to attain the CCSS expectations. Our book focuses on the means
for helping students arrive at the types of thinking and learning with texts
that the CCSS spell out. We argue that a rich combination of knowledge,
strategies, metacognition, and motivation all characterize the habits of
good readers. Seeing patterns of argument and language in text requires
knowledge; making inferences and getting to the gist requires strategies;
monitoring this process entails metacognition; and coordinating all of this
demands motivation.

Our book on reading comprehension is geared to any second- through eighth-grade teacher, or student of education, who is seeking to better understand the teaching of reading comprehension to improve classroom instruction. To help us in this task, we focused our writing on three teachers: Mr. Rodriguez, a second-grade teacher whose students are reading and learning about weather and communities; Ms. Fogel, a fourth-grade teacher who is teaching with a new basal reading program; and Mrs. Wilson, whose students are reading and responding to literature. Descriptions of their instruction were derived from the practices of talented teachers we observed or worked with over the years.

To enhance your use of this book, we now walk you through its organization. In Chapter 1, we explain the process of reading comprehension, describing how the mind makes sense of the page. A theory of comprehension is important because theory should inform a teacher's instructional decisions. We then move beyond the mental process of comprehension. In Chapter 2, we consider the texts that students read and the context of reading instruction. To help students develop reading comprehension, we explain how to select texts with care and, more important, how to understand what features of a text promote or inhibit reading comprehension. In Chapter 3, we discuss the basics of comprehension instruction. In this chapter we present a model of instruction that incorporates knowledge, strategies, metacognition, and motivation. We move beyond isolated strategy lessons to rich, varied discussions that promote understanding. We conclude the first part of our book with assessment, the focus of Chapter 4, presenting specific assessment techniques that can be employed in a classroom.

The next part of the book addresses comprehension instruction in the context of the three literacy frameworks. In paired chapters, we focus on planning and teaching comprehension with literature, informational text, and a basal reading program. The first of these paired chapters helps you to plan instruction, and the second chapter demonstrates how to put that planning into practice. Chapters 5 and 6 focus on teaching literature, Chapters 7 and 8 on information–inquiry, and Chapters 9 and 10 on basal reading programs.

Ours is not a book dedicated solely to comprehension strategies. However, they make up a good chunk of many chapters because they are instrumental in building understanding. Although you will not find separate chapters on individual strategies, they are integrated into our instructional chapters because they fit the comprehension and text problems that confront teachers and students. Similarly, we highlight several important approaches to discussion. The chart on the next page will help you find information on the teaching of specific comprehension strategies and powerful discussion techniques.

	Chapters 5 and 6	Chapters 7 and 8	Chapters 9 and 10
Comprehension strategies	• Narrative structure • Making inferences	• Expository structure • Self-questioning	• Determining importance and summarizing
Discussion techniques	• Literature circles and book clubs	• Transactional strategies instruction	• Questioning the author • Collaborative reasoning

Teaching comprehension is complicated because the act of comprehension is complex, involving knowledge, thinking strategies, metacognition, and motivation. When you have taught comprehension well, you have helped your students to build knowledge, kindle their interest in reading, employ strategies to negotiate the difficult bumps in the road, and monitor all they do so that reading becomes a self-teaching system (Share, 1995). Helping students grow as readers requires much more than teaching a finite list of discrete skills and strategies. It demands immersion in an exciting curriculum, study of important topics, and recognizing that reading will be, throughout one's life, a means of building knowledge, solving problems, tackling text-based tasks, and entering into exciting worlds. We hope that our book will start you down the road to appreciating the complex nature of reading comprehension and will provide you with some tools to ease your way.

Acknowledgments

FROM RACHEL

I am grateful to my coauthor, Peter Dewitz, whose dedication, hard work, and collegiality pushed me to think more thoughtfully about the teaching of comprehension. I always looked forward to our spirited conversations and benefited much from our equal partnership.

I appreciate my doctoral program mentors, including Linda Gambrell, John Guthrie, Peter Afflerbach, and John O'Flahavan, and my respected and treasured advisors, Michael Pressley and Ruth Garner, who left this earth far too soon—exceptional scholars and human beings both. They enriched my life in ways they probably never knew.

I thank all the colleagues, students, and classroom teachers I worked with, taught, and learned from over the years. They all helped me fashion a deeper understanding of that wonderfully complex endeavor of teaching comprehension. I also benefited from the insights, generosity, and advice of my dear friends and colleagues Janice Almasi, Laura Barden-Gabbei, Jonna Kulikowich, and Peggy Van Meter.

FROM PETER

Our book is a true collaboration between Rachel and me. It is the product of two people thinking, debating, and ultimately arriving at a shared vision for the teaching of reading comprehension.

The students, teachers, and administrators from Accomack County Schools, Madison Public Schools, and Augusta County School taught me about reading comprehension. Through working with them, my understanding of reading comprehension grew, and, most important, I learned what does *not* improve students' reading comprehension. I would also like to acknowledge my friend Michael Graves, who raised my appreciation of vocabulary and knowledge, and Laura Smolkin and our discussions about the nature of reading comprehension. Through both I learned that comprehension is more than strategies.

FROM BOTH OF US

We want to extend hearty thanks to Mariam Jean Dreher, who gave of her time and energy to review a previous version of this book. We also thank Nell K. Duke, who graciously consented to write the foreword. We both thank The Guilford Press team, Craig Thomas, Anna Nelson, and Mary Beth Anderson, who ushered this book through production with skill, patience, and enthusiasm. We also want to note Chris Jennison's interest and support.

We both take full, complete, and equal responsibility for the ideas and writing in this book.

Contents

CHAPTER 1

What Does Good Comprehension Look Like?

D o you ever think about how you read? Do you focus on your thinking during reading? Most of us are unaware of the complex processing we engage in during reading until we confront something challenging. When meaning eludes even the best of readers, resolving comprehension problems can feel like clasping a slippery fish with bare hands. But facing barriers to comprehension actually plays an important function. It forces us to slow down, take note, and initiate some corrective action. Hopefully, it also clues us in to the complexities of reading comprehension.

As you read through the poem below by Billy Collins (1988), attend closely to your thinking. Take on the role of detached observer. Do not critique the quality of your thinking; instead, just witness your inner monologue.

Introduction to Poetry

I ask them to take a poem
and hold it up to the light
like a color slide

or press an ear against its hive.

I say drop a mouse into a poem
and watch him probe his way out,

or walk inside the poem's room
and feel the walls for a light switch.

I want them to waterski
across the surface of a poem
waving at the author's name on the shore.

But all they want to do
is tie the poem to a chair with rope
and torture a confession out of it.

They begin beating it with a hose
to find out what it really means.

(p. 58)[*]

What first sprang to mind as you read this poem? Perhaps you translated the words into mental images. Or, you might have used clues in the poem to infer something that Collins didn't state explicitly, associating it to your own experiences or knowledge. Quite possibly, you paused to check your comprehension and asked yourself some questions when something was confusing. We also suspect that despite any difficulties you encountered, you were pretty confident that you could resolve them on your own. And most importantly, we hope you noticed how incredibly active your mind was during reading.

In this chapter, we explore the highly dynamic and complex nature of reading comprehension. We start this process by examining—to the extent that it is possible—the inner workings of the mind during comprehension. Since the brain's operations are not visible, the best we can do is draw inferences from the clues readers drop through their actions and self-reports of their thinking. The mental activity we can infer from introspection is incomplete because some of the text processing takes place beyond our awareness.

GOALS FOR THIS CHAPTER

✓ Take you into the mind of one fifth-grade teacher as she thinks aloud to help you understand the reading process.

✓ Outline the attributes of effective reading comprehension.

✓ Introduce four components of the good comprehender model and its implication for instruction.

✓ Present theoretical models of reading comprehension that inform instruction.

---

[*]From Billy Collins, "Introduction to Poetry" from *The Apple That Astonished Paris*. Copyright 1988, 1996 by Billy Collins. Reprinted with the permission of The Permissions Company, Inc., on behalf of the University of Arkansas Press, *www.uapress.com*.

A THINK-ALOUD OF A GOOD READER

Rosie, a fifth-grade teacher, read Billy Collins's poem as she concentrated on her thinking. She believed that tuning into her own thinking would help her understand comprehension, explain it to her students, and help them connect to their thinking. In Figure 1.1, we record the thoughts, feelings, and understandings that bubbled up into Rosie's awareness during thinking aloud and also highlight the mental acts she engaged in while reading.

When Rosie finished reading, she paraphrased the poem to double-check her understanding. She then shared her experiences thinking aloud with her students to begin a discussion of how we all need to be thoughtful and self-directing during reading. She explained that attending to one's thinking during reading is worthwhile and beneficial—even for very good readers.

Rosie's real-time processing of Collins's poem provides a concrete example of what good comprehenders do. Over several decades, researchers have studied good readers' practices by analyzing what these individuals report as they read texts that interest and challenge them (Pressley & Afflerbach, 1995; Shanahan & Shanahan, 2008). Chronicling good readers' claims about what they think and feel during reading has advanced our understanding of reading comprehension by making the normally invisible processing of texts more accessible.

Text from Poem	Rosie's Think-Aloud	Enacted Comprehension Strategies
I ask them to take a poem and hold it up to the light like a color slide	Who is the "them" Collins is referring to in the poem? I have an idea it might be students but I'll read on to see if this idea is confirmed.	Predicting
	Given the name of the poem, I'm thinking: hah—"slides." That's old technology. I wonder—how many students will know what these are? But why does Collins's use that imagery, that metaphor? Well, at first glance a slide is opaque and features can't be discerned until one holds it up to the light. Only then does the image become visible.	Questioning Connecting to knowledge base: text-to-world

(continued)

FIGURE 1.1. A sample of thinking aloud of Billy Collins's poem "Introduction to Poetry." Copyright 1988, 1996 by Billy Collins. Text from poem reprinted with permission of The Permissions Company, Inc., on behalf of The University of Arkansas Press, *www.uapress.com.*

Text from Poem	Rosie's Think-Aloud	Enacted Comprehension Strategies
	So does understanding or illumination relate to detailed, prolonged scrutiny?	**Questioning**
	I know Collins was a poet laureate. I also know other poems of his that I like, one of which I saw in another professional text on strategies instruction. His poems generally are quite approachable. . . . Okay, I'm stopping now to search about him on Google—to check and build up my background knowledge about him before reading in case it helps me construct the poem's meaning. Hmmm, on Google I see something about this poem on Project 180. So, browsing the Internet helped confirm my prediction that this poem can be used with students since it is the first poem selected by the Project 180 program.	**Connecting to, monitoring, and building knowledge base: text-to-world; text-to-text** **Verifying prediction**
or press an ear against its hive.	*Oh, I'm predicting that Collins intends to reference all of the senses. In the first stanza, he mentioned sight, then sound. . . . This tactic makes sense since typically poetry appeals to all the senses.*	**Predicting using text clues** **Connecting to knowledge base: text-to-text**
I say drop a mouse into a poem and watch him probe his way out,	*Okay—here I'm not as clear about what might be going on—seems like a break in the extended pattern the poet is setting up alluding to the five senses. Well, could dropping something be a type of touching?*	**Monitoring, questioning, and identifying confusion**
	Now, what do I know about mouse behavior that might help me understand what this means? I know in experiments mice have been dropped into a maze and then have an incentive to find their way out by smelling their food reward at the end of the route. . . . But I don't know if I like the reference to mice here—because I think we bring more resources to the task of understanding a poem than what a mouse enlists to find a piece of cheese . . . or maybe mice is a metaphor?	**Connecting to knowledge base: text-to-world** **Evaluating** **Questioning**
	Perhaps the author means that we have to work our way slowly through the poem—considering different possibilities, rejecting dead-ends, and heading in the direction of ideas that seem to lead somewhere.	**Inferring**

(continued)

FIGURE 1.1. *(continued)*

Text from Poem	Rosie's Think-Aloud	Enacted Comprehension Strategies
	Hmmm, Collins could have continued with his reference to the five senses by having the mouse "smell" his way toward his prize. I wonder why he used the word probe *instead. What is he up to here?*	**Evaluating** **Questioning**
or walk inside the poem's room and feel the walls for a light switch.	*Ah, here we are back to the sense of touch that I was expecting . . . but the poem doesn't seem to include anything about the "taste" or "smell" of the words.*	**Verifying prediction**
	"Feeling the walls" also makes me think of the times I've had to search for a light switch in a dark, unfamiliar location.	**Connecting to knowledge base: text-to-self**
	So I'm inferring that Collins means that you have to work your way tentatively through a poem. As awareness begins to emerge, you grope your way toward the "light" of meaning—allowing yourself to inhabit the entirety of the poem, experiencing it slowly rather than coming to some vague impression. Nuance comes with savoring, and not rushing, through the words.	**Inferring**
I want them to waterski across the surface of a poem waving at the author's name on the shore.	*I'm picturing in my mind an image of me skimming across the tops of the words, between the lines—the black squiggles on the page becoming little wavelets and the white spaces between them the sea foam and spray. . . .*	**Visualizing**
	But now I'm confused because the image of waterskiing makes me think of a more superficial involvement with the poem—just skimming above the surface of the poem instead of plunging deeply in the waters. This new image contradicts my earlier notion about the value of delving deeply into the poem. Hmmm—I need to think more about this. . . .	**Monitoring comprehension** **Problem solving**
	Now "waving at the author's name" is an interesting idea. The words make me think that despite the fact that the poet has crafted the poem—and probably had his own intentions in mind when writing it—as the reader, I can create my own meaning.	**Evaluating**

(continued)

FIGURE 1.1. *(continued)*

Text from Poem	Rosie's Think-Aloud	Enacted Comprehension Strategies
	This view is so different than the one held by my professor in a poetry course I took in college. When he returned my critique of a poem, he had scrawled that my interpretation was incorrect. He obviously did not buy into the idea that prior knowledge plays a huge role in the construction of meaning. An individual's unique experiences and knowledge can inspire a different, yet reasonable interpretation provided that information stated explicitly in the poem is not contradicted.	Connecting to knowledge base: text-to-self Evaluating
But all they want to do is tie the poem to a chair with rope and torture a confession out of it.	How funny! These words make me think that trying to force the meaning to come up with a "right" answer isn't going to work . . . reminds me of times when I'm trying to write a good lead or conclusion in a paper. The more I tussle with the words, the more I stay stuck. Instead, when I finally let go of the struggle, the words later spring to mind, of their own accord, when I'm taking a shower, drifting off to sleep, or going for a walk. . . .	Evaluating Connecting to knowledge base: text-to-self
They begin beating it with a hose to find out what it really means.	This sentence makes me think about my tendency to overanalyze everything—as if by putting in more and more effort, a true nugget of meaning will emerge. To me, "beating it with a hose" means overcritiquing, overanalyzing the poem, working way too hard to discern a precise meaning instead of enjoying the sensual experience, the lived and felt meaning of the poem. That it can become all too easy (as we get too analytic about poetry) to lose sight of the sheer sensual enjoyment of reading. Gee, what a great little poem. I really enjoyed the imagery and the message I gleaned from it.	Connecting to knowledge base: text-to-self Inferring Evaluating Evaluating

FIGURE 1.1. (continued)

ATTRIBUTES OF AN EFFECTIVE COMPREHENDER

When Rosie thought aloud, she exhibited many of the hallmarks of skilled reading. For one, she wrestled actively with text meaning. In fact, the word *comprehension* derives from the Latin root *prehens*, which means "to seize or grasp." But active "seizing" of meaning only describes Rosie's thinking in vague terms. In order to provide a finer-grained depiction of effective comprehension, we highlight below some of the processing that Rosie and other good readers engage in as they read (Pressley & Afflerbach, 1995; Duke, Pearson, Strachan & Billman, 2011):

- *Good readers set goals prior to and during reading and check to see if they are meeting those goals.*
  - Before reading, Rosie intentionally selected this poem to read for fun as well as for understanding.
  - She also wanted to see whether it would serve as a suitable resource to talk about her experiences with thinking aloud to her class.
- *Good readers often preview a text and examine its structure before reading.*
  - Rosie gave the text a good once-over before reading, checking its length and the way the words and lines were arranged on the page.
  - She noticed that the poem did not adopt a rhyming scheme.
- *Good readers use their prior knowledge to link ideas together and to make inferences.*
  - Rosie made associations between the poem and her personal, lived experiences.
  - She linked her accumulated conceptual knowledge and experiences to the poem.
- *Good readers raise questions before and while they are reading.*
  - Rosie questioned the text when she was curious.
  - She also raised questions when she was puzzled.
- *Good readers make predictions and confirm them as they read.*
  - Rosie guessed what might happen in the poem by drawing upon her existing knowledge and text information.
  - She noted when her hunches were confirmed by evidence.
- *Good readers, at times, visualize what they read.*
  - Rosie used the vivid words and imagery to conjure pictures in her mind.

- *Good readers are metacognitive; they identify confusions caused by unknown words or perplexing chunks of texts and work hard to resolve them.*
  - ♦ When reading the poem, Rosie recognized when meaning escaped her. She stopped when baffled, questioned the text, reread some lines, and rethought and revised her evolving interpretations.
  - ♦ She paraphrased the poem when she finished reading to conduct a final check on her understanding.
- *Good readers are thoughtful and emotive evaluators.*
  - ♦ Rosie evaluated whether the poem met the goals she set prior to reading. It did!
  - ♦ She noticed that the poem was chock-full of rich, sensory details, which appealed to her.
  - ♦ She appreciated the author's use of certain metaphors and word usages.
  - ♦ She decided that she not only really liked the poem but also considered its merits as a well-crafted piece.
- *Good readers are motivated.*
  - ♦ Rosie knew she could trust herself to interpret this poem given her past experiences successfully navigating other ones.
  - ♦ She knew she possessed the resources to construct a reasonable interpretation of a challenging text. What is more, she was willing to expend effort to do so.

Rosie used thinking processes that were well suited to understanding Collins's poem. She did not apply all strategic actions known to her, only those that were sensible to use in that specific context. Rosie also relied on her knowledge of colored slides, bee hives, mice, and water-skis to build her understanding of the poem. If she had read a more challenging text, she might have drawn on additional mental resources to construct meaning. If she had come across unknown words, she might have used various word-learning strategies to figure them out. Or, if she had selected an expository text, a magazine article, a research study, or a website instead of Collins's poem, she might have interacted quite differently with each material. And remember, we caught only a glimpse of Rosie's complex processing.

FOUR ATTRIBUTES OF A GOOD COMPREHENDER

We collapse the above characteristics of good readers into four broad attributes. Borrowing from Pressley, Borkowski, and Schneider's (1989) good information processing model, proficient readers (and capable learners in general) are *knowledgeable, metacognitive, strategic,* and *motivated.* A reader's effectiveness in large part depends upon the deft orchestration of these four broad attributes (Duke et al., 2011):

1. How extensive the reader's knowledge base is and how well he or she takes advantage of that information.
2. How motivated the reader is to read for various purposes and to put effort into completing tasks when reading different kinds of texts.
3. How successful the reader is in selecting and using appropriate strategies for reading with diverse texts and for varied purposes.
4. How well the reader understands personal academic strengths and needs as well as manages his or her comprehension and performance.

Good Readers Are Knowledgeable

Readers employ various types of knowledge to understand a text. They rely on knowledge from lived experiences; knowledge of words or vocabulary; knowledge of the world, facts, and concepts; and knowledge of genre and text structure. These types of knowledge are not mutually exclusive. Learning facts and concepts is intertwined with learning the words or labels for these concepts. You may have seen a giraffe at the zoo or a picture of one, but it is the word that cements the actual concept in memory (Stahl & Nagy, 2006). When Davis (1944) examined the components of reading comprehension, he found that word meanings had a great deal to do with a reader's success; vocabulary may account for 32% of comprehension. Also important are drawing inferences, understanding the structure of the passage, and the writer's techniques. For explanatory purposes, we will treat each of these overlapping types of knowledge separately below.

Personal Knowledge

Readers always make associations between the texts they read and their past experiences. They comprehend better when they relate what they are reading to something they have already experienced. Without prior exposure to similar situations or environments, comprehension is severely diminished. Such personal knowledge also includes *funds of knowledge* (Moll, Amanti, Neff, & Gonzalez, 1992), the social and cultural stores of knowledge that individuals accumulate through direct participation in their households and communities. Unfortunately, these rich resources of experiential knowledge, absorbed from family and neighborhood settings, often remain undervalued and underused in schools.

Conceptual Knowledge

Readers of all ages know much about the world and that knowledge is essential to comprehension. This type of knowledge refers to disciplinary or domain-specific information that individuals typically do not experience directly. This is our knowledge of history, physics, mathematics, and other areas of study. Imagine sitting down to read a book on microeconomics. Chances are that you know little about the topic, so, comprehension is difficult. Yet, what happens when someone encounters a more mundane text, a murder mystery? Most adult readers are better versed in the elements of crime than in microeconomics. This knowledge is readily available from television, movies, the news, and other novels. Such conceptual, or "world," knowledge is indispensable to making inferences that enhance comprehension.

Vocabulary Knowledge

Possessing a broad understanding of word meanings has been regularly linked to comprehension in both correlational and experimental studies. Vocabulary knowledge affects both word reading ability and comprehension (Ricketts, Nation, & Bishop, 2007). Students with larger vocabularies experience greater success decoding new words. They experience a mental "aha" moment when they decode a word they have heard or know that is impossible without that experience. Vocabulary also affects comprehension because the meaning of a passage is dependent on the understanding of the words. You simply can't fully understand a passage without knowing the meaning of words it contains (Graves, 2006). In turn, reading builds more vocabulary and world knowledge.

Textual Knowledge

Readers draw upon genre and text structure knowledge to understand a text. Someone with rich genre knowledge is better able to set purposes for reading by recognizing the particular purposes underlying each genre. For example, a book that falls within the science fiction genre can cue a reader that this text, occurring in the future, holds a possible hidden message for readers in the present. The reader's purpose then may be to simply enjoy a novel, entering into a new and unknown world, such as *The Martian Chronicles* (Bradbury, 1950a) or to look for connections between dilemmas and ethical issues in the future and in our times.

Knowledge of genre also means that the reader understands the structures that can underlie a text. The reader of realistic fiction knows that the story or novel will begin with the setting, characters, and the complication or problem. A series of events will unfold which heightens the conflict as the characters move to a solution. In informational text the reader knows that the facts are laid out in some organizational scheme depending on the topic describing, explaining, and illustrating particular concepts. The author may use introductions, headings, subheadings, and graphics to guide the reader through the discussion. Thus, genre and text structure knowledge act as an implicit map, supporting readers and helping them to anticipate what is to come (Goldman & Rakestraw, 2000).

Good Readers Are Metacognitive

Metacognition, which broadly can be thought of as "thinking about one's own thinking," actually refers to two separate but related components—awareness of one's capabilities as a reader *as well as* control over one's cognitive actions during reading. The self-knowledge piece involves (1) awareness of when comprehension breaks down; (2) awareness of personal strengths and shortcomings as a reader; (3) awareness of the demands placed on the reader from diverse reading tasks and purposes; and (4) awareness of when, where, and why to appropriately apply specific reading strategies (Flavell, 1976; Baker, 2002).

Managing cognitive resources during reading is complicated. Self-regulating readers set reading goals and make decisions about how to achieve those goals. They make choices based on task demands and the cognitive resources that they bring with them. Self-regulating readers monitor their comprehension to make sure that what they read makes sense. If attention wanders or confusions arise, they know how to rectify problems. They possess knowledge of powerful "fix-up" or repair reading strategies, which they deliberately apply to overcome glitches. Throughout—and at the conclusion of reading—self-directing readers judge whether they have met the goals they initially set. Finally, they evaluate their overall reading experience, using feedback to inform future decision making before, during, and after reading.

Good Readers Are Strategic

Reading for comprehension involves sophisticated and effortful coordination of several comprehension strategies or mental acts employed by a reader to build an understanding of a text. A reader is strategic when anticipating what might happen next in a story (*predicting*), when raising questions about a passage (*self-questioning*), when creating a mental image from printed words (*visualizing*), when deducing a relationship between two ideas or supplying information the author implies (*inferring*), when distinguishing between important facts and fascinating details (*determining importance*), when paraphrasing the gist of what's been learned (*summarizing*), and when relating personal experiences to a similar event experienced by a character (*making connections*). Strategies that good readers invoke for the purpose of building meaning are known as cognitive reading strategies (Duke et al., 2011).

Good readers also use strategies to repair blocks to comprehension. When a text is extremely challenging good readers deliberately think about how to free themselves from a tricky situation. For example, when grappling with a complex argument, good readers might notice their confusion and attempt to restate or summarize the ideas as a way of piecing together their understanding. These types of mental remedies, ones that good readers use to solve comprehension problems, are considered metacognitive reading strategies.

So, what distinguishes cognitive from metacognitive reading strategies? The difference lies in how a strategy is used. When a reading strategy is chosen to construct or retain meaning, it serves as a cognitive reading strategy. When a strategy eliminates comprehension problems and is used to assess whether preset goals have been met, the strategy performs a metacognitive function. Thus, the same strategy can serve dual purposes depending on its usage. For example, a reader can summarize to remember important information (a *cognitive* use) or briefly summarize to see if what was read makes sense (a *metacognitive* use). In this way a reader uses summarizing as a self-test. "If I can summarize it, then I am reasonably sure I understand it." In another instance, a reader can ask a question to show interest when reading something new ("Gee, I wonder why the rhinoceros has a horn?"—a *cognitive* use). Or questioning can be carried out when confusion arises ("So what exactly does this expression mean: 'There's a thousand-pound gorilla in the room'?"—a *metacognitive* use).

Many published reading curricula confusingly use the terms *skills* and *strategies* rather interchangeably. But this is not correct. Strategies can be contrasted with reading skills in two ways. First, strategies are performed with intentionality and awareness. The reader at some level of awareness chooses to visualize a scene or make a prediction. Skills, unlike strategies, are automatic mental activities that do not require conscious attention. The processes of summarizing and visualizing are invoked automatically without any conscious thought. Second, mental acts, when first learned, most assuredly start out as strategies. They are deliberate. However, with time and practice they become habitual and perhaps automatic; they become skills (Afflerbach, Pearson, & Paris, 2008). Yet, at any time during

BROWN, RACHEL.

BUILDING COMPREHENSION IN EVERY CLASSROOM:
INSTRUCTION WITH LITERATURE, INFORMATIONAL TEXTS,
AND BASAL PROGRAMS   Paper   286 P.
NEW YORK: GUILFORD, 2014

AUTH: SYRACUSE UNIVERSITY. GUIDEBOOK FOR
CLASSROOM TEACHERS.
LCCN 2013-20951
  ISBN 1462511201   **Library PO#** FIRM ORDERS

		List	30.00	USD
8395 NATIONAL UNIVERSITY LIBRAR		**Disc**	5.0%	
App. Date 8/27/14 SOE-K12 8214-08	**Net**	28.50	USD

SUBJ: 1. READING COMPREHENSION. 2. BASAL READING
INSTRUCTION.

CLASS LB1050.45   DEWEY# 372.47   LEVEL PROF

YBP Library Services

BROWN, RACHEL.

BUILDING COMPREHENSION IN EVERY CLASSROOM:
INSTRUCTION WITH LITERATURE, INFORMATIONAL TEXTS,
AND BASAL PROGRAMS   Paper   286 P.
NEW YORK: GUILFORD, 2014

AUTH: SYRACUSE UNIVERSITY. GUIDEBOOK FOR
CLASSROOM TEACHERS.
  LCCN 2013-20951
    ISBN 1462511201   **Library PO#** FIRM ORDERS

		List	30.00	USD
8395 NATIONAL UNIVERSITY LIBRAR		**Disc**	5.0%	
App. Date 8/27/14 SOE-K12 8214-08	**Net**	28.50	USD

SUBJ: 1. READING COMPREHENSION. 2. BASAL READING
INSTRUCTION.

CLASS LB1050.45   DEWEY# 372.47   LEVEL PROF

reading we can become deliberate and stop to think through what a word or passage means.

Good Readers Are Motivated

Motivation explains how actions are prompted (or not) by an individual's personal goals, values, and beliefs about the topics and outcomes of reading (Guthrie & Wigfield, 2000). Motivation should not be confused with the teacher creating interest in a specific book or task; instead, it is complex and internal and its impact is sizeable.

> Reading is an emotional domain, not a coldly cognitive enterprise. Reader motivation and affect are powerful forces in this journey toward competence. We may be able to move individuals into low levels of competence by attending only to their knowledge or strategic needs, but they will not have the personal interest to continue this journey, especially as the demands of text-based learning become greater and the text more complex, less predictable. (Alexander, 2003, p. 61)

Goals

Good readers read for fun and for learning (Guthrie & Wigfield, 2000). Prior to reading, individuals select goals with specific purposes in mind that may evolve over the course of a reading event. For example, good readers may start out with the intention of reading to learn. However, over the course of reading the purpose may change to include improving competence, having fun, or accomplishing a specific task. Poor readers often have superficial goals and read to complete an assignment as quickly as possible.

Values

Good readers find reading intrinsically satisfying. Whether for enjoyment or for learning, they find reading worthwhile. Good readers place personal value in reading, whether to appreciate the humor used by an author or to find the absolutely best tiramisu recipe. Even if that delectable tiramisu never gets prepared, the active search for the perfect recipe becomes a reward in itself. When good readers participate in something that is interesting and personally relevant they are more likely to process textual information at a deeper level, which leads to better recall, more complex representations of meaning, and an ability to answer more thoughtful questions (Eccles & Wigfield, 2002).

Beliefs

Good readers expect to do well when they perform reading tasks. They are confident that they possess the know-how to make sense of what they read. But just in case they get stuck, good readers believe that they can help themselves and do not blame their failures on external reasons. These readers have a sense of personal efficacy. Such confidence emanates from past experiences with using strategies effectively and noting that perseverance pays off.

A graphic depiction of the four components of the good comprehender model is presented in Figure 1.2. Although this schematic provides an overview of good comprehension (adapted from Almasi & Fullerton, 2012; Pressley et al., 1989), it does not detail what takes place inside the reader's mind during meaning construction. So how is it possible to capture the precise moment when the "click" of comprehension occurs (Pearson, 2009, p. 3)?

Eventually, this question may be answered by research in neuroscience that has implications for comprehension. Scientists have been studying brain activity through the direct use of brain scans and other data-collection tools, for example, positron emission tomography (PET), functional magnetic resonance imaging (fMRI), and event-related potentials (ERPs) (Tracey & Morrow, 2012). These technologies allow researchers to observe areas of neural activity, patterns of blood flow to parts of the brain, and speed of auditory and visual perception. Current studies are revealing more about the anatomy of the brain and its functioning while we are reading (Caine,

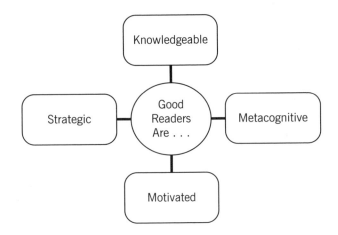

FIGURE 1.2. The good comprehender model.

2008; Hruby, 2009). However, it remains to be seen to what extent neuroscience can yield a comprehensive mapping of comprehension processing or contribute a set of pragmatic and cohesive guidelines to inform day-to-day instruction (Tracey & Morrow, 2012). So for now, our field does not have a definitive, biologically driven explanation of the brain's internal workings. Despite that, we know enough about reading comprehension from think alouds and other research to design effective instruction. In the next section we will explain how these understandings have been integrated into an effective model of reading comprehension.

THEORETICAL MODELS OF READING COMPREHENSION

Cognitive psychologists and educational researchers have long speculated about the mind's operations during reading. Their insights and research have led to explanations for what comprehension is and how it works. When the workings of the mind are spelled out into a solid explanation of the comprehension process we call the result a model or theory. Educators, psychologists, and literary theorists developed these models of comprehension and each model emphasizes different facets of the comprehension process. These models come and go, and sometimes they evolve as they are tested and new data suggests a revised look at how we comprehend.

Understanding models of reading comprehension will help you become a more insightful teacher whose instructional decisions are derived from sound principles, not the latest fad. If you understand that reading comprehension involves knowledge, strategies, metacognition, and motivation (i.e., the good comprehender model) you will not limit your instruction to the teaching of strategies. If a student struggles with reading comprehension, a good model can guide your attempt to understand your student's difficulties, exploring his or her decoding skills, fluency, metacognitive insights, and perhaps motivation. With a good model tucked in your head you will be able to evaluate new instructional programs and approaches that the latest experts in the field offer as a solution to all your problems. Models, in short, help us think clearly about learning and teaching—and help us evaluate our instructional options.

Given the large number of comprehension models, we decided to focus on just five. Each model that we selected focuses on one or more aspects of reading comprehension. The simple view emphasizes that reading begins with decoding and language comprehension. The construction–integration model reveals the complexity of the comprehension process and causes us to attend to many factors. Transactional theory reminds us that every person's response to the text is unique. Sociocultural theory points out that learning to think at multiple levels is acquired through interaction with others. Finally, the model of the engaged reader reminds us that motivation is critical to the whole act of reading comprehension. All these theories have provided researchers with powerful explanations that inform comprehension studies and instruction. In turn, solid research supports educators in providing better instruction in their classrooms. Stated another way, "Delivery of effective reading comprehension depends on research" (Israel & Duffy, 2009, p. xvii).

A Simple View of Reading

At the heart of the simple view of reading lies the assumption that reading comprehension consists of two components: decoding and language comprehension (Hoover & Gough, 1990). Decoding refers to automatically and correctly identifying words. Language comprehension involves the ability to understand the meaning of spoken words. According to the simple view, poor reading comprehension stems from difficulty with figuring out the written code or understanding oral language—or both components combined. The simple view reminds us to look to decoding as a major prerequisite to reading comprehension.

However, the critics of the simple view claim that this theory is way too simple (Pressley et al., 2009). While acknowledging the vital role of decoding and oral comprehension, detractors claim that deep reading comprehension entails so much more. First, there is a noticeable difference between reading and listening. During reading the reader exerts metacognitive control to accomplish his or her purpose, whereas the listener is more at the mercy of the speaker. Second reading requires knowledge of genres and text structures that rarely occur in oral discourse. Third, the simple view fails to address how the reader coordinates knowledge, specifically academic vocabulary, comprehension strategies, motivation, and the challenges of reading hypertext on the Internet (Cartwright, 2009; Hoffman, 2009; Pressley et al., 2009).

How does the simple view of reading compare to the good comprehender model? In practice, the simple view of reading has been used to support the intensive teaching of decoding in the early years, which transitions later on to comprehension instruction (Hoffman, 2009). In addition, this model has been cited as a way for teachers to spot readers' weaknesses, notably decoding, and then to use that information to provide remediation (Wren, 2006). However, the simple view has increasingly been critiqued because it suggests that all a teacher has to do to achieve good comprehension is to teach students decoding and oral language/listening comprehension skills.

In terms of the four broad attributes of good readers, the role of prior knowledge is addressed somewhat in the simple view because understanding spoken language is associated with vocabulary knowledge. Vocabulary names our experiences in the world and word meanings are stored in our knowledge base. However, under this theory, knowledge of academic vocabulary is not addressed, nor are other components related to skillful reading such as strategies use, metacognition, and motivation.

The Construction–Integration Model

Walter Kintsch's (1998, 2004) construction–integration model describes the mental processing involved in reading comprehension. According to this model, comprehension results when the reader constructs a mental representation of the text consisting of perceptual, cognitive, and affective factors. The model the reader builds contains images, thoughts, and feelings. This mental representation of the text requires several levels of processing, with the final level being "the way the mind views the world as a result of reading" (Kintsch, 2004, p. 1271). Comprehension begins with word identification (decoding in the simple view) and this allows the reader to access the meaning of words. Vocabulary or word meanings are essential for comprehension, and knowledge of grammar enables the reader to assign a grammatical function to words within sentences. Readers next construct their understanding by building coherence both within and across sentences, paragraphs, and larger units of text. For instance, readers link pronouns to nouns and use transitional words (*and, but, since, next, therefore*) to connect one idea to another. To build coherence across sentences, readers use their existing knowledge base to infer information not explicitly stated by the author. To connect larger units of text readers use their knowledge of text structure and genre. All of this processing is essential for readers to comprehend a text.

In the construction–integration model, Kintsch (2004) explains how text processing results in the formation of three types of mental representations or the way ideas are perceived and stored in the mind. However, you will never be aware of these three mental representations since most of the processing happens automatically and outside of awareness.

The first level, known as the *decoding* or *surface level,* refers to a fleeting representation of the text in memory (Kintsch & Kintsch, 2005). The surface level captures the exact wording of at least parts of the text. For our purposes this is the least important part of the model so we will move past it quickly and look at the next two stages as seen in Figure 1.3.

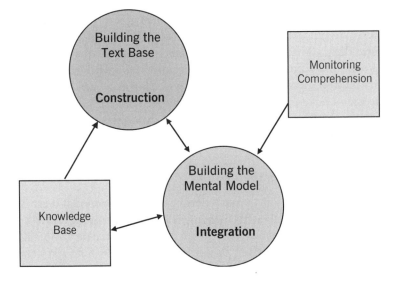

FIGURE 1.3. The construction–integration model of reading comprehension.

The Text Base

The second level of representation, the *text base,* moves beyond the mere duplication of the text. Instead, this level refers to a restructured, nonverbatim representation of the ideas conveyed by a text. In effect, the text base comprises multiple, associated idea units known as *propositions.* Although we are unaware of it, our mind represents everything we read as *propositions.* Consider the following sentence and the propositions within it:

> *Keith fell from the palm tree and injured his head.*
>
> Proposition 1: Keith exists.
>
> Proposition 2: The palm tree exists.
>
> Proposition 3: Keith is in the palm tree.
>
> Proposition 4: Keith fell from the tree.
>
> Proposition 5: Keith injured his head.

In the construction–integration model, the reader builds the text base by linking together the propositions and is left with the idea that Keith fell from the palm tree. As the reader comes across more sentences, additional propositions are formed and combined with previous ones. Sentence by sentence, onward and upward, a network of propositions is constructed that represents the text's meaning.

The ideas in the text are linked through the use of cohesive devices. The reader stitches the ideas together essentially working from the bottom up. At the lowest level of meaning, the reader continuously creates a series of relationships among ideas to construct the meaning of a text. For example, an author can increase coherence if the pronouns in the text link easily to the nouns (e.g., *he, she, it, they, some, few, many*), and cause-and-effect relationships are clear and heralded by signal words (e.g., *because, since, however, due to, hence, so*). The more connections there are among ideas, the more likely they will be remembered (van den Broek & Kremer, 2000).

Next the reader puzzles out the skeleton or organizational structure of a written piece—its underlying text structure. The text structure captures how the most important ideas, or the gist of a text, are put together. For example, a simple text structure for a story can consist of the character, setting, problem, and solution. In informational texts, propositions can be organized into other familiar patterns (e.g., cause–effect; compare–contrast; problem–solution; question–answer). When all of the small ideas are organized into an overarching text structure, the reader has constructed a *text base*. Remember, this *text base* is closely tied to the text but is not an exact replica of that text. Instead, it is a relatively superficial representation of meaning that does not involve deep understanding of the ideas.

The Mental Model

Kintsch's (1998) final level of text representation is the *mental model*, also called the situation model. This higher-order representation consists of the text base integrated with the reader's existing knowledge. Processing at this level is mainly interpretive and inferential. The reader elaborates the text content with personal knowledge and experiences, forming new connections, explanations and analogies, making unique comparisons, creating visual images, exploring consequences, and critically evaluating the material. Thus, the mental model is a "multidimensional meaning representation that may include visual, spatial, temporal, and emotional aspects, as well as abstractions implied by the text" (Caccamise, Snyder, & Kintsch, 2008, p. 84).

So why is this theory known as the construction–integration model? As readers read, they engage in two types of cognitive processing: *construction* and *integration*. According to Kintsch (1998), comprehension results from the building of several alternative meanings during the formation of the text base (*construction*), or what the text says. The reader then selects the most plausible of these possible meanings (*integration*) based on existing knowledge of the context and the specific situation to determine what the text means. We will remind you how *construction* and *integration* applies to relevant aspects of comprehension processing that we raise in this book. For instance, here's an example. Remember Keith falling from the palm tree? If you were able to integrate that sentence with your prior knowledge, you would know that we were referring to Keith Richards of the Rolling Stones and what happened to him during one holiday in the South Seas.

How does this model compare to the attributes of a good reader? What this model offers is a step-by-step explanation of what occurs as a reader moves from lower-level, shallow comprehension to higher-level, deep comprehension. Because of its specificity and its validation through research and mathematical modeling, the construction–integration model and its various offshoots continue to enjoy widespread appeal. Similar to many constructivist and cognitive theories, this model spotlights the highly active and constructive nature of comprehension.

Of the four attributes of a proficient reader, this model emphasizes the role of the knowledge base. Various sources of knowledge cued by the text and the context are involved in constructing meaning. However, in the construction–integration model, strategies play a role when knowledge does not. When the automatic construction of meaning falters, the reader employs strategies to bring ideas together (Duke et al., 2011). Motivation is briefly mentioned insofar as it relates to the level and quality of text representation achieved by different readers. Whether a mental model is created, whether it is highly developed, and whether old knowledge is integrated with new information in a text (e.g., learning) depends not only on the quality of readers' existing knowledge but also on their interests and goals for reading. Readers have different standards of coherence. For example, when reading fiction some readers might infer the motives of a character, whereas others do not feel compelled to do so.

Other psychologists have postulated an important role for both strategies and metacognition in the construction–integration model (Willingham, 2006) and even Kintsch (1998) has suggested possible additions to the model. The creation of the text base and the mental model happens largely outside our awareness; but we are more aware of the use of strategies especially when comprehension becomes difficult. When researchers attempted to crack open the comprehension process through protocol analysis by asking readers to think aloud while reading, they found strategies in the responses of their readers. The results of these analyses substantiated that readers predict, ask themselves questions, infer, and summarize. Willingham suggests that these cognitive strategies, although not the engine of comprehension, act as a guide and work interactively with metacognition. Figure 1.4 depicts how strategies affect the development of meaning. When the reader has difficulty building the text base, he or she might employ what he or she knows about story structure to organize the lower-level propositions into a narrative structure. When the mental model fails to come together, either the reader lacks the requisite knowledge or, for some reason, can't access it.

Metacognition is also essential to the construction–integration model even though Kintsch (1998) referred to it as problem solving. Consider first a conversation between two adults. At times the listener does not understand the speaker, but the listener can ask a question or look puzzled—both are indicators of metacognition. The speaker can reinforce the oral messages with gestures and facial expressions. However, during reading the reader must continue to monitor the message because questioning the author is not an option. The good reader monitors the developing message, rereading and engaging in other strategies to repair comprehension. The construction–integration model, therefore, must contain a problem-solving or metacognitive component, which Kintsch (1998), in *Comprehension: A Paradigm for Cognition*, identified as an area for future work.

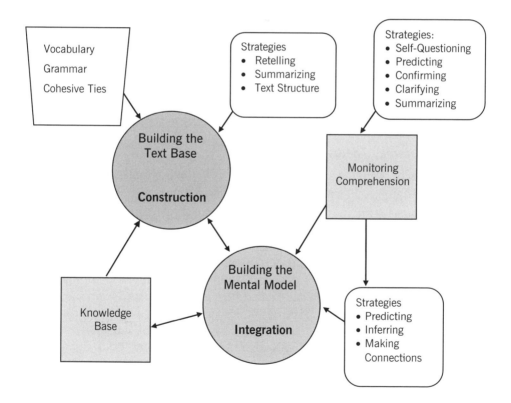

FIGURE 1.4. How strategies might influence the construction–integration model.

Transactional Theory

This perspective can be thought of as a "response to reading" theory (Rosenblatt, 1978/1994). Comprehension results from a "transaction" of a specific *reader* who responds in a given *moment* or *situation* to a particular *text*. The transaction among reader, text, and context yields a subjective unique interpretation. Readers do not construct identical meanings when reading the same text. Words on the page evoke unique associations for each person. These interpretive differences derive from variations in individuals' background knowledge, beliefs, and feelings, along with the moment in time and setting in which the transaction takes place. Thus, the notion of context begins to figure in the reading comprehension equation.

According to Rosenblatt (1978/1994), a reader's unique, contextualized relationship to a text falls along a continuum. A reader's motivation or intention for reading a particular text can range from reading for pleasure, an "aesthetic stance" or expressive stance, to reading for information, an "efferent stance." Over the course of a single transaction, a reader's stance toward a text can change. So we can switch back and forth between learning from a novel or taking delight in the well-reasoned argument of a historian. Knowing about the reader's stance will be important as we discuss the role of discussion in developing comprehension. Sometimes discussion focuses more on the aesthetic feelings generated by a text, and sometimes learning the stated ideas takes precedence. A third stance leads us to be critical and analytic.

Critical Literacy Theory

Stepping beyond Rosenblatt's (1978/1994) transactional theory are the critical literacy theories of Freire (1985), Luke (1995, 2004), and others. Critical literacy theories focus first on the social, cultural, and historical dimensions of reading. Social, cultural, historical, and political beliefs and values are bound within all texts. Reading can never be value free. Whether we know it or not, all texts sanction and perpetuate particular perspectives, stereotypes, agendas, biases, and power relations. Critical literacy approaches take note of this fact. They call on teachers and students to examine how texts position readers to buy into certain interpretations, which can then be accepted, rejected, or modified. Dialoguing about social, cultural, historical, and political implications of texts raises awareness of linkages among language, power, and social justice.

Critical literacy is important because we want readers to go beyond just understanding the text. We want them to engage in higher-order thinking and examine a text closely and decide on its message and how it might be influencing them. Today, in the United States 67% of fourth- and eighth-grade students can read at a basic level, meaning they can read grade-level texts, grasp the gist, and make basic inferences (National Center for Education Statistics, 2011). However, only a third reach a proficient level of reading where they can read critically and analytically. Complex modern life demands such abilities. We consider how to develop critical and analytic reading when we present other classroom discussion techniques.

Sociocultural Theory

Sociocultural theory moves beyond focusing on the internal process of building meaning to emphasize the importance of social interaction in learning to read and reading itself. According to Vygotsky (1978), children learn through direct contact with more knowledgeable and experienced others—parents, siblings, and teachers. Adult mentors or peers model the process of reading, explain it, and provide sufficient support so that younger and less proficient individuals can complete cognitive tasks that they normally could not achieve on their own. As novices become more competent, supports are gradually diminished. Over time and with continued practice these individuals become more confident and independent in applying their learning.

Reading aloud to young children is an ideal example of sociocultural theory in action. As the parent reads to the child, the child learns how to hold the book, how to turn the pages, and how to track print from left to right. Over time the child takes over some of the reading tasks—pointing to and naming the pictures, and reading some of the familiar parts. Later on, the child reads the book on his or her own, but the adult remains nearby to offer assistance. This same process of adult modeling and support translates well to a great deal of classroom instruction.

A major contribution of sociocultural theory, transactional theory, and critical literacy theory is the notion that one correct meaning does not exist in the text, awaiting release by the reader. Readers who transact with the same text will respond differently because of the unique constellation of personal experiences and general knowledge each person brings to the reading experience. These theories are important because they emphasize the role of discussion in the classroom. When students discuss the same text, they offer different, and at times, conflicting interpretations. It is through the negotiation of these differing views that critical and higher-level thinking occurs. In Chapters 6, 8, and 10 we highlight the important role of discussion in developing reading comprehension.

How do these models relate to the attributes of a good reader? Of the four attributes of good readers, motivation plays a larger role in transactional theory because the reader determines whether to take an efferent or aesthetic response. Motivation also comes into play when students have an opportunity to present and defend their views during animated discussions. In terms of knowledge, both personal, textual, and world knowledge are applied during the ongoing transaction between reader and text. Knowledge is vital in critical literacy theory, because we have to move beyond our knowledge of familiar contexts to discern and critique the assumptions of the author (R. Brown, 2008). However, the terms *metacognition* and *strategies* are not given high priority by educators concerned with critical literacy theory. Yet, it is easy to see how these attributes would be relevant. For instance, reading from a critical perspective means having to think about your own beliefs and assumptions and those of the authors. Furthermore, the use of cognitive reading strategies such as self-questioning, inferring, and making connections are essential when thinking about and responding to the hidden biases in texts.

The Engaged Reader and the Constructively Responsive Reader

When we turn our attention to two models of proficient reading: the engaged reader (Guthrie & Wigfield, 2000), and the constructively responsive reader (Pressley & Afflerbach, 1995), we gain some new insights about comprehension and the teaching of reading comprehension. The engaged model of proficient reading emphasizes the interaction of cognition and motivation (Guthrie, McGough, Bennett, & Rice, 1996). For even if children can read, they may decline to do so.

When embedded in an authentic context, using strategies becomes a tool to enhance comprehension and learning—and not an end in itself. Motivated and metacognitive readers tend to use strategies more than their disinterested, nonregulating counterparts. Students who select texts that are conceptually interesting but demanding are more likely to retain important ideas and persist longer than individuals who can't relate to the text. Furthermore, personally motivated reading for learning and pleasure, so central to engaged reading, is linked to reading achievement and even compensates for low family income and weak educational background (Guthrie, 2001).

The model of the constructively responsive reader (Pressley & Afflerbach, 1995) incorporates the four broad attributes of good readers presented earlier in this chapter (motivation, strategies, knowledge, and metacognition) to describe the complex nature of the reading process. Pressley and Afflerbach (1995) summarized 40 studies in which adult readers talked about their thinking. Because of the research they selected to review, they did not deal with comprehension processing that occurs outside of awareness, the intricacies of construction and integration of meaning, or the insights of young or developing readers. Mature readers think in deep and complex ways and it involves more than construction and integration. They seek information, evaluate information, and read in a strategic and passionate manner. These last two models remind us that creating highly engaged and thoughtful readers is a multifaceted, demanding process.

Why Models of Reading?

With the exception of the simple view of reading, all these theories form the foundation for the instructional guidelines in this book. For example, Kintsch's (1998) construction–integration theory underscores the necessity of making connections among ideas in a text and integrating them with prior knowledge. Transactional theory spotlights the unique contribution each individual brings to the construction of meaning. Sociocultural and critical theories demonstrate that reading fundamentally shapes and is shaped by the multitude of contexts in which literacy occurs. Finally, multidimensional models of proficient reading lie at the heart of this book. All these models provide educators with worthwhile goals to strive for during comprehension instruction. Of course, we know that not all students will become highly competent and responsive readers—even with the best of instruction. However, as educators, we can train our sights on this outcome. These models can chart our way as we steer toward our desired destination of the proficient reader.

LOOKING BACK, LOOKING FORWARD

This chapter illustrated the complex nature of reading comprehension by focusing on the many characteristics of good readers and the resources they draw upon in each reading experience. Good readers efficiently access and use relevant knowledge; they are aware of their strengths and needs as readers, they navigate the reading process with competence, they intentionally deploy strategies to build meaning and resolve confusions, and they are motivated to engage in the process. How each teacher understands the nature of comprehension influences instruction and assessment. We hope that the information provided in this and the remaining chapters in this book will help you with decisions about teaching comprehension in your classroom.

In the next chapter, we look beyond the reader and examine the role of text and the context in the comprehension process. Teachers need to understand how texts work to teach reading comprehension. They also need to attend to the powerful influences that home and classroom exert on literacy learning. Comprehension instruction also differs when the teacher constructs his or her own curriculum or is handed a published reading program.

APPLICATIONS AND EXPLORATIONS

1. Learn more about the theories described in this chapter. Share a recent comprehension lesson with your colleagues or classmates and discuss which theory supports your lesson. This will help you to begin tracking the interrelationships among theory, research, and practice. For additional information, consult *Lenses on Reading* by Diane Tracey and Lesley Mandel Morrow (2012).

2. Conduct a think-aloud with a good and a weak comprehender using texts that are appropriate for their reading level. This will give you some insight into how students comprehend and think when decoding the words is not a problem.

3. Compare and contrast the various theories mentioned in this chapter. Here's one idea to get started. Create a matrix with the names of various theories listed in the vertical column (e.g., transactional, construction–integration, engaged reader). Across the top of this matrix, list prominent characteristics of that theory (e.g., a theorist associated with the theory; key or distinguishing features; the ways the theory impacts instructional practice, such as the selection of texts and the roles and responsibilities of the teacher and students). Finally, fill in the cells of your matrix. This activity should help you better understand the similarities and differences among the theories that inform comprehension instruction.

CHAPTER 2

Beyond the Reader

Texts and Contexts of Comprehension

In the first chapter, we focused on what the reader brings to the comprehension process. We explored proficient reading by considering how meaning construction and integration hypothetically occurs. Now we move beyond the reader by linking the good comprehender model to instruction. Comprehension includes four elements that influence the construction of meaning:

1. The *reader,* who engages in the comprehension process.
2. The *text,* which is read for comprehension.
3. The *purpose, task,* or *activity,* which is undertaken for comprehension.
4. The *context,* which surrounds and also bounds the comprehending event.

Scholars hired by the RAND Corporation (Snow, 2002) developed this four-component model of reading comprehension. However, we feel it creates unnecessary complexity. We believe that the content of reading comprehension, and especially its instruction, cannot be considered separately from a reader's purpose or task for reading. Therefore, our revised model, in Figure 2.1, makes the task and purpose part of the context of the reading.

Imagine a fifth grader who selected the novel *Hatchet* (Paulsen, 1987) for summer beach reading. Basking in the sun, this reader becomes engrossed in the main character's repeated attempts to survive while dealing with the pain of his parents' divorce. Now read *Hatchet* in a classroom and surround it with graphic organizers and a computer-based Accelerated Reader assessment. The whole reading experience shifts. The purpose for reading

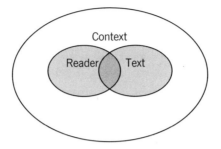

FIGURE 2.1. Elements of reading comprehension instruction.

is no longer aesthetic appreciation, getting lost in a good book; instead it becomes a means to achieve academic accountability. Context matters in literacy learning.

GOALS FOR THIS CHAPTER

✓ Explore reading habits and attitudes by profiling three students.

✓ Review the elements of comprehension.

✓ Think about selecting readable texts.

✓ Examine the contexts of reading comprehension.

A PROFILE OF THREE STUDENTS

Say hello to Miguel, Brody, and Tanisha. These students and their teachers will reappear throughout the book. We use them to illustrate how comprehension instruction must change with the context, materials, and abilities of the readers. Miguel, who is in Mrs. Wilson's sixth-grade classroom, is a member of a fantasy book club with five other students. Miguel, who reads above his grade level, is a third-generation American who grew up in a middle-class household where Spanish was spoken regularly. Although he is a fluent speaker of Spanish, he is equally facile with English. In his spare time, he enjoys reading, particularly fantasy, science fiction, and mysteries. He has traveled extensively with his educated parents.

Currently, Miguel is reading *Rowan of Rin* (Rodda, 2004) in preparation for a group meeting with Mrs. Wilson. The novel recounts the adventures of an initially timid Rowan who helps to save the villagers of mythical Rin from imminent disaster. As Miguel reads, he writes on a two-column chart the attributes and development of one of the main characters. In the first column, he notes the character's traits and personality. He also records any changes he observes in the character's thinking or feeling over time. In the second column, he substantiates each claim, citing proof from the text.

Brody, a student in Mr. Rodriguez's second-grade classroom, is studying weather, learning to describe it and to understand its causes and effects. Brody, who comes from a rural community, reads below grade level. He has been diagnosed with reading difficulties, is easily distracted, and has struggled with reading and writing since kindergarten. Decoding and spelling cause him considerable problems and he reads haltingly. Whenever possible, he avoids reading, both in and out of school.

Brody is working on an integrated social studies, science, and literacy unit. He is evaluating the usefulness of a website to answer a question about the weather. He reviews a website that Mr. Rodriguez bookmarked earlier. Brody begins by clicking the first link. He tries hard to understand what is on the page—but to no avail. He rereads the first passage but still can't tell whether the information on the page is useful. So he looks earnestly at the visuals, hoping that they will help him. Brody realizes this website is too difficult to read on his own. So, he selects another website that appears more promising.

Tanisha, a fourth-grader in Ms. Fogel's class, is reading a leveled book, from her basal reading program, with her teacher and other members of her small homogeneous reading group. Tanisha has grown up in a low-income, urban neighborhood. She can read most grade-level texts independently, but needs some support when reading science and social studies material. She much prefers fiction to nonfiction texts when given the choice, but in general, she dislikes reading in her spare time, both in and out of school.

Ms. Fogel assigned her on-grade students a leveled reader after they completed the main selection from the basal program. This leveled text reinforces vocabulary and provides additional practice in finding the main idea, the skill of the week. Tanisha dutifully completes her assigned work in the allotted time.

Although the ultimate goal of these three readers is to understand text, what they gain from their in-class reading will vary from one reader to the next. Each student lives and works in multiple contexts and each of these contexts influences his or her growth as a reader and writer. Over time, these children have developed personal views about the nature and purpose of reading and have established attitudes about the role that reading plays in their lives. Their beliefs are shaped by the materials and lessons in their classroom, the standards and goals of their school, and the current political context of reading instruction in the United States. For example, Miguel's instructional context emphasizes reading for pleasure and for learning literature concepts. In Brody's classroom, acquisition of knowledge drives instruction. For Tanisha, a primary learning objective is the mastery of comprehension skills and strategies. The instruction experienced by each student represents one of the three frameworks that we target in the book: literature-based instruction, inquiry learning with informational texts, and reading with a basal reading series. However, we want to make an important point here. Students whose literacy block is either literature based or inquiry oriented must read richly from literature and informational texts throughout the day and students working with a basal reading program must read beyond it.

THE ELEMENTS OF COMPREHENSION

Whether a *reader* successfully and deeply understands a text depends upon numerous factors:

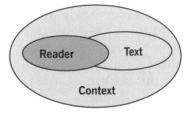

- *Cognitive and neurological abilities*: the biological inheritance that readers bring to reading, such as their capacities for perception, attention, memory, and language learning (Pressley et al., 1989).
- *Precursor skills*: knowledge of grammar, phonological awareness, decoding ability, sight-word recognition, which influences fluency, and in turn, comprehension.
- *Vocabulary knowledge*: word knowledge, which predicts reading comprehension (Davis, 1944) and accounts for much of a reader's comprehension ability.
- *Conceptual knowledge*: conceptual, disciplinary knowledge and associated vocabulary; familiarity with other texts, genres, and literary conventions.
- *Personal experiences*: the knowledge gained through living one's life and engaging in the world, including the narratives of our lives about love, loss, bravery, and reconciliation. Personal experiences also include knowledge obtained from direct home and community experiences, which includes literacy practices. These socially and culturally based "funds of knowledge" from out-of-school settings constitute a rich resource that often is overlooked, unacknowledged, or neglected in academic settings (Moll et al., 1992).
- *Strategic knowledge*: the knowledge of powerful tactics that supports meaning construction and integration; knowledge of what strategies

are and how to apply them, as well as why, when, and where to use them.

- *Interest and motivation*: individual preferences, the beliefs about ability and competence; expectations for success; goals motivating achievement, persistence, and performance; and values and internal or external reasons prompting choices and task completion.
- *Metacognition:* the knowledge of personal strengths and limitations as a reader and the ability to set purposes for reading, monitor comprehension, eliminate obstacles to comprehension, and to evaluate performance and understanding relative to goals.

Text is a second key element in teaching reading comprehension. Although text traditionally referred to printed words, the term now denotes anything that symbolically communicates information. In our swiftly changing digital world, text signifies not only traditional printed content but also digital material 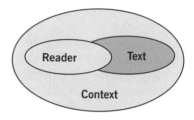 that communicates information through writing, still or moving images, sound, and the complex interplay of these forms on the Internet. Reading these texts requires multiliteracies and new literacies (Cope & Kalantzis, 2000; Leu et al., 2008).

DEFINING AND SELECTING READABLE TEXT

Text matters in reading comprehension instruction for two reasons. First, it is vital for teachers to know how to choose texts or to guide students when they make their own selections. The more a teacher knows about how a text works, the more professional judgment can be applied to matching a text to the needs and interests of a particular student. We introduce the factors involved in text selection now but expand upon them later when we consider teaching literature and informational text.

Second, teachers need to understand how a text works in order to plan and teach reading comprehension. Particular features of text can aid or thwart comprehension, including (1) the genre of a particular text, (2) the level of conceptual abstraction, (3) the transparency of the text's organization, (4) the clarity of sentence structure and syntax, (5) the difficulty of the vocabulary, and (6) the readability of the text.

The Common Core State Standards (CCSS; NGA & CCSSO, 2010), adopted by 45 states, describe the types of texts that students should be able to read. As students move up through the grades, they need to read a range of harder and more diverse texts. A third-grade student is expected to read mostly on-grade-level books but to occasionally venture into fourth-grade terrain. The difficulty of a text is important because one goal of the CCSS is to reverse the "general, steady decline . . . in the difficulty and likely also the sophistication of content of the texts students have been asked to read in school since 1962" (Appendix A, p. 2).

Matching Students and Texts

Part of improving comprehension instruction is picking the right book. Matching students to texts requires evaluating the texts, knowing your students, and considering the goals of your classroom activities. We strongly recommend examining the texts and considering their readability and accessibility. Readability is a measure of text difficulty; accessibility refers to other qualities of writing such as organization, clarity, and graphics. You must also consider the students' knowledge, backgrounds, capabilities, needs, and interests. Finally, it is important to think about instructional goals. Is the student reading this book independently or will he or she require some instructional support?

Readability formulas are the oldest quantitative tools we have to assess the difficulty of text. Included in this category are well-established tools like the Fry readability formula, the Flesch–Kincaid formula, and the Lexile system. Readability formulas use estimates of vocabulary difficulty and sentence complexity to determine the grade level of the text—or its readability level. Using the Fry readability formula (Fry, 1977) one counts the number of sentences and the number of syllables within a 100-word sample of a text. Fewer sentences mean longer sentences and often, greater complexity. More syllables mean more multisyllabic words and therefore more difficult vocabulary. These measures are then repeated several times across a long text with the results averaged. A chart plots the number of syllables against the number of sentences to indicate grade level of the text. In theory the grade level of the books can be matched to the reading level of the student, but such matches are always approximations that must be verified as the child reads.

You can also measure the readability of a text using Microsoft Word or readability formulae available on the Internet *(www.readabilityformulas.com)*. Microsoft Word uses the Flesch–Kincaid formula and it is found within the grammar tool on most versions of Microsoft Word.

The Lexile system is a newer, quantitative approach to determining readability. When using the Fry formula, one samples small segments of the text to produce the score. In the Lexile system, a computer analyzes entire books using estimates of vocabulary difficulty and sentence complexity as the measure of readability. This computer analysis yields a statistic for each text, known as a Lexile score, which ranges from 200L to 1500 + L, with a BR level for beginning readers. The Lexile score loosely corresponds to a grade-level designation. The Lexile website *(www.lexile.com)* lists the reading levels of tens of thousands of books. A book can be assigned a Lexile score or a student can receive a Lexile score, if he or she takes one of several reading tests. Many current reading tests, including the Gates–MacGinitie Reading Test (MacGinitie, MacGinitie, Maria, & Dryer, 2000) and the Qualitative Reading Inventory–5 (QRI-5; Leslie & Caldwell, 2010), now include a Lexile score along with grade level, percentile, and standard scores. Because both a student and a text are on the same scale, matching them is relatively easy.

Hiebert (2012) has suggested that the Lexile score alone is less useful in determining the difficulty of a book than the mean word frequency and the mean sentence length, which form the bases of the Lexile score. These two separate scores can be obtained by typing in 500 words of a book into the Lexile Analyzer *(www.lexile.com)*. With these results the teacher can determine if it is the difficulty of the vocabulary or just the sentence length that is contributing to the book's difficulty. A book with a modest vocabulary challenge but long sentences might not present difficulty to a given child.

Measures of readability are always imperfect because they fail to consider many factors of text difficulty and accessibility, including the reader's background knowledge and interests, the organization of the text, the clarity of the writing, and the author's voice. Book leveling, a system introduced by Irene Fountas and Gay Su Pinnell (2009) examines and ranks books on a scale from *A* and *B* for beginning readers up through *Z* for seventh- and eighth-grade readers. The book-leveling system considers the content of the book, the support provided by the illustrations, length, language structure, format, and the appropriateness of the text to the readers' experiences. Since many of these judgments are subjective, leveling can be used alongside the more objective readability formulas (Fry, 2002).

A more sophisticated analysis of text complexity is afforded by the Coh-Metrix procedure *(http://cohmetrix.memphis.edu/cohmetrixpr/index.html)*. The Coh-Metrix analysis begins with readability and then yields substantial information on text cohesion, or how clearly the ideas support and explain one another. This approach analyzes the way that different ideas in a text go together. Highly cohesive texts explicitly include text features that broadcast connections among words (signal words like *because* and *since*) and larger units of text. Thus, they scaffold the reader. Less cohesive texts, in contrast, present greater challenges because readers have to figure out how the distinct ideas in a text link together. All these quantitative measures are useful for evaluating text difficulty, but other factors come into play when selecting texts for comprehension instruction.

The CCSS (NGA & CCSSO, 2010) recommend three dimensions for selecting text: (a) quantitative, (b) qualitative, and (c) reader–text match. The quantitative dimension includes readability measures such as Lexile scores or grade levels computed from one of several readability formulae. Hiebert (2012) suggests that qualitative aspects of text can be determined by considering four factors as teachers examine a book. These factors are presented below in Figure 2.2, which is slightly adapted from Hiebert (2012).

The final step is matching the student and the text, always considering the purpose. For example, a text with a simple structure, a clear unambiguous theme, and minimal knowledge demands might be an excellent choice for independent reading. During teacher-guided instruction a more

Dimension	Stage 1	Stage 3	Stage 5
Levels of meaning	Single level of meaning (often supported by illustrations) Aims/themes explicitly stated (*The Bear's Toothache*, McPhail, 1988)	More than one level of meaning (*Frederick*, Lionni, 1973) a book about responsibility and the role of art Requires inferring of characters' motives and/or how text features may influence plot	Multiple levels require drawing extensively on reading/experiences from other sources Implicit purpose may be hidden or obscure (*Holes*, Sachar, 1998)
Structure	Texts follow structure of common genres (e.g., simple story structure or enumerative exposition) (*Baby Whales Drink Milk*, Esbensen, 1994)	More complex story structures, cause and effect relationships in exposition (*From Seed to Plant*, Gibbons, 1993)	Foreshadowing, flashback, multiple interacting plots or mixture structures (problem solution and description) in exposition
Language conventions and clarity	Literal language (*Frog and Toad*, Lobel, 1994)	Figurative language, irony (*Matilda*, Dahl, 1988)	Literary: high level of figurative, metaphorical language (*Out of the Dust*, Hesse, 1999)
Knowledge demands	Simple theme (*Frog and Toad*, Lobel, 1994)	Complex ideas interwoven (*Ramona Forever*, Cleary, 1995)	Interconnected themes (*The View from Saturday*, Konigsberg, 1996)

FIGURE 2.2. Qualitative dimensions of text complexity.

challenging text might be in order because the teacher can provide some of the required knowledge and assist the student with negotiating complex language, multiple themes, and different levels of meaning.

Range of Texts

Texts influence the growth of students' reading comprehension. To succeed in school and beyond, students need exposure to a wide range of literature and informational texts. Reading many easy books will build fluency; reading many challenging books will build vocabulary, knowledge, and comprehension. Students who stick to a narrow range of texts probably will find that material easy to understand, but they may not benefit from struggling with something new. Figure 2.3, from the CCSS (NGA & CCSSO, 2010), defines what students should be reading in school.

Literature

The broad category of literature includes several genres or categories, each of which can be divided into subgenres. Each genre conforms to a culturally accepted and conventional style, form, and content. A text belongs to a particular genre when it exhibits the features of other pieces of writing in the same group. Styles of homes can be likened to genres of literature. Each type has unique characteristics that make it recognizable. For instance,

---

COMMON CORE STATE STANDARDS

Over time, students are expected to comprehend a range of texts from a variety of cultures and historical periods. The range of materials specified by the CCSS includes both literature and informational texts.

Literature			Informational Text
Stories	*Dramas*	*Poetry*	*Literary Nonfiction, Historical, Scientific, and Technical Texts*
Includes children's adventure stories, folktales, legends, fables, fantasy, realistic fiction, and myth.	Includes staged dialogue and brief familiar scenes.	Includes nursery rhymes and the subgenres of the narrative poem, limerick, and free verse.	Includes biographies and autobiographies, history, social science, and the arts, technical texts, including directions, forms, and information displayed in graphic form and digital sources on a range of topics.

FIGURE 2.3. What students should be reading in school, according to the CCSS.

Tuscan-style homes, which look like villas, are built of pale stone or stucco, burnt-orange terra-cotta roofs, and graceful arching doorways. Thus, the genre of drama specifies a form of fiction that depicts a performance by actors speaking lines before an audience. A drama can be contemporary or historical, humorous or tragic. Familiarity with the broad genres of literature, drama, stories, and poetry clues you to their structure and organization. When readers know something about the characteristics and purposes of genres, their comprehension improves (Goldman & Rakestraw, 2000).

Knowledge of subgenres is even more beneficial. For example, stories can be divided into realistic fiction, historical fiction, fantasy, science fiction, and folktales. Each subgenre exhibits its own structure, purpose, and conventions. Realistic fiction includes short stories and novels that are set in current time and that involve real people who struggle with contemporary issues. Although written as a story, they help readers to empathize and relate to the entanglements of others who are just like them. In contrast, fantasy features improbable settings and characters that are often set in imaginary lands and times. Subgenres sometimes overlap. For example, fairytales are a type of folktale. They can share elements of fantasy—such as witches and fairy godmothers. Sonnets and haikus are both subgenres of poetry with different structures. Sonnets, which come from Europe, are 14-line poems, written in iambic pentameter, that follow a specific rhyming scheme. In contrast, haikus, which are associated with Japan, are descriptive, three-line poems that adopt a five-syllable, seven-syllable, and five-syllable structure.

The purpose of a text is reflected in its subgenre—and each one has its own conventions. Authors adopt a particular subgenre to best meet an intended purpose. A fable entertains young children with a short tale and conveys a moral or ethical principle. We also know that fables showcase the exploits and foibles of beasts that take on human attributes. Historical fiction entertains readers with common human themes but teaches important lessons about particular historical eras. We all know of fairytales that begin with the customary phrase *Once upon a time . . .* , and end with *. . . They lived happily ever after,* and showcase the triumph of good over evil, and the vindication of the powerless over the powerful.

Recognizing how an author organizes the ideas in a text, the *text structure,* improves comprehension. Ample research has documented that when children receive direct instruction in text structure, their comprehension grows because the structure serves as a map to the important ideas (Fitzgerald & Spiegel, 1983). The simplest literary stories follow a story grammar that includes the following elements: characters, setting, problem, goal, events, and solution. Instruction in story grammar, often called story mapping, guides students to analyze a story into its basic parts, keeping them in sequence. The knowledge of text structure helps students make predictions, remember key ideas, and retell what they have read (Armbruster, Anderson, & Ostertag, 1987; Gersten, Fuchs, Williams, & Baker, 2001; Williams, Stafford, Lauer, Hall, & Pollini, 2009).

As students move into the upper grades, the number of structural features of literature they encounter increases; and thus, simple story mapping inadequately reflects the complexity of novels and some short stories. While some elements like character and setting remain easy to identify, others may be subtler, requiring more inferential thinking. Noting a character's goals, motives, and feelings require greater interpretive skill. Literature also becomes more complex as each event in a story includes an action, a physical or mental response, and a consequence. Plot follows a series of rising actions; tension and suspense build until the climax is reached. Then, there is a gradual unfolding, or denouement, as problems untangle through a process of falling action.

In any given novel, there may be multiple subplots and conflicts to confront and resolve. Also, the author may employ additional plot devices that give a reader a glimpse into the future through foreshadowing or thrusts him or her into the past through flashbacks. All of these demands require the reader to develop a more nuanced view of the structure of literature.

In the upper elementary years, the problems in stories are often referred to as conflicts—individual versus individual, individual versus nature, individual versus self, individual versus technology. These various types of conflicts, as they are expressed in the development of the characters, are often a major clue to the underlying theme of the work. Theme is an expression of the big ideas in the story, a timeless view of human nature.

Below the text structure lie other text features that help or hinder the comprehension of literature. We refer here to the relational links that a reader must build between ideas, between pronouns and nouns, and between sentences. These mandatory connections help to form the text base, which we described in Chapter 1 when we introduced the construction–integration model. Consider this very short passage from the opening of *Sylvester and the Magic Pebble* (Steig, 1969):

> Sylvester Duncan lived with his mother and father at Acorn Road in Oatdale. One of his hobbies was collecting pebbles of unusual shape and size.
>
> On a rainy Saturday during vacation he found a quite extraordinary one. It was flaming red, shiny, and perfectly round, like a marble. As he was studying the remarkable pebble, he began to shiver, probably from excitement, and the rain felt cold on his back. "I wish it would stop raining," he said. (n.p.)

In this segment the reader must make some important connections. The phrase, *a quite extraordinary one*, must be linked to the pebbles in the first paragraph and then through the pronoun *it* to the pebble's description. Further on, the reader must link the descriptive words *extraordinary* to *remarkable* to build a full understanding of the pebble, because the illustration adds little to the author's description of the pebble.

Genre, text structure, and the myriad connections between ideas represent a silent contract between author and reader. The author selects particular genres, subgenres, and text structures to alert the reader to hold certain expectations during reading. This understanding between the author and reader supports the construction of meaning. How does it work? Experiences with the purposes and characteristics of various genres and subgenres can promote students' development of deep textual knowledge. Those with more knowledge about texts are better equipped to comprehend an array of literature. What is more, studying text structure and genre enables readers to predict what lies ahead and to zoom in on important ideas. In fact, one contribution to poor reading is the failure of readers to pick up on the cues and conventions that authors employ to aid readers in recognizing particular text structures and genres (Goldman & Rakestraw, 2000).

Informational Text

Comprehension of informational texts also requires an understanding of genre, text structure, and the same small connections necessary for coherence found in literature. Within the broad category of informational text there are the genres of literary nonfiction, historical, scientific, and technical texts. Literary nonfiction includes biography, autobiography, memoirs, and some historical accounts. These texts follow a narrative structure and typically include setting, characters, problems, conflict, plots, and resolution. Informational text, which also comes in a non-narrative or expository form, can be found in a science or social science textbook, newspaper, magazine, or the Internet.

The genres of historical, scientific, and technical texts follow several text structures. Authors select different text structures depending upon their purposes for writing—and a single chapter might contain several of them. There are distinct text structures for describing, expressing, explaining something, or persuading others to agree on a specific issue. It is unlikely that a teacher would teach all of these structures within an academic year, but there is ample evidence that a concentrated focus on one of these structures for 8 weeks or more will improve students' comprehension—even for struggling readers (Williams et al., 2002). The most common expository structures are listed in Figure 2.4.

Structure	Description	Example	Common Signal Words
Description	What something looks, feels, smells, sounds, tastes like, or is composed of	Characteristics of a hurricane	*Characteristics, features, to illustrate, for example, for instance, such as, is like, looks like*
Sequence	When or in what order things happen	How a seed becomes a plant	*First, next, then, finally, first, second, third, before, after, when, now*
Problem–solution	What went wrong and how it was or could be fixed	The Exxon Valdez sank and spilled oil all over the bay, requiring a community-wide and corporate clean-up	*Problem is, because, in order to, so that, trouble was, if/then, solved, puzzle/answer*
Cause–effect	How one event or a series of events lead to another	The Civil War and its causes; the aftermath of the war and its effects	*Because, therefore, cause, effect, so, as a result, consequently, hence, due to, thus, this led to, brought about, produce, trigger, affect*
Compare–contrast	How things, people, and events are alike and different	Compare and contrast sedimentary, igneous, and metamorphic rocks	*Both, alike, unalike, but, however, than, on the other hand, but, similarly, although, also, in contrast, in comparison, same, different, either/or, just like*

FIGURE 2.4. Expository text structures in nonfiction.

In addition to using familiar patterns, or text structures, to organize ideas, authors of informational text can strive to make a text "considerate" to help a reader locate and retain important information (T. H. Anderson & Armbruster, 1984). A considerate text has topic sentences, clear headings, and subheadings that foretell information to come. They also include bold-facing of key facts and concepts, visuals that support text content, hyper-links in digital text that connect to background information or definitions, and chapter-ending summaries that restate important topics. All of these textual devices act as a map making it easier for the reader to follow the author's ideas and arguments. However, considerateness alone does not ensure better comprehension. Not all easy-to-comprehend informational texts include all these features. For example, the books of Seymour Simon lack most textual features like headings, subheading, and bolding, but instead feature rich photographs that provide text support. Furthermore, even when textbooks contain many features of considerateness, they may still be difficult to understand (Beck, McKeown, Sinatra, & Loxterman, 1991).

The clarity and engagement of the writing will affect comprehension. Remember the construction–integration model that has guided our discussion of comprehension? It requires that a reader forge connections among ideas, words, and sentences and then integrate those understandings with prior knowledge. A text becomes more comprehensible when it is easier to make connections among ideas and when the burden of prior knowledge is eased. This is especially true when reading science, geography, civics, or history—a situation in which the reader's prior knowledge may be lacking. So an informational text that supports comprehension should include the following cohesive devices:

- Spelled-out relationships between pronouns and nouns.
- Sufficient explanation to compensate for a lack of prior knowledge.
- Clear links between new concepts and previous ideas.
- Obvious cause-and-effect relationships among ideas.

Isabel Beck and her colleagues adopted these guidelines and revised fourth-grade social studies texts (Beck et al., 1991). In rewriting the originals, the researchers ensured that all cohesive devices were clear. For example, they added nouns when the pronoun–noun relationships were vague and incorporated knowledge that many readers might lack. Such changes made the revised texts longer. They also raised readability levels by 1 year. Yet, students' comprehension improved despite the added length and increasing reading level.

The final text feature that affects comprehension is the way an author speaks to the reader, or the *voice* an author uses to communicate thoughts and feelings. A text with voice does not have the "leaded, impersonal tone" (Ravitch, 1989, p. 27) that attempts to convey objectivity by eliminating any personal touches. Instead, an author uses language that shows that the topic is personally meaningful—and invites the reader to think so too. In Figure 2.5, compare the short passage from a traditional textbook (Sample 1, Davidson & Stoff, 2011) to a second one (Sample 2, Hakim, 2003) that we think is more engaging.

To add voice to historical texts Hakim (2003) uses several techniques. First, her writing is vivid with far more sensory details. Second, she eases the burden of prior knowledge by including potentially unknown details. Third, there is an element of humor in her writing. Adding voice to a textbook potentially makes information more memorable and enhances a student's ability to answer comprehension questions correctly (Beck et al.,

---

Sample 1

The first colonist arrived in Virginia in the spring of 1607. About 100 men sailed into Chesapeake Bay and built a fort they called Jamestown. It would prove to be England's first permanent settlement in North America.

Jamestown barely survived its first year. It was located on a swampy peninsula where insects thrived in warm weather. During the first summer, many colonists caught diseases such as malaria, and died.

The colony had another serious problem. Many of the colonists had no intention of doing the hard farmwork needed to grow crops. Those men who came to the colony were not farmers. They were skilled in other trades.

Sample 2

When the first colonists arrived, there were no friends to greet them. No houses were ready for them. They had to start from scratch—and I do mean scratch, as in scratching. The early colonists often had to live in huts of branches and dirt, or Indian wigwams, or even caves, and none of those places was bug-proof. And, of course, they had to scratch a living out of the ground.

Later colonists lived in small wooden houses with one or two rooms. Eventually, some lived in fine houses. A few lived in mansions, with beautiful furniture and paintings and dishes and silver. But no one had a bathroom like you have, or electric lights, or a furnace, or running water, or kitchen appliances. And very few people lived in mansions anyway.

FIGURE 2.5. A comparison of two American history textbooks. Sample 1 is from Davidson and Stoff (2011); Sample 2 is from Hakim (2003).

1991). What's more, voice turns writing into something far more enticing for readers.

Our discussion of text points out many of the factors that must be considered in selecting and using a text to develop reading comprehension. First, the text used to teach reading should be at the students' instructional level. Various leveling systems make it easy to find out the readability of many books and match them to individual students. However, don't stop with readability. It is also important to consider the level of meaning, the knowledge demands, the clarity of structure, and the quality of writing. For younger and less adept readers, texts with a clearly defined structure are preferable. While a clear structure benefits young and struggling readers, stronger readers should be challenged to read materials with less transparent text structure (McNamara, Kintsch, Butler-Songer, & Kintsch, 1996).

A final thought about text is really about instruction. Student choice is vital in developing comprehension. When Cathy Collins Block and her colleagues created and studied successful comprehension intervention programs, they found that choice was an essential factor (Block, Parris, Reed, Whiteley, & Cleveland, 2009). Once the teacher and the students defined the topic or the theme, the students selected one of several books to read. Choice gives students some control over learning, thereby promoting motivation.

THE CONTEXTS OF READING COMPREHENSION

The final element of comprehension, the *context*, can be defined as the external circumstances surrounding the reading act. Without question, in recent decades there has been an increasing emphasis on the importance of context in comprehension instruction. Much of the increased

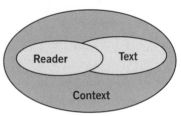

emphasis on the social context of reading can be traced to the theoretical work of Lev Vygotsky, whose work was introduced in Chapter 1. Context has been conceptualized far more broadly to encompass the numerous ways that it affects a reader's meaning construction.

There are three major assumptions that underlie Vygotsky's (1978) sociocultural theory. First, learning happens through social interactions, with language being the tool that enables those interactions. Adults explain and model how to do and think, and the child internalizes the oral language of the adults. Then, the child uses the internalized oral language to guide behavior. For example, imagine a parent teaching a child to make scrambled eggs. The adult explains and models the process (Break the egg over the bowl; beat the eggs completely . . .). When this language is internalized, the child silently repeats these words to guide his or her actions when the adult is no longer present.

The first Vygotskian assumption connects to the second one—that learning requires a knowledgeable parent, mentor, peer, or teacher. More experienced or knowledgeable people are in a position to help others. This notion, in turn, leads us to the third Vygotskian assumption—the zone of proximal development (ZPD).

At the core of the ZPD is the notion that carefully calibrated support given by more experienced individuals enables learners to accomplish far more than they ever could on their own. At the bottom of the zone is the child's actual developmental level—or what that child can manage individually without help. The rest of the zone represents what the child can do when provided with adequate guidance. Initially, the child needs more support; but later, far less is required as skill develops.

When Vygotsky's sociocultural theory is applied to literacy practices, the social context is front and center (Heath, 1983). Parents, grandparents, siblings, and preschool teachers serve as sources of initial support for young children. By participating with others in early, out-of-school literacy practices, children bring vastly different experiences and knowledge about literacy to school (Snow, 2002, p. 16). When these children enter kindergarten it is the job of the teacher to model and provide the support to move the children from where they are to higher levels of achievement. Teachers, aides, and even other children can provide the necessary support.

Think of the context as a series of concentric rings that expand outward from the reader. The first and most obvious ring surrounding the reader is the classroom—and the messages that a teacher sends about reading instruction. The next ring is the school and school district, which exert an influence on reading above and beyond the classroom (Taylor, Pearson, Clark, & Walpole, 2000). Researchers have clearly documented that the school, and specifically the principal, affect the development of reading ability. Next comes the political climate in which reading instruction takes place. The most obvious political contexts impacting instruction today are No Child Left Behind (2002) and Race to the Top (2011). These political initiatives have prompted the high stakes testing regime that determines the rating of a school, and soon, a teacher's evaluation and compensation. The final ring is the social and cultural context, which spans the home and local neighborhood to the global community.

The Classroom

In this book, we focus on three literacy instructional frameworks: reading literature, reading informational texts to inquire, and reading with a basal reading program. These three frameworks can be found in any classroom. At times students read literature, selecting their own books and sharing with others. Often, students read to learn, using textbooks, trade books, and the Internet to build knowledge. Frequently, students receive their comprehension instruction via a basal reading program, as is the case in 74% of U.S. classrooms (Education Market Research, 2010). We briefly examine each of these contexts to observe how they influence the nature of reading comprehension and its instruction.

Literature-Based Reading Instruction

The most common model for literature-based instruction is the readers' workshop where students select their own books and read independently. Typically at the beginning of the readers' workshop, the teacher provides a lesson that introduces an important skill, strategy, or literary concept. Then students read independently or with a partner, work on short-response projects or longer writing tasks. While students are reading, the teacher confers with individuals to assess their needs, discuss problems, provide support, and suggest the next book. Later, students share their reading experiences with each other. Within the literature-based classroom teachers may employ small-group discussion, like literature circles (Daniels, 1996) or book clubs (McMahon & Raphael, 1997), in which students share their thinking and personal responses to texts.

The context of literature-based classrooms is individual choice and personal response. Although this structure is sufficiently flexible to promote various attributes of good comprehension, the emphasis on motivation is what first springs to mind. The teaching and learning of reading strategies is individualized and responds to the needs of the group and the individual. There is no preset sequence of instruction. Strategies may be taught to the whole group or reinforced individually during reading conferences. When functioning at their best, literature-based approaches engage students in ever-deepening cycles of describing, explaining, connecting, interpreting, and judging (Beach & Marshall, 1991).

In a literature-based framework, the teacher does not control the curriculum through a series of texts prescribed by a publisher. Instead the students determine what they want to read within the guidelines established by the teacher. The teacher may develop lists or tubs of leveled books from which the students may choose. He or she may designate themes like friendship, survival, or tolerance that students explore during the school year (Block, Parris, Reed, Whiteley, & Cleveland, 2009). Within these themes, students learn to choose books that match their reading abilities.

Classroom discussions, whether in small groups or with the entire class, constitute an important contextual factor. During discussion, students' social and cultural characteristics, knowledge, and backgrounds come into play as they jointly grapple with meaning and provide unique perspectives. We know that when we see a movie with others and then share our interpretations, we typically leave with deeper understandings than if we had not shared at all. Our views are consolidated or changed by negotiating meaning with individuals with alternative viewpoints. When many minds converge on the same topic, interpretations are likely to become more nuanced and elaborate than when they are developed on our own.

Inquiry-Oriented Reading Instruction

Inquiring to learn creates another context for comprehension instruction. More emphasis is placed on informational text, especially trade books, periodicals, and the Internet. Novels may be included in the inquiry class-room, especially historical fiction. Novels give depth and voice when facts alone cannot capture a battle, a political fight, or social changes in a given era. In the inquiry classroom, a teacher often begins with a common text that all students read. After the topic has been defined, students choose to read other books, articles, and Internet resources to learn more about a selected topic.

In this instructional framework, the goal of reading is to identify key facts, discern ideas, discuss thinking, and apply new learning. Comprehension strategies are useful cognitive tools in the inquiry classroom because sometimes the informational texts are difficult and the students lack prior knowledge. The teacher may develop strategies with the whole class or work with small groups of students. Students often collaborate. They construct meaning together, sharing perspectives and gaining insight. Students are motivated to learn and evaluate new ideas, not simply to become better readers.

Basal Reading Programs

Basal reading programs follow a routine that is dictated by the pacing of units, the structure of lessons, and the scope and sequence of instructional skills and strategies (Chambliss & Calfee, 1998). Basal reading programs are divided into six or more instructional units per year, which in turn are divided into weekly lessons. Both short literature and informational texts appear in the basal program, but literature predominates, especially in programs published prior to 2008. The goal of the program is to follow the curriculum, finish the lessons and the units, and by doing so, students will make progress in learning to read.

With some variation among programs, the lessons follow a set routine. Each week the teacher engages the students in a read-aloud to develop interest and activate prior knowledge. He or she then teaches a number of phonics, vocabulary, and comprehension skills targeted by the reading program. The students then read two or three selections, one from the main anthology and others from leveled books as the teacher asks page-by-page questions. Toward the end of the week, the teacher reviews previous skills, then moving on to grammar and writing. All this culminates with an end-of-week assessment on the vocabulary and skills covered that week.

Within a basal reading program, comprehension is predominantly about skill and strategy instruction and page-by-page guided reading. One or two skills are taught each week and a few are reviewed. Basal reading programs are less about developing knowledge or fostering motivation, and more about acquiring skills and strategies. This context drives many of the decisions the teacher makes. It influences the selection of materials because workbook practice takes precedence over extended reading of novels and nonfiction trade books. Skill proficiency takes precedence over personal response to literature. The programs foster a teacher-directed environment, where the teacher does most of the talking and the students respond. Generally speaking, developing students' individual initiative and self-monitored control of the comprehension process are not explicit goals.

Looking across Frameworks

In each reading framework, students sometimes set different purposes or goals for reading. They read for enjoyment, for longer-term learning, for critical evaluation, for gathering information, and for completing assignments. But often, the purpose for reading is dictated by the instructional framework itself. The literature-based framework encourages personal choice and response. Within the inquiry framework many students set personal goals and become deeply engaged with the text. Even within the basal classroom, many students still find the space to engage literature and informational text on their own terms.

The School, the District, and the State

Classroom teachers, especially those in public schools, do not operate as self-employed entrepreneurs; they work within a system that is influenced by the federal government, interpreted by the state, and then put into practice by the school district and their principal. In most public schools, accountability standards create a context for reading instruction that no teacher can ignore. Current political mandates require that all students must be assessed annually in reading and mathematics, starting in third grade. States then establish standards of performance and create assessments to measure these standards. Each school must achieve adequate yearly progress (AYP), which means that currently 86% of all students, including 86% of subgroups like African Americans, Hispanics, and special education students must pass their state test at a proficient level, although waivers to these rules have recently been granted to many states. This creates tremendous pressure especially in schools in high-poverty areas. If a school fails to make AYP, a series of punitive measures are put in place including mandated school reform, transfers of students to better schools, and eventually, total school reorganization. In some states performance on these tests is now linked to teacher evaluations and merit pay.

The instructional response to this political climate is teaching to the test (Shepard, 2010). State-mandated high-stakes tests spawn interim district tests or benchmark tests that drive data analysis and instructional decisions. The results of these interim assessments cause teachers to focus their work on specific standards (e.g., finding the main idea, or making an inference) until students demonstrate mastery. In fact, a flood of workbooks and test-taking practice books are published specifically to help teachers teach to the test. Schools spend literally hundreds of hours practicing giving tests, practicing test taking, and meeting to discuss test results (Goren, 2010). Thus, the context of reading comprehension becomes the state standards and the specific task of passing the test more than immersing students in activities that build their knowledge, strategies, metacognition, and intrinsic motivation. Because skills development is the dominant feature of the curriculum, the students experience reading as a series of short, unrelated passages and answering questions instead of using longer, more complex trade books and novels for learning. Teaching to the test squeezes out time for the appreciation of literature or reading for inquiry.

This bleak view varies from one public school to another depending on the influence of the principal and other leaders in and outside the school. In some schools the test dictates instructional practices; in others, the test is viewed as important but the leaders believe that a range of instructional practices builds literate students, with tests representing just one genre of instruction (Hornof, 2008).

Culture and Society

At the outer edge of our concentric rings of context is the culture and society in which the students live. Just consider the differences between Miguel's and Brody's neighborhoods. Miguel lives in an upper-middle-class community; Brody resides in a rural, working-class one. Miguel grows up with the clear expectation that he will go to college. His parents read all the time for a variety of reasons. Books, magazines, and newspapers pepper their home. They browse for information on iPads, send e-mails on smart phones, and read novels on their e-book readers.

Brody's family runs a farm on a shoestring budget. Although he is still young, this second grader is expected to enter the family business when he graduates from high school. The adults read little at home, but sometimes they read to Brody. They obtain their news from television and use the Internet regularly to maintain their business accounts and communicate via e-mail. The parents, who are concerned about their farm's viability, want Brody to do well and value education. However, their expectations for him do not extend to higher education. Reading for pleasure and information is not modeled at home compared to Miguel's household. With the lack of available printed texts coupled with his reading difficulties, Brody does not seek out books as a regular source of pleasure, escape, or information, partly because reading is difficult for him.

The peer group also exerts a strong influence on students' reading attitudes and behavior. Peer groups set their own standards about reading and books. Some elementary children get caught up in the latest book fad— *Harry Potter and the Sorcerer's Stone* (Rowling, 1999) or *Diary of a Wimpy Kid* (Kinney, 2006)—and urge each other on through competition while marveling at the next book in the series. However, with other groups it is not the norm for students, regardless of ability, to be seen reading or carrying books. If you saw the movie *Stand and Deliver*, the main character required three math textbooks. One book he kept at home, one in study hall, and one in his math classroom. He was willing, eventually eager, to learn math, but he would not carry a book. The book or the backpack would set him apart from his peers and they would then hassle him. Peter Dewitz (coauthor of this book) witnessed the same thing when he taught sixth-grade reading. Students simply would not carry books, even self-selected, attractive paperbacks. When the culture of the school and the culture of the peer group collide, the teacher must sensitively and creatively navigate the gulf between the two by leading children to a literate experience, but not at the expense of alienating them from their culture.

LOOKING BACK, LOOKING FORWARD

The elements of comprehension, the reader, the text, and the context are mutually interdependent. In the first chapter we concentrated primarily on the reader, whereas here we focused more on the text and the context. All are vital to creating a successful comprehension program.

As a teacher of reading comprehension you need to select texts with considerable care. You need to know the characteristics of comprehensible texts so you can match them to the needs of your students. Understanding concepts like genre, text structure, coherence, and voice will help you choose texts that will help your students learn well and develop their comprehension. Understanding texts will also help you plan your comprehension lessons. If you know where and why a text is difficult, you will know when to intervene and how to support your students. The more you understand about texts, the better you will be able to assist your students.

Context plays an important role in the development of reading comprehension. Some social contexts stimulate students' growth in reading, whereas others squelch it. Consider a literature-based classroom where children select their own books and engage in spirited discussions. However, this U.S. classroom, especially in public schools, does not operate independently of federal reform efforts and political agendas, including the current culture of high-stakes testing and accountability.

Reading comprehension is also affected by out-of-school contexts. The home, the neighborhood, and broader society influence what and how often children read. Although parents and guardians value reading and education, some facilitate it more vigorously than others for varied reasons. When the literacy practices at home are compatible with those in school, learning to read is easier than when the culture of the school and the home or peer group clash. Thus, it is important for any teacher of reading comprehension to know more about the intersecting contexts that encircle a reader and a text.

APPLICATIONS AND EXPLORATIONS

1. Select three fiction books and examine their readability using three methods: the Fry formula *(www.readabilityformulas.com/fry-graph-readability-formula.php)*, the Lexile level *(www.lexile.com)*, and the guided reading level (see Fountas & Pinnell, 2009). What do these three systems reveal? You might also enter a portion of the text into the Coh-Metrix system.

2. Select three texts on the same nonfiction topic and make sure one is a textbook. Examine these texts and look at the clarity of their structure, the cohesiveness of the language, the presence or absence of necessary prior knowledge, and the voice of the writer.

3. Find out how high-stakes testing is driving instruction in local public schools. If possible, interview a few public school teachers. See if you can compare the answers of a teacher who works in a high-poverty school to those of a teacher in an upper-middle-class school.

4. Interview a few children from one classroom and find out who reads at home and what they read. Extend that interview by asking students about the reading habits and preferences of their family and friends.

CHAPTER 3

Teaching Comprehension

In Mrs. Wilson's sixth-grade classroom the students begin their literacy block by watching a movie about a character named Hiccup, who struggles to become a brave warrior. Before the film starts, the students are given a graphic organizer about character development, and the teacher directs them to note Hiccup's appearance, actions and reactions, speech, and thoughts—as well as what the other characters in the feature-length cartoon have to say about him. The students will compare Hiccup to a character in their self-selected novel. This focus lesson lasts about 20 minutes and then the students disperse to various activities. Most students begin to read independently. As they do, Mrs. Wilson meets with the fantasy group, six students who are concentrating on the works of Emily Rodda. Later, Mrs. Wilson will get to her humor group if the students can bear to put down *Diary of a Wimpy Kid* (Kinney, 2002).

Mr. Rodriguez is teaching the topic of weather to his second graders. The students have been keeping weather charts recording temperature, precipitation, and wind speed. The teacher and the students generate a list of weather conditions on the board—rain, high winds, dark clouds, fog, and sunshine. Next, he asks students to develop a list of questions they have about weather because they have been focusing on the strategy of self-questioning. He wants the students to ask questions before, during, and after reading. Most want to discuss severe weather conditions and to know whether hurricanes and tornadoes can happen where they live in New York State. Mr. Rodriguez then introduces a series of trade books about severe weather to the students but asks them where else they might learn about weather. The whole class immediately suggests that they look on the Internet.

Ms. Fogel's fourth graders sit quietly while she reviews the learning center rotations for the day. She wants to see her yellow group first while the other students read in the classroom library or complete worksheets from the basal on cause and effect, reference sources, and synonyms/antonyms. Other students will develop a story in the writing center or partner-read to build their oral reading fluency. When the yellow group meets with the teacher they are supposed to bring their leveled book, *Animals on the Move*, from their basal program. She begins by previewing the illustrations in the book and reminds the students to complete their concept map about migration. While the students read the story with their partners, the teacher asks a few factual questions and helps them complete the cause-and-effect worksheet.

All of these teachers are working to develop their students' reading comprehension. Each is working from a different framework and a different set of instructional beliefs. Mrs. Wilson is committed to a literature-based framework, Mr. Rodriguez is focusing much of his energy on inquiry and the reading of nonfiction, while Ms. Fogel is working with the new basal program purchased by her school district. In this chapter we discuss the common elements that underlie each of these frameworks and consider the roles that knowledge acquisition, strategies use, metacognition, and motivation play in them. We discuss the practical application of research when we describe how to develop comprehension in three dominant instructional frameworks: literature (Chapters 5 and 6), information and inquiry (Chapters 7 and 8), and basal reading programs (Chapters 9 and 10).

GOALS FOR THIS CHAPTER

✓ Describe theories of comprehension instruction from teaching individual strategies to teacher- and student-guided discussion.

✓ Discuss close reading as a goal for comprehension instruction.

✓ Explore comprehension strategies as a tool for knowledge development.

✓ Explain a model of comprehension instruction that integrates strategies, knowledge, motivation, and metacognition—the gradual release of responsibility model in context.

THEORIES OF COMPREHENSION INSTRUCTION

Since the 1980s the standard model of comprehension instruction has been the gradual release of responsibility model (GRRM). First outlined by Pearson and Gallagher (1983), the model consists of several interrelated instructional phases. In Figure 3.1 we have reproduced a recent version (Duke & Pearson, 2002; Duke et al., 2011). The GRRM begins with the teacher doing all the work of explaining and modeling how to comprehend. This is the direct explanation part of the model (Duffy, 2009). Gradually the teacher brings the students into the act. They begin to do the thinking; they try out the tasks. The teacher is an active participant who helps the students to implement the tasks especially when they go off track. This part of the model is called guided practice, because the teacher is acting as a guide, scaffolding the process. Scaffolding consists of anything that the teacher might do to help the students—ask a question, provide a hint, give directions, or model the task again. Eventually, as the students' skill improves, the teacher's role diminishes, and the students are able to conduct the task independently.

The preceding paragraph is purposefully incomplete because we explained the process of teaching reading comprehension and purposefully ignored the content of this instruction. We did not tell you that a teacher could teach a strategy, multiple strategies, and other components of the good comprehender model through the GRRM. When the GRRM first burst

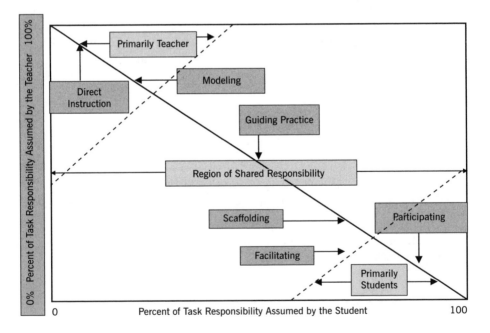

FIGURE 3.1. Gradual release of responsibility model. From Duke and Pearson (2002). Copyright 2002 by the International Reading Association. Reprinted by permission.

on the scene in the mid-1980s, research in comprehension focused mainly on the teaching of individual strategies, such as finding the main idea (Baumann, 1984), summarizing (Taylor & Beach, 1984), and making inferences (Dewitz, Carr, & Patberg, 1987). Obviously the model had merit because all of these studies produced gains in the students' ability to use the comprehension strategies and increased their reading ability.

Multiple Strategies Instruction

Good readers, however, do not plod along using one strategy at a time. The good comprehender model that we developed in Chapter 1 explicitly states that readers orchestrate a number of strategies as they work to construct meaning. So researchers began to design comprehension instruction in terms of teaching multiple strategies, which could be taught using a process of gradual release. The most prominent of these multiple strategies approaches are reciprocal teaching (RT; Palincsar & Brown, 1984), collaborative strategic reading (CSR; Klingner, Vaughn, & Schumm, 1998; Klingner & Vaughn, 1999), and transactional strategies instruction (TSI; Pressley et al., 1992).

Reciprocal Teaching

This instructional approach was developed as a means of fostering reading comprehension and comprehension monitoring. RT begins with the teacher introducing and modeling four strategies—self-questioning, clarifying, summarizing, and predicting. After a portion of the text is read, the teacher asks questions, clarifies difficult words or phrases, summarizes, and makes predictions. Next, one of the students leads the group using the same four strategies. The teacher scaffolds the student's attempt, helping him or her formulate questions and summaries and intervening to keep the discussion on track. The role of leader then shifts to the other students in the small group. Every time the students meet they take on more of the responsibility for reading and running the group.

   RT has proven to be successful. The approach has been applied at the primary level up through junior college with various forms of implementation (Rosenshine & Meister, 1994; Hacker & Tenant, 2002). The students who have participated in RT have demonstrated strong comprehension gains on tests developed by the researchers and somewhat lesser gains on standardized tests. RT can become too procedural. In the wrong hands the implementation of the strategies can take on more importance than the ideas in the text. The teacher and the students can become so intent on asking a question or developing a summary that they neglect the content of the passage. Hacker and Tenant demonstrated that a variety of implementations, whole-class discussion, small-group discussion, and a combination of both lead to success.

Collaborative Strategic Reading

An adaptation of RT, CSR (Klingner et al., 1998; Klingner & Vaughn, 1999) added some strategies and structured the students' independent work. The four basic RT strategies were modified to include the following:

- Preview the text, use brainstorming to activate knowledge, and make predictions.
- Monitor comprehension through a *click* and *clunk* activity. One student is responsible for noting when ideas make sense (click) and another when they do not (clunk).
- Getting the gist. The students identify the main ideas by asking themselves questions like "Who or what is this about?"
- Wrap-up. The students review important ideas and then generate questions.

Some of the work in CSR is done in a whole group, but the bulk is conducted in cooperative, small groups borrowing some ideas from literature circles (Daniels, 1996). Each student is assigned a role (leader, clunk expert, click expert, gist, announcer), cue cards, and learning logs to help them remember how to use the strategies. CSR has been shown to improve students' comprehension especially when it has been implemented within social studies instruction (Klingner et al., 1998).

Transactional Strategies Instruction

TSI (Pressley et al., 1992) is the most comprehensive of the multiple strategies approaches. TSI softened some of the edges of RT, and increased its flexibility. Pressley and his university and public school colleagues expanded the set of cognitive strategies and added an emphasis on interpretative, collaborative discussion. That is, students used a coordinated set of strategies as they engaged in more fluid and lively discussions of texts.

The results of TSI are quite impressive. The second graders who received the instruction improved their reading comprehension and their word recognition significantly over a comparison group (R. Brown, Pressley, Van Meter, & Schuder, 1996). Additional studies by C. Collins (1991) and V. Anderson (1992) showed that students in the upper grades made substantial improvements on standardized tests. The TSI students also talked more cogently about the reading process and realized that successful reading involved more than decoding and practice. More recently, a study using TSI with informational texts found that a multiple strategies approach had more impact on students' learning than teaching single strategies spread out over time (Reutzel, Smith, & Fawson, 2005).

In RT, CSR, and TSI, the teachers and students follow the GRRM. The content of comprehension instruction is a repertoire of strategies. The composition of this repertoire differs from one approach to another, but all share a metacognitive focus and the need to synthesize what has been read. TSI is the most different of the three having the strongest focus on interpretation and discussion.

The three approaches also differ in how the teacher hands off the responsibility for strategy use to the students. In RT, the teacher executes the release by giving the students the task of leading the discussion with the teacher providing support and guidance. As the students develop more skill, the teacher does less. Hacker and Tenant (2002) demonstrated that with no loss in effectiveness, some roles like summarizing could be completed in a whole-class setting, while others could be conducted with a partner. The partners then come together to create a small group. In CSR, the release of responsibility is achieved by giving students specific roles. If your job is to ask the questions, a role card guides you through that part of the activity. In TSI the release of responsibility is accomplished in small reading groups where an extended discussion emphasizes the use of reading strategies. Unlike RT, the script of following just four strategies is not fixed, but teachers and students employ strategies as needed to solve comprehension problems. Over time, some teachers try to limit their impact on students' thinking by transferring to the students the task of leading the discussions. The GRRM also means that, with practice, the explicit teaching of strategies is phased out, giving way to longer episodes of rich talk in which strategies are seamlessly woven into discussion. In effect, the over-arching goal of TSI is to teach comprehension strategies just long enough to help students construct solid interpretations during discussion.

Discussion and the Development of Comprehension

The most current wave of comprehension instruction research stresses the important role of discussion (Wilkinson & Son, 2011). An engaging, interactive classroom discussion shares many of the attributes of TSI, but without the explicit emphasis on strategies. In a classroom discussion, students have the opportunity to make their views known, consider alternative perspectives proposed by their peers, and reconcile these viewpoints. By hearing and considering different points of view students can reach high levels of thinking. Through discussion, students' literal and inferential comprehension grows, and sometimes critical thinking or reasoning (Murphy, Wilkinson, Soter, Hennessey, & Alexander, 2009). It appears that discussion has its greatest benefits for average and below-average readers because many strong readers do not need help in understanding texts (Murphy et al., 2009), but they do need assistance with critical, analytic thinking (Chinn, Anderson, & Waggoner, 2001).

To describe a discussion we need to consider four attributes—the stance, the interpretative authority, the control over turn taking, and the control over topic. The concept of stance refers to Rosenblatt's (1937/1978) distinction between aesthetic and efferent reading (see Chapter 1). We can also add a third stance, becoming a critical and analytic reader, but most discussions adopt a mixture of stances. The second factor, interpretative authority, refers to whose voice counts most. In many classrooms, the teacher asks all the questions and acknowledges who is correct. This interactional exchange is known as a recitation. In other classrooms the teachers and students share interpretative authority. Often the teacher controls the topic and the flow of discussion, whereas in other contexts, control is shared between the teacher and the students. Finally, in some discussions the teacher controls the turn taking, and in others students join in whenever they want, without needing to raise their hand for recognition. Figure 3.2 (derived from Chinn et al., 2001) takes the four types of discussion that are topics in our book and lists the attributes of each and the chapters in which these explanations can be found.

These various types of discussions do not represent a complete break from multiple strategies instruction; rather, we view them as an unbroken continuum. As teacher and students move from multiple strategies instruction to discussion, the strategies become less important and the ideas in the text become more important. While students may be engaged in strategic thinking their comments often do not carry a strategy label, and the teacher rarely says, "Good inference, Bill," or "Can you summarize, Marge?" As we show, this focus on content and ideas is critical to developing strategic readers.

CLOSE READING

The CCSS want all students to engage in close reading of text "to determine what the text says explicitly and to make logical inferences from it: cite specific textual evidence when writing or speaking to support conclusions drawn from the text" (NGA & CCSS, 2010, p. 10). For many, close reading is a new term, but not a new concept. We have all engaged in close reading.

Discussion Approach	Stance	Interpretative Authority	Control over Turns	Control over Topic
Literature circles; book clubs (Chapters 6 and 10)	Primarily aesthetic, partly efferent	Held by students	Controlled by students	Controlled by students
Questioning the author (Chapter 10)	Primarily efferent, but some critical/analytic	Shared by teacher and students, but students are expected to do more	Controlled by the teacher	Shared by teacher and students, but teacher exerts control through questioning
Transactional strategies instruction (Chapter 8)	Efferent, aesthetic, and critical/analytic	Shared by teacher and students, but shifting to students	Shared by teacher and students	Shared by teacher and students, but over time the students exert more control
Collaborative reasoning (Chapter 10)	Primarily critical/analytic	Students are completely responsible for the positions they take	Students are free to speak whenever they want, but teacher can exert control through questioning	Shared by students and teachers

FIGURE 3.2. Profile of key attributes during different approaches to discussion.

After that last thunderstorm toppled the large oak tree into your garage, you engaged in a close reading of your insurance policy to see if you were covered. In college you read your biology text closely to determine the exact role of mitochondria in the cell's nucleus. When you read in Shakespeare's *Henry VI, Part 2,* "The first thing we do, let's kill all the lawyers" you had to decide if that was a literal statement of intent or a figurative way of considering a society that was less constrained by endless petty rules. Close reading is a very purposeful style of reading, one that asks the reader to delve into the text, analyze it, determine the important ideas, and consider how the author's choice of structure and language facilitated his or her purpose. It also often requires multiple readings of a text and considerable discussion.

Close reading has its origins in the literary criticism of I. A. Richards who developed the field of literary criticism in the 1920s. Richards and his colleague, C. K. Ogden, argued in their New Criticism that a literary work be considered in its own right free from preconceived biases, beliefs, and prior knowledge. He had his university students read and interpret poems without knowing when they were written and who wrote them. This allowed Richards to probe how students interpreted the text itself and how they considered the vocabulary, figurative language, symbolism, and structure of the text.

Richards' works stand in contrast to the reader response theories of Louise Rosenblatt (1937, 1978) discussed in Chapter 1. Rosenblatt believed that each reader brings his or her background knowledge, beliefs, and experiences to a text and creates his or her own interpretations. In the transaction between the reader and the text different experiences and insights occur for each reader. To Rosenblatt there is no one correct reading of a text, while to Richards there is only one correct reading. Rosenblatt also advanced the view that there were different types of reading or stances that exist on a continuum. In the aesthetic stance the reader reads for the experience and enjoyment of reading, while in the efferent stance the reader reads to learn. The CCSS, however, are pushing the efferent stance and diminishing the value of aesthetic reading, while we maintain that both stances are equally important—reading is both a search for ideas and meaning and joyful experience.

The CCSS are emphasizing close reading because they object to instructional practices that diminish the efforts and the initiative of the reader. "Preteaching" or frontloading the students with too much background information makes it unnecessary for the students to grapple with the text's meaning. Not every text requires a picture walk, but comprehension does require knowledge and teachers must build what students lack. When students struggle and teachers quickly provide their interpretation of the text, students do not have to think hard or reread to develop their own understanding. Instead, teachers should turn students back to the text and guide them to understand the author's language. Reading at times requires hard thinking. When teachers focus too much on the students' personal response to the text, the students miss the wonder of the author's language, structure, and stylistic skills.

Close reading is not literal comprehension. As we will develop in this chapter and others, reading always requires making inferences. We infer the pronoun–noun connections, cause-and-effect relationships. We infer character traits, motives, and feeling. And we infer main ideas and themes. All of these inferences require prior knowledge. Try a close reading of quantum theory and you will quickly appreciate the vital importance of prior knowledge. Close reading simply says don't preteach knowledge that the students can construct for themselves.

Many of the instructional practices in our book are completely consistent with close reading, but some are deliberately not. The interpretative discussions of TSI (R. Brown et al., 1996) require a close examination of the text. The queries of questioning the author, text-dependent questions in CCSS jargon, demand a close reading of the text and an interrogation of the author (Beck, McKeown, Hamilton, & Kucan, 1997). Collaborative reasoning of Anderson and his colleagues (R. C. Anderson, 1998) requires a close reading of the text, and a consideration of evidence and reasoning to support interpretations. Many of the dialogues in Chapters 6 and 8 show the teacher returning the students to the text to explore the author's purpose and language. We do believe there is a place for the aesthetic response. Not all reading requires a close reading, and advocating so would undermine the pleasure that many students derive from reading J. K. Rowling, Rick Riordan, Jeff Kinney, and Roald Dahl. Literature circles, book clubs, and independent reading encourage the aesthetic response. Comprehension strategies, our next topic, are tools for helping the reader engage in close reading.

STRATEGY INSTRUCTION: A TOOL FOR KNOWLEDGE DEVELOPMENT

When we developed our good comprehender model in Chapter 1, we stressed the importance of knowledge, strategies, metacognition, and motivation. By focusing exclusively on the strategies of the comprehension process, some educators have neglected the important roles of knowledge and motivation. Many popular books have unduly focused attention on strategies at the expense of knowledge and motivation. We should not teach skills for the sake of skills, nor strategies for the sake of strategies. Strategies must be tools that are employed within a real-learning context where readers build knowledge or engage with literature.

There is a definite link between strategy use and knowledge; unfortunately the relationship between the two is not totally clear. Let's take two instances both supported by research. First is a middle-grade student who is reading a history chapter about the Civil War. We can guess that this reading task is difficult for this student who knows little about the Civil War. He has to read closely, stop often, and use headings and subheadings to search for information. He is slowly putting the ideas together to form a model of the text.

Another student in the same class has a depth of knowledge. His parents are Civil War buffs and they have taken their children to battlefields and reenactments across the South. His rich knowledge makes reading easier: he does not need to use as many fix-up strategies, and his ability to infer and evaluate is enhanced (Bråten & Samuelstuen, 2004). Strategies may be more necessary when the reader's knowledge base is slim, but others argue that a deep knowledge base enables the reader to think more flexibly and strategically (Bråten & Samuelstuen, 2004). Strategies use does play a role in reading comprehension, but only after taking into account a student's word-recognition skills, general verbal ability, and prior knowledge (Cain, Oakhill, Barnes, & Bryant, 2001).

Making strategies the tool of building knowledge was the goal of two research efforts—concept-oriented reading instruction (CORI; Guthrie, Wigfield, & Perencevich, 2004) and in-depth expanded application of science (IDEAS; Romance & Vitale, 2001). In both research programs, comprehension strategies instruction was situated within science instruction to build content knowledge, improve strategic thinking, and, in the case of CORI, to boost students' motivation. CORI includes strategies like activating prior knowledge, questioning, searching for information, summarizing, and organizing information graphically. In a series of studies, Guthrie and his colleagues reported that CORI improved reading comprehension abilities significantly compared to more traditional approaches of comprehension strategies instruction (see Guthrie, McRae, & Klauda, 2007). The IDEAS program (Romance & Vitale, 2001) also embedded reading and language arts instruction within science instruction. In a series of studies, Romance and Vitale (2001) demonstrated that students achieved greater comprehension when strategy instruction is embedded in science learning compared to more traditional methods. In these approaches, as with TSI, the strategies served as tools to support the important work of building knowledge and learning concepts. Thus, the goal of comprehension instruction did not end with just teaching the tools.

A MORE COMPREHENSIVE MODEL
OF COMPREHENSION INSTRUCTION

Because comprehension requires knowledge, strategies, metacognition, and motivation we have redesigned the GRRM and situated it within a real context: reading literature and informational texts for enjoyment and learning, and in our case, doing so within different instructional frameworks. We changed the model because comprehension instruction must be more than the explicit explanation of strategies and carefully guided reading. Teachers must integrate comprehension strategies instruction in a meaningful context that provides the motivation to learn. Figure 3.3 presents our revised version of the GRRM. For shorthand, we refer to our model as the gradual release of responsibility model in context (GRRM-C).

Our revised GRRM-C begins with a content to be explored and real texts to be read. The teacher begins the process with more knowledge than

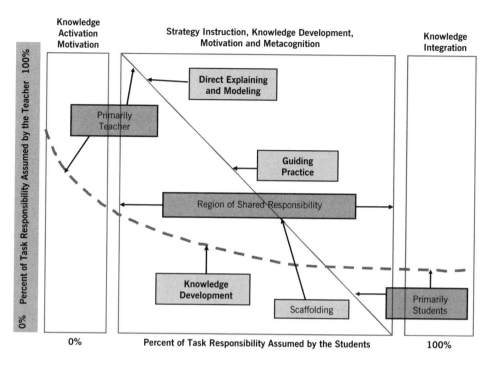

FIGURE 3.3. Gradual release of responsibility model in context.

the students and he or she activates and builds the students' knowledge. Together the teacher and the students set a purpose for the reading. The beginning of the GRRM-C shares much in common with the prereading stages of the directed reading activity (Betts, 1946) or the scaffolded reading experience (SRE; Graves & Graves, 2003). During this prereading phase (knowledge activation/motivation) the teacher develops the students' knowledge, introduces and explains vocabulary necessary for comprehension, previews the text, and sets a purpose for reading.

Consider a group of fifth graders getting ready to read a chapter on the Civil War. The teacher might begin by asking children to brainstorm what they know, really an informal assessment, but also a knowledge activation and motivation activity. Then the teacher might show a segment of Ken Burns's (1990) PBS television special about life in the North and the South just prior to the war, adding information to a graphic organizer, which is a knowledge development activity. Next, the teacher explains specific vocabulary words—*secession, slavery, states' rights,* and so forth.

When we move into the middle, larger phase of the model (strategy instruction/knowledge development) the teacher and the students are working on building knowledge and using comprehension strategies to do so. As students read, they employ strategies to find important ideas, make inferences, and summarize what they are learning. The teacher essentially moves to parallel tracks, at times learning about the Civil War and at other times helping the students to employ comprehension and metacognitive strategies. For a lesson or two the content takes a backseat to the strategies. The teacher allocates a few lessons to explain and model the use of comprehension strategies; as the students gain expertise in the use of the strategies, the teacher helps less. The strategies are used to solve the comprehension problems that arise while reading and learning. The teacher's role now shifts to supporting the students as they read; it is a shared responsibility. Over time the use of strategies and the building of knowledge becomes more and more the responsibility of the students.

In the last phase of the process (knowledge integration) the students consolidate what they have learned. They may complete a graphic organizer, write about what they have read, or develop a multimedia project. The teacher is still providing assistance; we do not assume that the student/learner is ever free from the need for support. The amount of support any group of students will need depends on their comprehension ability, their level of knowledge, and the difficulty of the text. Also, additional support is required as the teacher continues to deepen students' existing knowledge, metacognition, motivation, and strategies use.

Direct Explanation of Strategies

In our GRRM-C, the teacher explains the strategies, models their use, and thinks aloud while he or she does so. The teacher is the expert who explains how to read strategically. Gerald Duffy and his colleagues developed specific criteria for direct and explicit explanations of comprehension strategies (Duffy et al., 1986). Duffy et al.'s work stresses the importance of providing students with *declarative knowledge*, what they will learn to do; *procedural knowledge*, how they should implement the strategies, the thinking process; and *conditional knowledge*, why strategies are important and when to use them. When referring to this kind of direct teaching in the remainder of this book, we prefer the term *direct explanation* because we feel the term is more self-evident. A direct explanation lesson should meet the following criteria and you will find examples of these lessons in Chapter 6 (making inferences), Chapter 8 (self-questioning), and Chapter 10 (determining importance and summarizing).

- Identify the strategy and discuss its purpose.
- Provide a clear explanation of the mental process underlying the

strategy, including the text features and clues that support the strategy.

- Explain how the strategy will help the reader and when it should be used.
- Model the strategy and think aloud until the students no longer need the support.

Students do not require as much teacher-standing-in-front-of-the-class explicit explanation as you might think. In one comprehensive look at RT (Palincsar & Brown, 1984) the researchers found minimal differences between an approach to RT that began with four to six explicit strategy lessons and another approach that plunged students right into dialogue in which strategies instruction was interwoven (Rosenshine & Meister, 1994). Other researchers found that the dialogue of TSI produced greater results with second graders than did explicit instruction with one strategy at a time (Reutzel et al., 2005). We would argue that one or two clearly articulated lessons on strategies may be necessary but then students should be moved quickly into dialogue, where guided practice occurs. The amount of direct and explicit instruction also can vary with different students and strategies. Introducing third graders to the task of determining importance with informational text can be quite challenging, but focusing on making inferences with a gifted group of sixth graders will take minimal instruction, if any.

One of the most confounding problems in strategy instruction is the lack of consensus on the process that underlies each of the major strategies. "How strategies should be taught is not easily derived from the research . . . what goes on under a strategy label is not consistent from study to study" (McKeown, Beck, & Blake, 2009, p. 221). For example, the experts concur that summarizing what you read will help improve comprehension, but how best to teach summarizing is open to debate because the process of constructing a summary varies from one study to another. In one study students were taught to delete details and redundant information, categorize details (plum, apple, orange = fruit), search for main ideas or topic sentences, and finally, if needed, generate their main idea (A. L. Brown & Day, 1983). What was left is integrated into a summary. In another study students read sections of a text and then generated a one-sentence summary statement (Taylor & Beach, 1984). These one-sentence statements were combined into an overall summary. In Chapter 10, where we focus on a biography, we have chosen the text structure approach to summarizing (Taylor & Beach, 1984) because it is more consistent with our goals than the more rule-governed approach of Brown and Day. Each time we introduce a strategy we discuss why we chose that specific approach.

Guiding the Discussion and the Learning

Guided reading is that phase of comprehension instruction where the teacher acts as a guide to develop the students' thinking and understanding. At the outset we want to make it clear that guided reading is more than just asking questions. It is not a gentle inquisition but more often resembles a grand conversation (Eeds & Wells, 1989). The problem that all teachers face is how to guide the discussion to build comprehension of the text at hand, develop knowledge, and promote students' thinking so that their comprehension abilities transfer to other texts.

The goals are achieved through scaffolding, "a process that enables a child or novice to solve a problem, carry out a task, or achieve a goal which would be beyond his unassisted efforts" (Wood, Bruner, & Ross, 1976, p. 91). A teacher has a number of tools that can be used to scaffold the students' comprehension:

• Graphic organizers, and even Post-it notes, can guide students' learning; they provide a place to record thinking, ask questions, or record key ideas. These response forms and notes remind students to use strategies and attend to what they are learning. (We tackle graphic organizers in Chapter 10.)

• Collaborative learning, in which partners or small groups assist one another, supports the use of strategies and students' learning. When two students work together to develop questions or write a summary, they assist each other with comprehension and learning.

• Moment-to-moment verbal support and teacher modeling provide hints and redirection when comprehension breaks down. The questions, comments, directives, and modeling of the teacher forms the bulk of what we refer to as scaffolding.

• Reduce the complexity of the task and the text. Students can contribute to the common instructional goal, but in different ways, often reading easier text.

Guided reading should take place during small-group discussions led by the teacher or by the students with teacher assistance. Evidence suggests that effective teachers spend more time in small-group instruction than do ineffective teachers (Taylor et al., 2000). Carol Connor and her colleagues demonstrate that these effective teachers tailor the small-group experience to the needs of students. Struggling readers need more time with the teacher while strong readers require less (Connor, Jakobsons, Crowe, & Meadows, 2009). Activities like book clubs (McMahon & Raphael, 1997) and literature circles (Daniels, 1996) are ideal for stronger readers who need less teacher support, thereby freeing the teacher to work with other students who need additional support.

While the nature of the dialogues in guided reading is open to debate, there are some necessary elements in all discussions. These include:

- Asking questions that elicit a high level of thinking.
- Encouraging students to elaborate on their responses.
- Supporting, acknowledging their ideas, and elaborating on them.
- Fostering connections among ideas.
- Prompting explanations that employ evidence from the text (Goldenberg & Patthey-Chaves, 1995; Murphy et al., 2009).

We review several studies that examine the process of leading a teacher-guided discussion, but remember there are other discussion formats like literature circles (Daniels, 1996) or collaborative reasoning (Chinn et al., 2001) where the students assume more control. In a recent study, McKeown et al. (2009) compared a content approach to a strategies approach for guided comprehension lessons. In the content approach, questioning the author (QtA; Beck et al., 1997), the teacher had the students read a portion of the text and then stopped them to discuss the selection. QtA rests on the premise that the author is fallible and the reader must inquire critically. The discussion is initiated with general questions: "What is the author trying to tell us?" and "What is this passage about?" The students then talk about the passage, and the teacher encourages additional comments from other students. If the students miss major ideas, the teacher directs them to reexamine the text. Sometimes students are asked to connect one idea in a passage to another through queries like "How does this connect with what the author told us before?" or "Why do you think the author tells us this now?" Some evaluative queries are asked, such as "Did the author explain this clearly?" and "Does this make sense with what the author told us before?" At all times the discussion focuses on the ideas in the passage. QtA is a close reading of the text.

McKeown and her colleagues (2009) contrasted this content approach to a strategies approach. In the strategies approach the teacher periodically stopped the students' reading to focus on problems in the text and helped them select and apply strategies to solve these problems. The researchers developed their own strategies approach, validated by experts, rather than employing one of the known, researched approaches like RT (Palincsar & Brown, 1984) or TSI (R. Brown et al., 1996). In the strategies approach, the teacher initiated the discussion by having the students focus on problems in the text and then asked the students what strategy might be used to solve the problem. At other times in the discussion the teacher commented on students' use of a given strategy (e.g., "I like the inference you just made"), or asked them to use a given strategy ("Who can clarify what we just read?"). The results of the study confirmed that the content approach led to greater comprehension than did the strategies approach, with these effects transferring to passages that students read without teacher support. Since the results of this study were not straightforward, we examine yet another approach to better understand what constitutes a strong, guided reading lesson.

In Figure 3.4 we present dialogues for three approaches—a strategy approach, a content approach (QtA), and RT. In both the content approach and the strategy approach, the students read a story titled "The Fun They Had" (Asimov, 2005), taken from the McKeown et al. (2009) study. In the story two children, living in the year 2157, come across a book for the first time; they wonder just how it works. In the RT excerpt (Palincsar & Brown, 1984), the five students and the teacher discuss a nonfiction article on the history of salt. In RT the students take turns leading the discussion. The students in this dialogue have been practicing RT for 13 days.

What can we conclude from these three dialogues? In both the content and the RT approaches, the students and teacher spend more time actually discussing the content of the passage than in the strategy approach. Even though RT has a specific goal of having students learn to use four strategies, they still persistently discuss the main ideas and details of the salt article. All of the teacher's statements reflect how well the students understand the content. In the content approach the students grapple with details of the story, specifically the setting. In the strategy approach the focus is on the strategies, or on the process of asking the students to use a specific strategy, or labeling the student's comments as an example of using a strategy ("You made an inference").

How the teacher directs or supports the dialogue also differs across the three examples. In the content approach the teacher begins the discussion by asking the students "What is going on here?" In effect, the discussion begins with a summary without ever using the word *summary*. Strategies are used but are not labeled. The students' comments are long and clearly ideas are being put together. In the RT approach the students also summarize, and ask questions and predict, but the students and the teacher label the strategies. It appears that there is nothing inherently wrong with using strategy labels and there may be something good about it. A strategy label—summarizing, predicting—may help remind the students that there is a process they can follow. For example, asking students to summarize a portion of a story may help them recall that this kind of summary has to contain a setting, characters, an event, and a reaction.

A Strategies Approach (McKeown, Beck, & Blake, 2009, p. 238)	A Content Approach (McKeown, Beck, & Blake, 2009, p. 239)	Reciprocal Teaching (Palincsar & Brown, 1984, p. 162)
TEACHER: Oh, good. Stop here, Holly. This is a good place to stop and check our understanding. What might be confusing here? Holly? HOLLY: On the page headed May 17, 2157. TEACHER: Oh, 2157. That might be confusing to a person reading this. What could you do to help yourself understand 2157? STUDENT: Ask a question. KYLE: Maybe you could like to tell if it's a date or what. Just like if it's a date, you could, um, see how many years from now it is. TEACHER: So, you think this story takes place in the future, good. You made an inference. Did the author once say this is taking place in the future? Did the author state that? STUDENTS: No. TEACHER: But yet you knew it, didn't you, Kyle? KYLE: Yeah. TEACHER: Based on what you read. And then you even did some work in your mind, trying to figure out how far into the future it was, so that was good. Is anyone in the room confused about anything we read here? What did you think about the business with the books having print?	TEACHER: So what's, what's this all about? What's going on? Tajae, what's going on? TAJAE: Tommy found a book and they're looking in it, and they're saying the pages are crinkly and stuff, and they're thinking that if you read the book, you can go back in and it will be totally different about it, but it's all still the same, and they say that after you read it one time, you might as well throw it away cause you'll, cause if you read it and you know what it's about, if [inaudible], TV one cause if you turn on the TV and then you watch something, the next day, it won't be the same. TEACHER: Yeah, all that's very true. Catherine? CATHERINE: It's in the future. It says that it's 2157, so the book is really old because now, like in the future, it's saying that they don't read books. They read like on television screens and they're shocked because the book is really old and stuff. TEACHER: Yeah, and you, you added to what Tajae already said. Yeah, this is set in the future. And the book and the screen are two totally different things.	CHARLES: Name three different basic methods how salt is produced. ANGELA: Evaporation, mining, evaporation . . . artificial heat evaporation. CHARLES: Correct, very good. My summary on this paragraph is about ways that salt is being produced. TEACHER: Very good. Could you select the next teacher? *(Another paragraph about salt mining is read.)* LUCAS: Name two words that often describe mining salt in the old days. KYLE: Back to the salt mines. LUCAS: No. Angela? ANGELA: Dangerous and difficult. LUCAS: Correct. This paragraph is all about comparing the old mining of salt and today's mining of salt. TEACHER: Beautiful! LUCAS: I have a prediction to make. TEACHER: Good. LUCAS: I think it might tell when salt was first discovered, well, it might tell what salt is made of and how it's made.

FIGURE 3.4. Three types of guided reading.

One part of the comprehension process is sometimes neglected in all three of these dialogues; that is, the need to make connections among phrases and sentences within the passage to build cohesion. This process coincides with the construction phase of comprehension that we presented in Chapter 1 as part of the construction–integration model. QtA promotes these connections when the teacher asks, "How is that connected to what we already read?" Although not all readers have difficulty with this basic aspect of comprehension, a teacher must be aware of the potential problem and be ready to address it. Consider the passage that was used to elicit the discussion for the McKeown study (McKeown et al., 2009), the story by Asimov (2005).

> Marie even wrote about it that night in her diary. On the page headed May 17, 2157, she wrote, "Today Tommy found a real book!"
>
> It was a very old book. Marie's grandfather once said that when he was a little boy his grandfather told him that there was a time when all stories were printed on paper.
>
> They turned the pages, which were yellow and crinkly, and it was awfully funny to read words that stood still instead of moving the way they were supposed to—on a screen, you know. (p. 27)

One thing that makes this short passage difficult to comprehend is the pronoun–noun relationships. A second occurs because the author takes the reader back multiple generations, a time–sequence link. The reader must sort out whose grandfather is being discussed. Then comes the phrase "They turned the pages . . . ," and the reader must connect the word *they* to Marie and Tommy. These comprehension problems might become apparent when the students are asked to retell the passage. If students do have these problems, the teacher can ask students about these relationships: "In the last paragraph, who is the author describing when he uses the word *they*? How can we figure out who 'they' are?" Since texts present comprehension problems for readers, like the ones described above, successful teaching depends upon careful planning and close reading.

Planning Guided Discussions

Planning guided comprehension is challenging. It demands selecting texts thoughtfully and then reading closely to determine potential comprehension problems. Without a thorough understanding of the text and its potential problems, teachers will not formulate the right questions and will not understand why students' comprehension is impaired. In fact, some teachers do not anticipate stumbling blocks that might trip students up when reading. A recent study of fourth- and fifth-grade teachers found that 85% of teachers were unable to analyze a text and determine when and why students might have comprehension difficulties (Kucan, Hapgood, & Palincsar, 2011). These teachers believed that comprehension problems stemmed primarily from vocabulary difficulties or weak text features—headings, bold print, and subheadings. These teachers were unaware of what makes a text coherent, what makes the "ideas hang together in a meaningful and organized manner" (Graesser, McNamara, & Louwerse, 2003, p. 83).

Planning comprehension instruction begins with selecting texts. Text selection should be guided by a few key principles:

1. The teacher, the students, and sometimes both can select the texts.
2. Texts should be selected because they contribute to the content goal of the lesson. So, if your class is learning about mysteries, select good books of that genre.
3. Select texts that students can read at their instructional level: a level where the students read with 90% accuracy or better.
4. Select texts where there is a match between the clarity of the text's structure and the comprehension ability of the students.
5. Select texts where there is some cognitive challenge, something to think about. A text that is so bland, without any challenge or voice, will not engage the reader; nor will it provide students the opportunity to think strategically or critically.

Effective guided practice cannot be conducted on the fly; it must be planned. The first step in planning is to read the text closely. We recommend that you read it twice. The first time you read the text, your goal is simply to understand it on your own terms. The second reading is designed to examine the text closely to look for potential comprehension problems. You want to enter into the minds of your students and try to anticipate how they think and what might cause them difficulty. Your comprehension skills are so developed that you will often fail to note problems that will stump the average student in your class (Kucan et al., 2011). Examining the text from this text-processing perspective is critical to developing an effective guided lesson. Anticipating where the comprehension problems are likely to occur helps you to frame your questions and know when to stop and support your students.

In any guided comprehension lesson it is important to decide where and how often to stop and discuss the text. We do not advocate the basal practice of asking comprehension questions on each page of the text. Doing so is likely to disrupt comprehension. Instead, we suggest that you stop as infrequently as possible; the more of the text that the reader has inside his or her head, the more likely he or she is to make connections among ideas and build a personal model (van den Broek & Kremer, 2000). It also is likely the younger and more inexperienced readers should stop less often so that their memory for each text segment is not disrupted. Better readers accommodate frequent interruptions to the reading process.

Implementing Teacher-Guided Discussion

A strong teacher-guided discussion encourages students to summarize what they have read and elaborate on their initial understanding. During the discussion the students should look for and solve text-processing problems, make inferences, generate questions, and work to understand the text. Even though the teacher is in the lead, the result is a discussion—and not oral assessment. When comprehension presents a problem, the teacher or one of the students can take the lead, modeling strategies to resolve the misunderstanding. These are our guidelines for teachers:

• *Summarize or paraphrase.* Ask the students to summarize what the text was about either at the beginning or end of reading—or both. This summary compels the students to put ideas together, serves as a metacognitive check, and reminds students to focus on the text and not just the strategies. This summary is useful because it gives you insight into what the students have comprehended, what they can express about their understanding, and whether any reteaching is in order. Plus, summarizing addresses the first standard in the CCSS (NGA & CCSSO, 2010).

• *Solve problems.* Help the students with the difficult parts of the text. At all times the teacher should direct the students to look back into the text to either locate information or to justify an answer. This is a vital move for successful comprehension because it prevents students from relying on their prior knowledge when the information is in the text. Weak comprehenders overrely on prior knowledge and do not adequately attend to the text (Dewitz & Dewitz, 2003; Neuman, 1990).

• *Make inferences.* All texts are incomplete and the author counts on the readers to supply information that he or she only implied. There are many types of inferences. We infer cause and effect, themes, main ideas, and characters' feelings, traits, and motives.

• *Standards.* In many schools, teacher-guided discussion must accommodate the specific standards of the district. It is useful to ask a few questions that address those standards. In a guided reading lesson you might ask a question about author's purpose, fact or opinion, or cause and effect because it gives students specific practice with the skills assessed at the end of the year.

CLOSE READING

The CCSS urge teachers and students to engage in close reading of the text. For practical purposes a close reading is a slightly more intense version of what we have been describing. A close read has the following characteristics (Fisher & Frey, 2012):

- The students read short passages, typically a few paragraphs, excerpted from a novel, news articles, textbook, or a short poem.
- A close reading requires a difficult text, complex ideas, something to chew over, and it can be conducted any time that a particular chunk of text is difficult and presents comprehension difficulties. A close reading demands hard thinking about words, phrases, and figurative language. In the guidelines for questioning the author, Beck and her colleagues (1997) suggest that even one complex sentence can be a target for close reading.
- Close reading typically requires multiple readings of the text with each reading taking the students deeper into the text. With each rereading of the text the students are able to apply a bit more knowledge to the text. Teachers can direct students to specific words, phrases, and sentences that present comprehension difficulty.
- In a close reading there is limited frontloading of prior knowledge. The teacher avoids telling students what they should be able to derive from reading the text. Yet, without prior knowledge comprehension is very difficult and at times impossible. Test this out by reading any book on quantum theory. The CCSS did not repeal the schema view of comprehension (Anderson & Pearson, 1984) nor does the knowledge that is necessary to drive the construction–integration process (Kintsch, 1998) become unnecessary during a close reading.
- During a close reading teachers ask text-dependent questions. The phrase "text dependent" is simply a new label for "Right There, Think and Search," and "Author and Me" questions (Raphael, 1986). A text-dependent question is not an "On My Own" question that causes the reader to speculate or wonder. During a close reading the teachers also question and discuss specific words, phrases, and literary devices.
- During a close reading the students underline, highlight, and take

margin notes. They cite from the text to bolster their arguments, and the teacher frequently asks them to justify their answers from the text.

Because the CCSS hold considerable influence, there will be a push to engage all students in a close reading of the text. However, the overall impact of close reading on the development of reading comprehension is yet to be determined. Since close reading shares characteristics with QtA (Beck et al., 1997) and TSI (R. Brown et al., 1996), we can speculate that engaging students in close reading will improve their reading comprehension. When and how often students should read and discuss closely is an open question. It will require research to determine if close reading will build skill and motivation (S. Brown & Kappes, 2012).

Student-Guided Discussions

As students' comprehension develops and their social skills improve they can begin to lead their own discussions, relying less on teacher guidance. The research confirms that classroom discussions enhance students' comprehension and higher-level thinking and reasoning (Murphy et al., 2009). As many theorists proposed and as the research confirms, learning to think and reason improves through a dialogue with others as varying points of view and knowledge are brought to the text (Bakhtin, 1981; Piaget, 1928; Vygotsky, 1978). Depending on the goals, a teacher can employ a technique like literature circles (Short & Pierce, 1990; Daniels, 1996) or book clubs (McMahon & Raphael, 1992) to build an aesthetic or expressive response, or try collaborative reasoning (R. C. Anderson, Chinn, Waggoner, & Nguyen, 1998) focusing on critical/analytic thinking. The teacher-led approaches we presented in the previous section, including QtA (Beck et al., 1997) are more efferent in nature—stressing the important ideas in the text.

Janice Almasi (1995) documented that peer-led discussions developed comprehension as effectively, if not more so, than did teacher-led discussions. In the peer-led discussions the students tended to ask more questions, their responses were more elaborate, and the students tended to generate more text interpretations. Literature circles improve students' ability to discuss books, employ strategies like predicting and questioning, raise comprehension, and heighten motivation to read independently (B. H. Davis, Resta, Davis, & Camacho, 2001; Marin, 1998). Book clubs have been shown to increase reading vocabulary and the use of metacognitive strategies like self-questioning and summarizing. TSI (R. Brown, 2008; Pressley et al., 1989). They start out as teacher guided and can transition to peer-led talk that accommodates aesthetic, efferent, and critical/analytic discussions of text.

Knowledge Expansion, Integration, and Application

Our model of comprehension instruction situates the explanation and practice of reading strategies within a context where students are reading and writing for a purpose greater than strategies attainment. They are reading a novel to learn about important big ideas or themes, or reading nonfiction to expand their knowledge of the world. So while students are employing strategies, they are also working with their teachers (1) to consolidate, reorganize, and reflect upon what they are learning; or (2) to experience a text at a deeper level. Knowledge expansion, integration, and application can take place throughout the GRRM-C cycle. It does not happen only at the end.

Knowledge expansion can take many different forms. Students might be taking notes from a science text, or keeping a journal of their reactions to a novel. These notes and thoughts reflect their growing knowledge and insight. Students might create graphic representations, concept maps, or semantic maps to integrate these emerging ideas and represent them in a new way. To really know means to transform. Discussion promotes the development of knowledge as students share viewpoints and consider the arguments of others. We are now at the end of the GRRM-C cycle. At this point, students have built knowledge and become more strategic (in terms of cognition and metacognition) in their reading and thinking. Topical interest and motivation to read has propelled them through the cycle, and continues to spark their curiosity.

Independent Reading

Comprehension development continues when students read independently because wide reading of many texts and genres has been shown to improve comprehension (Kuhn, 2004; Schwanenflugel et al., 2006). We do not advocate traditional sustained silent reading where children read silently and the teacher acts as a model reading at his or her desk. This practice does not promote engaged reading and accountability because teachers do not monitor what the students are doing (Manning, Lewis, & Lewis, 2010). Kelly and Clausen-Grace (2006) recommend a procedure called R[5] where students read, relax, reflect, respond, and rap. Read and relax are the first step; the students read a book of their choice (teacher guidance is essential) and relax in any part of the room. Students reflect by keeping a reading log or writing in a personal response journal. Finally, students respond and rap by sharing with a partner what they have read. Ray Reutzel and his colleagues (Reutzel, Jones, Fawson, & Smith, 2008) recommend regular reading conferences where teachers guide children's book choices and conduct brief reading conferences where students discuss the main points of the book. This practice improves students' fluency and recall.

LOOKING BACK, LOOKING FORWARD

As we documented in the first chapter, reading comprehension is a highly complex cognitive activity. It is impossible to explain and model exactly the kind of thinking that actually goes on during strategic reading. What teachers demonstrate in the classroom are instructional approximations of the real act (Resnick, 1987). At best, we can support students through explaining and modeling, asking questions to propel the reader to act, and even pointing out which ideas should be connected to make an inference or create a summary. However, teaching this kind of thinking does not ensure that students will be sufficiently motivated to apply it. That desire is fueled by a meaningful curriculum, interesting tasks, student choice, and the reader's values, beliefs, and goals.

In this chapter we outlined some very successful instructional approaches—RT, CSR, QtA, and TSI. From these and other studies, we extracted the essentials of comprehension instruction as viewed through an augmented version of the GRRM, which incorporates the development of knowledge, motivation, metacognition, and strategy instruction. Comprehension instruction must be grounded in a rich and exciting context that provides interest and builds motivation. Strategies, both cognitive and metacognitive, are tools that serve two overarching goals—enjoyment and learning.

In Chapters 5 and 6 we apply these concepts of comprehension instruction to the reading of literature. In Chapters 7 and 8, we reintroduce them in the context of reading informational text. In Chapters 9 and 10, we observe how they function in a basal reading program. Up to this point, we largely have provided foundational information; in the following chapters, we apply these concepts to specific texts and students. However, before examining the teaching of knowledge, strategies use, metacognition, and motivation in three frameworks, we turn first to the topic of assessment in Chapter 4. Assessment is fundamental to effective teaching in all three instructional frameworks.

APPLICATIONS AND EXPLORATIONS

1. Select two texts you use often, one narrative and one informational, and analyze their text-processing problems. Imagine one of your weaker readers. What would cause him or her to have comprehension problems? Look beyond the obvious vocabulary problems and prior knowledge issues to explore where sentence structure, cohesive ties, and inferences must be made.

2. Observe a friend/colleague leading a small-group discussion. Note the type of questions that are asked, the sequencing of those questions, the responses given to students, and the types of provided support. Together, discuss the lesson and determine what makes it effective.

3. Read further about RT, CSR, and TSI. Identify the common elements that define their success.

CHAPTER 4

Assessment

A teacher asks students to read a selection and then answer some related questions on a worksheet. One student reads the first question and identifies a few key words. She proceeds to the beginning of the text, scans and finds the key ideas, varies the wording, and jots down an answer. Using the same tactic, she zips through the remaining questions. She never actually reads the text.

A teacher assigns a project based on the Civil War book, *Pink and Say* (Polacco, 1994). The student decides to write a newspaper article based on events in the book. He asks his mother for help. She promptly takes charge, writing most of the article herself.

A teacher administers a standardized comprehension test to a class. One student comes upon a passage about a race between a pineapple and a hare (Hartocollis, 2012). He reads it quickly and then rereads it more slowly. "This makes no sense," he mutters. Panicked, he arbitrarily selects answers to the eight multiple-choice questions.

How well has each of these assessments worked? What did we learn about the comprehension of these students? Are our interpretations about their understanding and their strategies appropriate? Nobody ever said comprehension assessment was easy. In fact, one frequently asked question from colleagues and teachers we know is "How do you assess comprehension?" In some schools it is the most pressing issue.

Currently, two educational trends drive this concern for assessments—high-stakes testing and response to intervention (RTI). The high-stakes testing movement, bolstered by government initiatives, such as No Child Left

Behind (2002) and Race to the Top (2011), has pushed almost every state to adopt the mandatory testing of reading in grades 3 through 10. States have rushed to buy or create tests that both predict students' performance and provide diagnostic information. So, at various points in the school year, you want to predict which students will most likely pass the high-stakes test. Your challenge is to find or construct a test that will yield an accurate prediction. This raises many questions. What kind of passages will students read? How is it possible to account for students' prior knowledge when selecting the passages? What should be assessed in comprehension—students' content understanding, their use of comprehension skills or strategies—or both? These are just a sampling of questions that need to be considered when designing or selecting tests.

RTI, an approach that attempts to head off reading problems early in a child's schooling, requires students who receive intervention to be retested periodically to see whether they are improving. Such progress monitoring involves giving students a test every week or two and then tracking their growth on a graph. Although assessing letter recognition or phonemic awareness is relatively straightforward, the assessment of comprehension is exceedingly complex (Paris, 2005). What is the definition of growth? A child who is an expert on skateboarding will excel on a passage about the development of freestyle sports. However, if the next passage focuses on the vanishing bee population, that student's results may decline. Raising or lowering the reading level of each passage by a year also could cause the results to vary.

Fundamental questions about the assessment of reading comprehension are raised when we consider the two educational imperatives of high-stakes testing and RTI. Imagine what happens when we broaden our scope to include other forms of assessment intended for use at the school and classroom levels. How do we add, without overwhelming students and teachers, placement, periodic screening, and diagnostic tests? How do we select the most suitable assessments to guide daily instruction? And most important, how do we find time for all this testing while still maintaining the integrity of instruction?

When we think about issues such as these, we venture into complex and contested terrain. Yet, we acknowledge one core issue that undergirds the entire assessment process—how can we assess readers' comprehension performance as it varies across texts, tasks, and purposes? When we mull over the complexity of assessment, we soon realize that these are the same factors we need to consider during instruction. In this chapter, our intent is to address some of the complexities of assessment and then provide guidelines for dealing with them.

GOALS FOR THIS CHAPTER

✓ Become aware of the purposes and audiences of reading assessments and how these purposes differ for various audiences.

✓ Observe how the process of assessment differs in the three instructional frameworks—literature, inquiry, and basal reading.

✓ Understand the connection between the CCSS and assessment.

✓ Describe general classroom-based approaches to assessing students' comprehension in literature, inquiry, and basal reading settings.

✓ Learn how to assess students' knowledge, motivation, cognitive and metacognitive strategies use, and motivation for reading.

✓ Consider the role of diagnostic assessment.

THE AUDIENCES OF ASSESSMENT

Multiple audiences have a stake in student performance and assessment (Afflerbach, 2007), with each group wanting to know something slightly different.

1. Administrators are primarily concerned with assessment *of* learning, in particular what students in a school, grade, or classroom have accomplished. Also called *summative* assessment, this approach emphasizes a formal appraisal of student achievement as indicated by a score on a standardized comprehension test. In this high-stakes environment, business leaders, politicians, and the voting public have an interest in the performance of students because of their tax dollars being spent.

2. Teachers are increasingly concerned with high-stakes assessment now that part of their evaluation is geared to student growth. They also focus in the classroom on assessment *for* learning, otherwise known as *formative* assessment. The purpose of formative assessment is to provide feedback on instruction and to track students' interim progress.

3. Parents or guardians want answers to three, overarching questions: How is my child doing when compared to some basic standard of reading? Is my child developing appropriately as a reader? How does my child compare to others in his or her classroom?

4. Students want to know how they are reading (i.e., "What grade am I going to get?"). They desire information about how teachers gauge their

progress. However, we believe that students need to take responsibility for assessing themselves by becoming increasingly aware of themselves as readers, evaluating various aspects of their reading, and judging which books are suitable matches for their abilities, interests, and needs. We also believe that students should reflect on their processes of reading as they work to monitor and control them.

Although a veritable maelstrom of "item-by-item teaching" (Shepard, 2010) currently swirls around us, spawned by the high-stakes assessment environment, we believe there are other important assessments that will help teachers evaluate and guide their students' comprehension. Notice that embedded in the word *evaluate* is the root, *value*. Unquestionably, we evaluate what we value (R. Brown, 2002) and at this time, what we see most clearly on the horizon is high-stakes testing. Thus, in many schools, teachers will allocate considerable time to prepare for and practice standardized tests rather than understanding students' everyday construction, integration, and application of meaning and their enjoyment of reading.

The reality of teaching the test cannot be ignored. All teachers need to find time for instruction and other forms of classroom assessment in an environment of mandated state testing, particularly in public schools. Even we grappled with this issue as we wrote this book. Although we recognize the need to prepare students to take standardized comprehension tests (if only to familiarize them with directions, formats, and conventions associated with the demands and expectations of the genre [Guthrie, 2002]), we opted to emphasize assessments that support teachers' day-to-day instructional planning and decision making because these too are required of you. We begin this process by exploring how various assessments are threaded into three literacy frameworks.

THE ASSESSMENT PROCESS IN THREE CLASSROOMS

Our book regularly takes you into three reading classrooms: literacy, inquiry, and basal reading programs. This will be the case in this chapter as well. The brief vignettes illustrate how each teacher incorporates different assessments within a particular framework to track students' comprehension. We focus on informal measures, those designed by teachers for their own purposes. That is not to say that these are the only, or even the most suitable, assessments to embed within each instructional framework.

Literature-Based Framework

Book clubs are a constant feature of Mrs. Wilson's sixth-grade classroom. To identify topics and titles for the groups, Mrs. Wilson distributes an *interest inventory* at the beginning of the year. During the peer-led book club discussions, this teacher listens to students' talk and records *anecdotal notes* for future reference. Mrs. Wilson also relies heavily upon a variety of *visual representations*, such as graphic organizers, that reveal students' knowledge, understanding, and reactions before, during, and after reading. Short *written responses* (e.g., quickwrites, exit slips, response journals) and longer projects provide further evidence of student growth. She also puts a premium on student *self-evaluation*. Whether reading or discussing a literature circle book, students regularly are asked to evaluate their levels of participation, to consider their use of strategies, and to reflect on their progress. *Conferring* is an integral part of her assessment tool kit; Mrs. Wilson meets regularly with students to push their thinking deeper, to provide a focus lesson for individuals or groups, and to see how well they monitor and evaluate their understanding; all are key factors in promoting independence. Finally, students take a mandated *standardized reading comprehension test* in the late spring. In preparation for this test the school has designed three benchmark, or interim assessments, that are administered in November, January, and March.

Inquiry-Based Framework

Mr. Rodriguez has several assessment goals for his second-grade integrated unit on communities and weather. At the beginning of the year, he gives students *screening tests* to make grouping decisions and to identify the range of texts students need for conducting their inquiries.

Mr. Rodriguez assesses students' knowledge and strategy use throughout the inquiry unit. He creates a *brainstorming chart* at the beginning of the inquiry unit to assess what students already know about the topics. He reviews students' *written responses* to learn more about their understanding, vocabulary knowledge, and strategies use. During research, students take simple notes on a *graphic organizer,* which helps Mr. Rodriguez know how well his students can glean relevant facts from unimportant details in printed or online texts. He regularly *confers* with individuals to gauge their progress and learning. Since he wants to foster metacognitive habits and positive dispositions, Mr. Rodriguez has students fill out short *self-assessments* to help them monitor their own attitudes and work. Students also complete an inquiry *project* that demonstrates their learning of science and social studies content at the end of the thematic, integrated subject-area unit. Periodically, he employs *running records* of students' oral reading to track the progress of those who need extra attention.

Basal Reading Framework

Ms. Fogel's fourth-grade literacy instruction revolves around a basal reading program. The program contains weekly and unit tests of the content read and the vocabulary and comprehension skills students have learned. The program also contains placement tests, informal reading inventories, and biannual vocabulary and comprehension tests. Of these, Ms. Fogel regularly uses the *weekly test* and the *unit test*, which she gives approximately every 6 weeks.

Implementing instruction and assessment according to the basal program's pacing guidelines leaves little time for anything else in the literacy block. Still, Ms. Fogel supplements her basal reading assessments with some easily integrated assessment tools. For instance, during guided small-group reading, she uses the students' *retellings, question responses,* and *discussion comments* to check understanding. Toward the end of the year, she administers the state-mandated *vocabulary and comprehension standardized tests.*

All three of these teachers take the position that the district- and state-mandated assessments are necessary and that they assist their students to do well. However, most of the assessment information they find valuable comes from the comments and written work of the students. In these three classrooms assessment and instruction are not separate, rather, assessment flows from instruction.

ASSESSMENTS AND THE CCSS

Increasingly comprehension assessment will be linked to CCSS grade-level objectives (Valencia, Pearson, & Wixson, 2011). In some ways, the notion of evaluating the dimensions of good comprehending is compatible with the CCSS's vision of a successful college- and career-bound student. For instance, new standardized tests will assess students' ability to understand key ideas and details, to integrate knowledge and ideas across text and genres, and to perceive how the author's craft and structure affect meaning, as seen in Figure 4.1.

The assessment of the CCSS will require new assessment tools that go beyond the traditional reading of a few passages and the answering of multiple-choice comprehension questions. Hearkening back to the New Standards Project, which stressed the use of authentic texts, performance activities, and portfolios, the developers of the new assessments will attempt

COMMON CORE STATE STANDARDS

The CCSS have a slim to negligible chance of making a difference unless new assessments are devised to address stepped-up expectations for readers (Pearson, 2011). These new tests must be able to show how students:

- Understand informational and narrative texts of increasing complexity.
- Contend with a wide range of author's purposes, genres, styles, and text structures.
- Analyze and evaluate the information and viewpoints found in printed and digital texts.
- Use varied types of text to build world and academic knowledge.
- Cite textual evidence to support their inferences and interpretations.
- Compare, contrast, and synthesize information and viewpoints on the same topic found in multiple texts.

FIGURE 4.1. New assessments need to align with the CCSS.

to find better ways to assess the interpretations, analysis, and intertextual connections the CCSS expect of our students (National Center on Education and the Economy, 1998).

INFORMAL CLASSROOM ASSESSMENTS

Just as views toward literacy and instructional practices have changed over time, so too, have attitudes toward assessment. Current definitions of literacy point to multiple dimensions of comprehension. No single assessment can adequately measure its complexity (Pearson & Hamm, 2005). To determine whether students are becoming better readers, evidence in the classroom should be gathered on students' knowledge, metacognition, strategies use, and motivation. Evidence for each of these components can be collected from informal assessment, designed by the teacher, by listening to what students say and reading what they write. Informal or formative assessment is not a testing instrument but a process where teachers and students continually reflect on learning (Black & Wiliam, 1998).

Oral Responses and Discussion

Teachers can draw on students' answers to questions, retellings, and dialogue to inform instruction. Each of these practices can be employed to collect information about students' knowledge, use of comprehension strategies, metacognition, and motivation. Teachers can ask questions that probe students' strategic and metacognitive awareness, their knowledge of what they read, and their reasons for not engaging thoughtfully with a text during independent reading. By keeping your eyes and ears open, you can learn a lot.

Questioning

The oldest and most frequently used practice for assessing comprehension is questioning (Afflerbach, 2007). Provided in published materials or generated by a teacher, questions serve to assess knowledge or to scaffold thinking so that students can achieve with assistance what is impossible on their own.

Teachers need to bear in mind that different types of questions fulfill different purposes. One widely used system of questioning is called Bloom's taxonomy (Bloom, 1956), which has been revised more than once. The most current version (see L. W. Anderson & Krathwohl, 2001) includes the following six levels of cognitive processes: (1) *remember*—defining and recalling information, (2) *understand*—paraphrasing or explaining ideas, (3) *apply*—using knowledge in a new way, (4) *analyze*—integrating and distinguishing concepts, (5) *evaluate*—appraising and defending views, and (6) *create*—formulating or writing new viewpoints. There is also a knowledge dimension that can explore students' factual, conceptual, procedural, and metacognitive knowledge. Teachers can generate questions that correspond to each of these levels of cognitive processing or knowledge dimensions.

Consider the questions in Figure 4.2. Bloom's taxonomy has strengths and weaknesses for developing comprehension questions. In terms of strengths, the taxonomy reminds teachers to ask increasingly complex questions rather than to depend on ones beginning with *who, what, where,* and *when.* One weakness of the taxonomy is its failure to break down the

Questions	Dimension
Where did the story take place?	Cognitive—remember
How did the character feel when he won the contest?	Cognitive—understanding
What are the themes in the story?	Cognitive—analysis
Did the author make you believe that the character was truthful?	Cognitive—evaluate
How did you determine a main idea?	Knowledge—procedural
Did that strategy help you summarize the story?	Knowledge—metacognitive

FIGURE 4.2. Sample questions based on the new Bloom's taxonomy.

understanding category into the many levels of inferences necessary for comprehension. As we developed in Chapter 1 with the construction–integration model and as we expand in Chapter 6, the process of understanding is complex and requires many strategies and different types of inferences.

We recommend a simpler system for developing questions: the question–answer–relationship (QAR) scheme, proposed by Taffy Raphael (1986). Like Bloom's taxonomy, the QAR reminds teachers to ask a range of questions. However, it also calls attention to the connections between various types of questions and the kinds of thinking in which students should engage. The QAR identifies four types of questions:

1. *Right there.* Questions focus on answers that are stated verbatim in the text.
2. *Think and search.* Questions focus on answers that require the reader to draw upon or compare and contrast information directly stated in several parts of the text.
3. *Author and you.* Questions focus on inferential thinking. To answer these questions, the reader must think about what he or she already knows and then use this information to complete what the author implied. In effect, students have to "read between the lines."
4. *On my own.* Questions focus on answers that are not dependent on the text. Students need to state an opinion, provide a personal reaction, or draw on knowledge.

In the following example, a fifth-grade teacher prepares several questions in advance of teaching a nonfiction selection on the *Hindenburg* disaster using the QAR guidelines. We provide a short excerpt from that small-group lesson, followed by what a teacher can learn about students' comprehension by analyzing their responses.

MR. WILLIAMS: Here's a question for you. So, does what happened to the Hindenburg remind you of anything else? [e.g., *On my own*)

OLIVIA: Yeah, the *Titanic*.

ALL: Yeah.

EMILY: You can now see the movie in 3D.

MR. WILLIAMS: In what ways are the disasters of the *Hindenburg* and the *Titanic* alike and how are they different? [e.g., *On my own*]

OLIVIA: They were a new kind of transportation.

CATORI: And they were in a disaster; but, the *Titanic* sank and the *Hindenburg* blew up.

MR. WILLIAMS: Yes, that's true. So, why do you think people wanted to travel on the *Hindenburg* in the first place? [e.g., *Author and you*]

EMILY: They didn't know there was going to be a problem.

OLIVIA: It was like an airplane.

CATORI: But it wasn't an airplane, really.

MR. WILLIAMS: What do you mean? [e.g., *Author and you*]

CATORI: Airplanes go lots faster.

OLIVIA: Yeah, well, even though the airplane goes faster than the *Hindenburg*, it still traveled faster than if they went by boat. It says here in the book that it took the *Hindenburg* 2½ days to cross the Atlantic and boats took between 5 and 10 days. If it were me, I'd rather take something that went faster.

EVAN: It also was like, you know, people always want to be the first to try something new. You know, like when Apple puts out something, everyone wants to get it.

MR. WILLIAMS: Oh, so you are saying you think people wanted to travel on the *Hindenburg* because the new technology meant they could get to America faster and that people also wanted to show that they would be among the first to try it out? Like celebrities? [e.g., *Author and you*]

So how does knowing something about the *Titanic* or even seeing the movie help you better understand what you read about the *Hindenburg*? [e.g., *Author and you*]

EVAN: Well, it's like what we've been talking about—making text-to-text connections.

MR. WILLIAMS: Can you say more about this? [e.g., *Author and you*]

EVAN: Well, I thought about how people felt about going on the *Titanic* and that helped me know what it was like going on the *Hindenburg*.

This line of questioning reveals worthwhile information. It appears that students possess a basic understanding of the text since they can engage in a discussion about its contents. Furthermore, the students know how to connect their personal knowledge to information presented in the text. A few can even use that knowledge to defend their interpretations. Mr. Williams also garners several bits of information likely to have implications for teaching. For one, the group did not spontaneously make a connection linking the *Hindenburg* with the *Titanic*; they had to be prompted. In addition, Mr. Williams will need to watch Emily more closely because her comments seemed off topic. Finally, Evan was able to express why it made sense to make a text-to-text connection in this instance—providing a rationale for its use.

Listening, Observing, and Keeping Records

While listening and observing students, teachers can monitor knowledge, strategies, metacognition, and motivation. Although listening and observing yield immediately useful information, it often is more productive to create records for future use. Thus, for a particular text, task, or purpose a teacher needs to decide in advance: Does it make sense to make a bulleted list of notes, to use a targeted checklist found on the Internet, or to write an anecdotal narrative description?

Because small-group discussions move quickly, taking notes is impractical; thus, using a checklist is preferable. For recording purposes, we devised the following checklist to track the strategies and connections students display during small-group discussions (see Figure 4.3). At the top of the chart, there is a place to record the students' names and the date. As the discussion proceeds, a teacher can write a plus sign (+) when the student initiates a strategy on his or her own, a check mark (✓) if the strategy is used when prompted, and a nought sign (◯) if a student is unable to use the strategy even with prompting. At the end of the day or the week, a teacher can look over the notes to decide what to reteach or work on next.

In Figure 4.3, the students in the small group were meeting with the teacher to discuss the first three chapters of *Holes* (Sachar, 1998). According to this checklist, Tia is making the most progress in terms of using strategies without prompting. She summarizes what has been read, and spontaneously makes predictions, inferences, and connections to personal experiences and to other texts. None of the other students were successful in summarizing the entire selection, but they did make connections to their personal experiences. Several students in the group—Julie, Molly, and Darius—would benefit from more explicit instruction in generating inferences, and focusing on character traits and motives. Finally, the teacher plans whole-class instruction on summarizing the chapters. Evaluating needs to wait until more of the novel has been read.

Conferring

Teachers confer with students for many reasons. One purpose is to check on students' status and progress. A short reading conference provides insights

Group Snapshot: Comprehension Strategies and Responses								
Date: Week of December 3, 2012		**Student Names**						
Text: *Holes*; Chapters 1–3 **Strategies**		Julia	Cassie	Merzhad	Molly	Darius	Tia
P—Makes predictions		✓	✓	+	✓	✓	+
VP—Verifies predictions		✓	✓	✓	✓	✓	+
S—Determines importance and summarizes what has been read	Beginning of selection						
	End of Selection						
	Whole Selection	⊘	⊘	⊘	⊘	⊘	✓
CT—Connects ideas to other text							+
CS—Connects ideas to personal experience		+	+	+	+	+	+
CW—Connects ideas to world event or issue		✓	⊘	⊘	⊘	⊘	⊘
IF—Inference fiction: makes inferences about characters' feelings, motives, and traits		⊘	✓	✓	⊘	⊘	+
IN—Inference nonfiction: makes inferences about cause and effect, problems, importance		NA	NA	NA	NA	NA	NA
V—Visualizing		✓	⊘	+	⊘	⊘	+
E—Evaluating quality, usefulness, and credibility		⊘	⊘	⊘	⊘	⊘	⊘
SQ—Student generates questions		✓	✓	+	✓	⊘	+
M—Monitors comprehension, detects problem, and takes action (i.e., rereads, skips)		✓	⊘	+	✓	✓	+

Use the markings below to characterize the students' use of the strategies.

⊘ The student is unable to use the strategy even when prompted by the teacher.

✓ The student is able to use the strategy when prompted by the teacher.

+ The student initiates the use of the strategy without teacher prompting.

When the small-group lessons are completed, reflect on what strategies should be the focus of the next lesson.

FIGURE 4.3. Tracking students' comprehension moves during a discussion.

into their decoding, fluency, and comprehension. As part of a teacher–student conference, you may listen to a student read and think aloud, you may question the child about his or her motivation to read, and you can set goals and make book suggestions to motivate reading. Although conferences can be impromptu, we recommend scheduling them at regular, rotating intervals. We suggest the following guidelines:

1. Keep conferences focused.
2. Keep them 5 to 7 minutes in length.
3. Keep the number of conferences per day manageable (i.e., three to five students).
4. Keep notes to preserve a record of the meeting for monitoring progress and responsive teaching.

Ray Reutzel and his colleagues (2008) developed a simple format for conducting a reading conference. During the conference, the teacher conducts a running record of the book the student is currently reading and notes the student's rate and accuracy. First, the student retells a portion of the book and the teacher follows up with questions about story elements or topics, main ideas, and informational explanations. Second, the teacher and the student set goals for a future conference, and identify another book to read. Third, the teacher and the student decide how the book will be shared with the class.

Retelling within a Conference or during a Discussion

Analyzing a retelling of a story can be as simple as noting whether the child mentioned the setting, the main character(s), the problem facing the character(s), and how that problem was solved. For a more detailed description of how students can use story grammar to identify the key aspects of a narrative for retelling and summarization, see Chapter 5.

The retelling of nonfiction should also focus on its structural elements, such as main ideas, supporting details, procedures, and explanations. Although teachers often know how to assess students' comprehension of fiction, they are less familiar with using retellings for informational texts. In preparation for nonfiction retellings, students learn some basic expository structures that authors use to organize their writing. After laying this foundation, a teacher models retelling when reading aloud from informational trade books. Practice continues until students understand how retelling works. Nonfiction retellings can be assessed using some type of rubric.

(See Moss, 2004, for a detailed description of this multistep process, as well as a criteria/rubric to assess nonfiction retellings.)

Using an Interview in a Conference

A short interview during a conference can reveal the extent of a student's knowledge, interests, attitudes, goals, perceived competence, and strategies use. A teacher can find an existing interview form (see McKenna & Stahl, 2009) or create targeted questions. Tips for conducting interviews parallel those for retellings in that they should be short and students' responses should be noted.

Here is an example of an interview that focuses on metacognition with a second grader:

Ms. TAYLOR: What do good readers do?

MAYA: They read the whole thing.

Ms. TAYLOR: What do good readers do before they begin to read?

MAYA: They look at the words on the cover.

Ms. TAYLOR: What's one thing a good reader does during reading?

MAYA: Read the story fast.

Ms. TAYLOR: Do you think you are a good reader?

MAYA: Yes.

Ms. TAYLOR: Why do you say that?

MAYA: Because I can read all the words.

Ms. TAYLOR: What do you do when you read something you just don't understand?

MAYA: I ask someone to tell me the words or I get a dictionary.

From this interview we learn that Maya associates reading with decoding words rather than with making meaning. She does not appear to apply comprehension strategies, such as using picture clues to activate knowledge. Maya does have some metacognitive knowledge (i.e., "fix-up" strategies), but her repertoire needs expanding. From this interview, Ms. Taylor can reinforce that good readers are thinkers who focus on building meaning and not just word calling. To encourage monitoring, she can ask the student after reading: "Does what you just read make sense?" The evidence also suggests that Maya would benefit from explicit cognitive and metacognitive strategies instruction, starting with predicting and making connections.

Thinking Aloud

Another way to assess knowledge, cognitive and metacognitive strategies, and motivation is to have students think out loud as they read in a conference or in a small-group lesson. When students talk about their thinking, teachers glimpse how well students use strategies to construct and defend their interpretations (Bereiter & Bird, 1985; Davey, 1983). For example, compare the two responses provided by fourth-grade students when asked, "What are you thinking?" at the end of reading a selection about the Wright brothers.

- Justin: "I am thinking about how the plane lands. There are no wheels. The brothers might be millionaires for being the first to fly an airplane."

- Corinne: "That was an interesting story. During that first time of flight it must have been really exciting. Also, I found out aviation started a long time ago. They did a great thing that helped in the past and that's why I can fly in a plane now. I am thinking about how they invented the plane, how they made it, and how they got a plane in the air to fly it. But what is a sand dune?"

Justin's think-aloud focused on a specific, interesting, but nonessential detail. He also expressed an opinion, although his comment did not demonstrate understanding of the important issues in the text. In contrast, Corinne expressed an opinion and then provided support for why she found the text interesting. She made a causal inference linking her knowledge of the original flight to her ability to fly now (Graesser et al., 2002). As part of her think-aloud, Corinne summarized the gist and asked a question for clarification. Thus, her short response indicated how adept she was at employing various strategies to understand the text.

Small-group reading instruction, reading conferences, and shared reading experiences provide good opportunities for using think-alouds. To start, it is wise to explain the purpose for thinking aloud and to model its use. Then, give students a chance to practice. Stop them at the end of a section or page and ask, "What are/were you thinking?" If a student responds to the query with a simple retelling, prompt further, "So what do you think of that?" In general, whoever is reading takes a first crack at thinking aloud; thereafter, other students can chime in with their interpretations. At the beginning, expect to cue students to talk about their thinking during reading. However, with practice, many of them will grasp how to do so without prompting.

Written Responses and Work Products

Students complete a great deal of written work in class and this paper trail provides insights into the students' knowledge, thinking, and work habits. Over a week's time a student can complete graphic organizers, record thoughts in a response journal, and answer an open-ended question about a text selection. Graphic organizers give some insight into the students' understanding of text structures; response journals reveal students' ability to summarize, infer, and make connections to prior knowledge. Long-term projects yield evidence of students' research skills, resourcefulness, and diligence.

Graphic Organizers and Other Idea Trackers

Graphic organizers support comprehension and learning by highlighting the structure of texts and the interrelationships among ideas; they also provide a window into children's comprehension (Moore & Readence, 1984). (In Chapter 9 we describe how to use graphic organizers, whereas here we focus on their assessment value.) When students complete story maps we acquire a glimpse into their knowledge of narrative structure. Those students who struggle to complete the map are probably in need of further instruction and attention. A cause-and-effect graphic organizer on the American Revolution suggests that this particular student is struggling to understand the basic causes of the nation's beginning. Figure 4.4 indicates an understanding of taxation and representation as an underlying factor in the revolution, but the student who completed this graphic organizer failed to remember that the geographic distance between the colonies and Great Britain and their 100-year history of self-government through colonial legislatures contributed to the causes of the revolution.

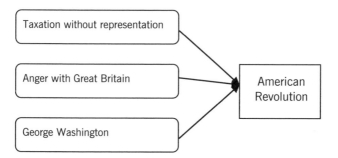

FIGURE 4.4. Graphic organizer: Causes of the American Revolution.

Another type of idea tracker, the popular K-W-L chart helps teachers explore students' prior knowledge and their ability to generate questions (Ogle, 1986). After students complete the K ("what I know") portion of the graphic organizer, the teacher can gauge the students' prior knowledge and then develop what the students do not know. The L ("what I learned") portion is a measure of knowledge gained at the end of the lesson or unit.

Good readers are thinkers. Teachers can follow the "tracks" of students' thinking and strategic processing through their use of margin notes or codes, annotations, or think sheets—all of which have been popularized by Harvey and Goudvis (2007). We distinguish here between graphic organizers and think sheets, although some people lump them together. Both types of tools stimulate and scaffold thinking—and provide teachers with assessment information. However, graphic organizers are visual tools that support learning, keep students focused, and facilitate understanding of specific text structures and concepts. Students do not explicitly record their reasoning on these organizers; instead, good thinking occurs behind the scenes. What's more, some students complete graphic organizers without ever necessarily perceiving why or how they foster comprehension.

Think sheets, in contrast, are not just repositories for structured facts or ideas. They push students to explicitly take note of their thinking and allow teachers to assess it. In addition, students are taught that such tools can be used to support their own comprehension and learning. Figure 4.5 illustrates differences between a traditional worksheet and a think sheet.

Written and Expressive Products

Students' writing and even artistic representations can be used to assess various elements of comprehension. Work samples can include written responses, drawings, collages, reports, role playing, and projects. In Mrs. Wilson's sixth-grade class the students are provided with several weekly opportunities to write about their independent and assigned reading. Sometimes the teacher directs what the students will write; at other times, as is the case with response and dialogue journals, students often decide how to respond. Below is an example of one boy's response to *Diary of a Wimpy Kid* (Kinney, 2002). Prior to writing, the teacher tells students that each response should include a summary of the events in the story, inferences about the characters' feelings and motives, and a connection to their personal experiences or to another story.

Greg invites Rowley to the house and while his brother has band practice they go in his room and look for stuff. They find a horror movie and later

Worksheet	Think Sheet
Comprehension Skill: *Main Idea or Detail*	**Important or Interesting?** *Sifting Out Important from Interesting Information*

Worksheet	Think Sheet
Directions: Read each set of three sentences. In the blank space, write either an *M* for the *main idea* or *D* for the two *details*. ____ Often they hide so they can sneak up on their prey. ____ Animals use camouflage to blend into where they live. ____ Some creatures hide so they won't be eaten. ____ Animals use camouflage in several ways. ____ Their coats take on the same color as the objects near them. ____ They look like, or mimic, other objects. ____ The arctic fox uses color to blend in with its environment. ____ In the winter, it turns white and in the summer it turns brown. ____ Some animals change color with the season. ____ When the animals eat something else, their color changes to match the new food. ____ Some animals change color because of the food they eat. ____ The food changes the color of their skin.	*Directions:* From the nonfiction text on animal camouflage, choose at least five facts. Ask yourself: Is this information something important to remember? • If so, then write it down in the Important column. • If not, but it is interesting, put it in the Interesting column. • In the third column, explain how you decided whether the detail was important or interesting. Something to think about: • Can a detail or fact be both important and interesting?

Important Detail	Interesting Detail	Your Thinking

FIGURE 4.5. Comparing Worksheets and Think Sheets.

while Greg's parents are asleep and his brother is staying with a friend, they watch the movie. They must sneak the movie back into his brother's room without messing anything up.

This response shows that the student, Robert, has a basic understanding of the story. He can summarize what he read, but the summary contains no inferences about the character's feelings or motives for breaking into his brother's room. Furthermore, Robert appears to make no connection to his own experiences or to other theme-related books. Mrs. Wilson makes note of this and will discuss it with him in their next conference. If enough students are having difficulty with inferences, then a new or refresher strategy lesson might be in order for a small group or even the whole class.

An important part of assessing work samples is providing constructive feedback to students. By doing so, they know what is needed to improve in the future. Feedback also conveys the message that the work is being taken seriously; it is not busywork. Feedback can be oral or written, but commonly, guidance is provided through rubrics. Rubrics are particularly beneficial because:

1. They inform students about the criteria for assessment.
2. They provide a framework and the language for discussing the features of outstanding, good, mediocre, and unacceptable work.
3. They can assess both product and process. Thus, rubric criteria can address a student's metacognition, strategies use, and motivation in addition to evaluating knowledge development and learning.

DIAGNOSTIC ASSESSMENT: FOR STUDENTS WHO FIND IT DIFFICULT TO COMPREHEND

In every class there will be a few students who find comprehension difficult. Observing them as they read and discuss in small groups and studying their class work will give you some insights into their difficulties; but often, you need to go beyond these methods and conduct a diagnostic assessment. The first goal of diagnostic assessment is distinguishing comprehension problems from decoding and fluency deficiencies. It is not unusual to confuse the two problems, because poor word-recognition skills and weak fluency can undermine comprehension. When a student focuses on the words, there is less attention available for decoding (Cartwright, 2010). A good first tool for diagnosing comprehension problems is an informal reading inventory like the Qualitative Reading Inventory–5 (QRI-5; Leslie & Caldwell, 2010).

The QRI-5, like any informal reading inventory, consists of graded word lists, reading passages, retelling guide, and comprehension questions. How these tools are used affects the information that is gained. The skill of the teacher administering and interpreting the inventory determines its effectiveness. To diagnose effectively, the teacher needs to have a model of reading in mind to guide his or her inquiry. Use the following directions and questions to guide your diagnostic thinking.

1. *Look first for problems with decoding and fluency*:
   - Is the student able to read grade-level material with an accurate rate above 94%? Is the student's reading at an instructional level for word-recognition accuracy?
   - Can the student read grade-level material with a fluency rate above the 30th percentile, according to national fluency norms? (See *www.readnaturally.com/pdf/oralreadingfluency.pdf.*)

2. *If word recognition and fluency are established, think about the following causes of comprehension difficulties:*
   - How does vocabulary knowledge affect the student's comprehension? Are there critical words in the passages that the student does not know?
   - Is the student's comprehension difficulty affected by passage type? Does the student fare better when reading narrative versus informational text?
   - How is the student's comprehension affected by prior knowledge? Does lack of prior knowledge prevent the student from making needed inferences?
   - Does the student have difficulty with gleaning information from the passage, making inferences, or both?
   - Does the student employ comprehension strategies when reading? Does the lack of strategies use impact comprehension?

Using Informal Reading Inventories to Understand Comprehension

The standard administration of an informal reading inventory begins with assessing a student's word knowledge on a graded word list. From this assessment the teacher obtains a good estimate of where to begin the reading of graded passages. In the next part of an informal reading inventory the student reads a series of graded passages as the teacher attempts to find the student's independent, instructional, and frustration levels, with those levels defined by both word-recognition accuracy and comprehension. Each informal reading inventory is a bit different. For our purposes, we focus on the QRI-5 because it provides many features for assessing comprehension difficulties.

Before a student reads any passage, the teacher asks him or her three or four concept questions to assess prior knowledge and to determine if the passage is suitable. If the student has no prior knowledge of the topic, the manual suggests selecting another passage. With the first passage selected, the teacher has the student read it orally while recording miscues and noting reading rate. Upon completion, the student either retells the story, answers a series of comprehension questions, or both. If the student's performance is satisfactory (i.e., the child reads at an instructional level), the teacher proceeds to the next higher-graded passage and keeps doing so until a frustration level is reached. However, if the initial passage is too difficult, the teacher may try easier passages until the student's instructional level is attained. The teacher can further explore a student's comprehension problems by comparing his or her performance on narrative and expository text and on silent versus oral reading.

You can develop a deeper understanding of students' reading comprehension by conducting a close analysis of the questions missed on the QRI-5 (Dewitz & Dewitz, 2003). Look for the following problems:

- Can the student make causal inferences and infer the effect of an action if the cause is given?
- Can the student connect several ideas to determine the main idea?
- Does the student's comprehension break down because he or she fails to connect pronouns to nouns?
- Does the student overuse prior knowledge and excessively elaborate with information that is not pertinent to the text or that is simply wrong? Poor readers tend to overuse prior knowledge (Oakhill & Cain, 2007).
- Does the student fail to answer the question because he or she didn't know critical vocabulary?

Categorize each wrong answer using one of the above five reasons. Then determine the primary reasons for a student's comprehension problems. Many students rely too much on prior knowledge; others fail to make causal inferences; still others lack the necessary vocabulary (Neuman, 1990; Dewitz & Dewitz, 2003). The QRI-5 also provides a think-aloud procedure to assess a student's use of comprehension strategies.

Assessing Students' Motivation and Strategy Knowledge

At the beginning of the year, it makes sense to screen students on their metacognition, strategies use, and motivation to read. Every teacher knows the importance of motivation. Yet, outside of providing choice, sparking enthusiasm for a specific book or project, and providing points and pizza for reading, teachers typically overlook other aspects of motivation—social interaction, and self-efficacy (Afflerbach, 2007). One way to obtain information beyond observing students' actions or inferring attitudes through body language is the Motivation for Reading Questionnaire (MRQ; Baker & Wigfield, 1999; Gambrell, Palmer, Codling, & Mazzoni, 1996). This 54-item assessment requires students to rate themselves on a scale of 1 to 4 on 11 facets of motivation, shown in Figure 4.6.

Three schools that one of us (Peter Dewitz) worked with used the MRQ to guide their instruction. The results of the survey revealed that most students reported no social reasons for reading. They did not talk about books with their friends or family. Additionally, many students avoided challenging books. The teachers used these results to design new experiences in the classroom and the school. Students conducted book talks in the library and over the public address system. Students shared new books that they enjoyed and teachers helped students get started with more challenging texts.

Motivation Factor	Sample Questionnaire Item
Self-efficacy beliefs	I am a good reader.
Challenge	I like hard, challenging books.
Work avoidance	Complicated stories are no fun to read.
Curiosity	I read to learn new information about topics that interest me.
Involvement	I enjoy a long, involved story or fiction book.
Importance	It is important to me to be a good reader.
Recognition	I am happy when someone *recognizes* my reading.
Grades	I read to improve my grades.
Competition	I am willing to work hard to read better than my friends.
Social	I talk to my friends about what I am reading.
Compliance	Finishing every reading assignment is very important to me.

FIGURE 4.6. The factors within the Motivation for Reading Questionnaire. The specific items that comprise this survey can be found at *www.msu.edu/~dwong/ CEP991/CEP991Resources/Baker%26Wigfield-MotivRdng.pdf.*

I have a purpose in mind when I read.	Global
I think about what I know to help me understand what I read.	Global
I discuss what I read with others to check my understanding.	Supplemental
I underline or circle information in the text to help me remember it.	Supplemental
When a text becomes difficult, I reread to increase my understanding.	Problem solving
I try to get back on track when I lose my concentration.	Problem solving

FIGURE 4.7. Sample items for the Metacognitive Awareness of Reading Strategies.

Surveys are available to assess students' metacognitive awareness of reading strategies. The Metacognitive Awareness of Reading Strategies (Mokhtari & Reichard, 2002) yields information about students' use of global, supplemental, and problem-solving strategies. Figure 4.7 provides samples from the 30 items on the survey. The students complete the survey by indicating how often they use each strategy—(5) I always or almost always do this to (1) I never or almost never do this.

The survey questions we developed in Figure 4.8 can help you probe more deeply into the students' knowledge of reading strategies. The survey

Please answer the questions below with as much detail as you can.

1. What makes someone a good reader?
2. When you read, how can you tell the difference between what's important and what isn't important?
3. Do you ever make a picture in your mind from what you are reading? Why can this be helpful?
4. What kinds of questions do you ask yourself when you are reading?
5. What does it mean to "evaluate" the information in a text?
6. What information do you use to guess what is going to happen next when reading? Is it a problem if your guess is wrong?
7. What clues can an author leave in a text to help you figure out what information is important?
8. Why do good readers need to "infer" what's going on in a text?
9. Why do you and your classmates have different understandings/draw different conclusions/come up with different ideas/when you read the same text?
10. How can making a connection between books you've already read and your personal experiences help you better understand the book you are reading now?

FIGURE 4.8. A sample reading strategies interview.

begins very generally ("What makes someone a good reader?"), and then focuses on specific strategies and their use. We recommend using these questions as part of a reading conference or within a small-group comprehension lesson. Such a survey can indicate which students need more tailored support so you can provide additional support to the students who need it (Duffy, 2009).

These surveys, while valuable, tell you what students report and not what they do. They are more valuable for older students who can more easily understand the questions and have the insight to respond. Any survey must be supported by direct evidence of metacognition and strategy use. Since both of these key components are hidden from view, we urge caution in interpreting results. If classroom discussions and written work also suggest that students lack metacognition and reading strategies, a teacher can be more confident in using the data.

LOOKING BACK, LOOKING FORWARD

In a personal communication, a testing director mentioned that schools in her district were spending 61 days a year out of a 180-day school year for giving tests, preparing for tests, reviewing results, or rewarding students for strong test performance. We suspect that this is not an isolated case. As the emphasis on assessment and accountability continues, juggling the demands of outstanding comprehension instruction with proliferating and mandated testing will remain no small feat.

Nevertheless, the importance of assessment should not be minimized. What counts is assessing what truly matters. That means obtaining a clear profile of each student's knowledge, metacognition, strategic processing, and motivation—as well as keeping tabs on their growth. We believe that every teacher should continually ask the question: Will the results of this assessment provide me with worthwhile evidence that can inform my teaching? If the answer is *no,* it is time to reconsider that assessment and examine if there is a better alternative. Grading is not the only reason we assess.

What does the common statement "Assessment drives instruction" mean? To us, it refers to viewing assessment through the lens of the GRRM-C. Ongoing, informal assessment provides the basis for day-to-day instructional decision making. Pairing principled teaching with well-chosen assessments is necessary for developing self-reliant, mindful, and capable readers.

That brings us to the end of the first half of our book. In the second half, we take the various concepts and guidelines we introduced earlier and apply them in the context of three literacy instructional frameworks. Chapters 5 and 6 focus on the teaching of comprehension in a literature-based reading program. We then portray the teaching of comprehension with informational texts in the context of inquiry-based instruction in Chapters 7 and 8. Finally, in Chapters 9 and 10, we describe the teaching of comprehension in a basal reading program.

APPLICATIONS AND EXPLORATIONS

1. List the assessments you currently use (or are familiar with) and then decide whether they address knowledge, motivation, strategies, and metacognition. If you have a gap, what assessments can you add, especially considering the informal actions you can take in the classroom?

2. Administer the QRI-5 or another informal reading inventory and consider what the assessment reveals about that student's knowledge, strategies, motivation, and metacognition. What else would you need to add to assess this student?

3. Teaching students to become good comprehenders is demanding, and so is preparing students for success on the high-stakes assessment. What can you think of to balance the two and do credit to both? Review with your colleagues or classmates the work by Guthrie (2002) and Hornof (2008).

CHAPTER 5

Planning Comprehension Instruction in a Literature-Based Framework

The telling of stories has been characteristic of all people for thousands of years. Some 3,500 years ago the Sumerians wrote down the first story, the *Epic of Gilgamesh*, the tale of a leader bent on saving his city. Since then we have continued to tell stories, write and read stories, record stories, broadcast stories, and film stories. Some have argued that the narrative is the way we make sense of the world—it's how we define who we are (Gallagher, 2000). The narrative may be rooted in our basic cognitive functions and we use it to communicate, convince, explain, and entertain. For Bruner (1986) the narrative is a distinct form of thought different from the linear, analytic thinking of science or technology.

Reading fiction provides many benefits besides its sheer entertainment; it is an aesthetic experience (Rosenblatt, 1978/1994). The story or the narrative schools us in the lives of other people. Reading stories helps us understand other people, empathize with them, and see the world from other's perspectives. Raymond Mar and Keith Oatley (2008) have demonstrated through brain imaging that fiction produces a vivid simulation of reality. When we read fiction we activate in our brain the same sensory centers that real experiences would trigger. Reading that "LeBron James hit a three-point jumper from the corner" stimulates the motor centers of the brain and metaphors like Tormé's "velvet voice" activates the auditory part of the brain. These recent brain imaging studies document the reality of the "lived through experience" that Rosenblatt (1937) described many years ago.

As students proceed through school, fiction hopefully continues to elicit this aesthetic experience even as it becomes a topic of study. The Common Core State Standards require the reading of fiction and view it as an object of study, just like planets, nations, and triangles. Starting in the primary grades, children study the characteristics of various fictional genres, the structure and elements of fiction, and the language of fiction. They learn strategies to retell, summarize, make inferences, and determine the theme of fiction. The skillful teachers walk a tightrope, helping students to understand and appreciate the structure and meaning of literature without squelching students' aesthetic response. That is our goal as well.

In this chapter and the next, we consider how to help students comprehend fiction. Following the theme of our book, fiction requires knowledge, motivation, metacognition, and strategic thinking. In Chapter 5, we focus more on planning instruction, discussing knowledge development, and motivation. In Chapter 6, we present "live-action" teaching of fiction from real classrooms focusing on strategic thinking, metacognition, and knowledge development through moment-to-moment decision making.

GOALS FOR THIS CHAPTER

✓ Consider two approaches for teaching literature.

✓ Align the good comprehender model with literature instruction.

✓ Discuss the influence of the CCSS.

✓ Build knowledge by constructing units of instruction.

✓ Develop knowledge for individual texts.

✓ Build knowledge of vocabulary and figurative language.

✓ Motivate students through independent reading.

TWO APPROACHES FOR TEACHING LITERATURE

The Anthology Approach

Two major frameworks have dominated the teaching of literature for decades: the literature anthology and the reading workshop. In the first approach the teacher assigns specific selections for the whole class or small groups to read. The selections may come from an actual anthology or they may be chapter books or novels. Often these selections are organized in some thematic fashion. The teacher introduces the selections, develops some knowledge and vocabulary, and then the students read. The teacher then engages in a discussion, asking questions to develop students' insights and assess their understanding. After reading the student might complete a graphic organizer or write a response to his or her reading. Periodically, the teacher might introduce and model a comprehension strategy such as predicting, summarizing, or determining the theme. One selection follows another as the class moves through the anthology or onto the next novel.

The Reading Workshop Approach

In contrast to this teacher-centered model is the reading workshop approach developed by Nancie Atwell (1998). The reading workshop centers on students' self-selected reading, but does not prohibit a group of students from reading the same selection. The typical reading workshop begins with a teacher-sharing time as he or she reads and discusses a poem, short story, or novel. The shared text might illustrate a theme the class is discussing, focus on a particular aspect of the author's craft, or tie to the history or science curriculum. If the class is studying the Civil War, the teacher might read and discuss *Pink and Say* (Polacco, 1994), the story of a young Southern white soldier assisting a Northern black soldier after a battle.

Next, the teacher introduces a focus lesson on a topic or strategy that students need. Early in the year the focus lessons cover the procedures of the reading workshop. When the procedures flow well, the focus lessons shift to literary concepts and comprehension strategies. The core of the reading workshop is self-selected reading, student response, and teacher conferences. For 30 to 40 minutes a day the students read independently, write about what they are reading, and confer with the teacher. Both the written responses and the conferences provide an opportunity for the teacher to assess students' learning and to guide their comprehension. At the close of each workshop, a few students share what they have read, and by relating their experience, they motivate the others in the class.

THE GOOD COMPREHENDER MODEL
IN LITERATURE INSTRUCTION

The anthology approach and the reading workshop are two frameworks for organizing the reading of literature and developing students' comprehension. We view them not as opposites but as alternatives that teachers should employ depending on their goals and the needs of their students. Yet, we need to consider both of these frameworks from the perspective of the good comprehender model (see Chapter 1, Figure 1.2, p. 14).

Good readers are knowledgeable, motivated, strategic, and metacognitive. To read literature, the reader must bring to the page general knowledge of the world and knowledge of the structure and elements of fiction. The anthology approach allows teachers to develop the same knowledge for the whole class because there is a common text. In the workshop approach knowledge development is an individual concern. The good comprehender is strategic and metacognitive—and that means the teacher should allocate time to explain and model cognitive and metacognitive strategies, and employ discussions guiding students to apply those strategies. For students who struggle with strategies and metacognition, more teacher direction is probably required. The anthology framework affords more opportunity to do so especially if the teacher works with small groups of students all reading a common text. To achieve the same end, a teacher in the workshop approach must either assign common texts or focus on strategies during individual reading conferences.

Readers must be motivated and that means choice. The reading workshop approach is organized around choice to promote motivation. Teachers who use an anthology approach must include some choice.

THE COMMON CORE STANDARDS

The CCSS will have a considerable influence on how we develop students' reading comprehension and what it means to be a reader of literature. These are the literature standards expressed as broad goals not specific to a grade level, as seen in Figure 5.1.

According to the CCSS,

> Students who meet the Standards readily undertake the close, attentive reading that is at the heart of understanding and enjoying complex works of literature. . . . They actively seek the wide, deep, and thoughtful engagement with high-quality literary and informational texts that builds knowledge, enlarges experience, and broadens worldviews.

But, we must caution—the best readers in the world are not always thoughtfully engaged with high-quality literature. Instead of reading literature that is good for them, they read literature that tastes good (Krystal, 2012). The best readers in the world read pulp fiction, at the beach, and revel in its stereotypical characters and hackneyed plots. Our goal is to create thoughtful *and* avid readers.

The CCSS describe the increasing difficulty of the texts students should be able to read and the insights and understanding they should be able to develop from those texts. To achieve these goals, we must provide an exciting, rich curriculum and promote the habit of independent reading. Before we look at the teaching of comprehension, we will return to Mrs. Wilson's sixth-grade literature classroom that is a hybrid of the anthology and the reading workshop models.

	COMMON CORE STATE STANDARDS

Key Ideas and Details

1. Read closely to determine what the text says explicitly and to make logical inferences.
2. Determine the central ideas or themes of a text and analyze their development, summarizing the key supporting details and ideas.
3. Analyze how individual events and ideas develop and interact over the course of a text.

Craft and Structure

4. Interpret words and phrases as they are used in a text including determining technical language, connotative and figurative meanings, and analyze how specific word choices shape meaning or tone.
5. Analyze the structure of texts including how specific sentences, paragraphs, and larger portions of texts (section or chapter) relate to each other and the whole.
6. Assess how point of view or purpose shapes the content and the style of a text.

Integration of Knowledge and Ideas

7. Integrate and evaluate content presented in diverse media and formats including illustrations with a text.
8. Standard does not apply to literature.
9. Analyze how two or more texts address similar themes or topics in order to build knowledge or to compare the approaches the authors take.
10. Read and comprehend complex literary texts independently and proficiently.

FIGURE 5.1. CCSS for literature.

Looking inside Mrs. Wilson's Sixth-Grade Classroom

Mrs. Wilson, the sixth-grade teacher we have been following, has constructed a two-part reading experience for her students. Each day the students are reading, discussing, and analyzing the texts she has selected, sometimes in small groups and other times with the whole class. Currently they are studying the concepts of plot, which constitutes the varied ways that authors construct their stories. She begins with three novels: *Hatchet* (Paulsen, 1987), *The View from Saturday* (Konigsburg, 1996), and *Holes* (Sachar, 1998). *Hatchet* has a chronological plot; the action begins with a plane crash and then moves forward, with just a few flashbacks, as the main character works to survive in the wild. *The View from Saturday* tells the separate stories of four sixth graders, full of problems and doubt, as they prepare for a quiz-bowl championship. At the end of the novel these stories are woven together and the interactions of the characters are revealed. *Holes* has a complex structure with several ambiguous flashbacks that tell the background of the story. All of these background elements come together at the end of the book, making the characters' present actions sensible. Each group in the class reads one of these novels and then there is a large sharing time where plots are compared and discussed.

The second part of Mrs. Wilson's curriculum involves free-choice reading and literature circles. The students are expected to read widely in school and out. Mrs. Wilson confers weekly with each student to review the reading, discuss problems, provide encouragement, and suggest new books. The students also participate in literature circles where a group of four or five students choose to read the same book and meet regularly to discuss it. Literature circles happen when the students are not working on whole-class projects like plot or character study.

CCSS Standard R10: Texts in grades 2–12 must be gradually more complex by the end of each school year with the teacher providing support as needed.

During the literature circles the teacher observes and supports the students' discussions.

The CCSS imply that the teacher must exercise authority over text selection to ensure students read widely and deeply to build knowledge and skill. To create avid readers, however, the students must exercise considerable authority over what they will read. An anthology or a whole-class novel can only be the starting point for a successful comprehension program (Dewitz & Wolskee, 2012). Mrs. Wilson also provides the time and the structure to promote student self-selected, independent reading. We first discuss how to create units of instruction, for it is through these units that knowledge is built. Next, we consider how to build knowledge for individual selections.

BUILDING KNOWLEDGE: CREATING UNITS OF INSTRUCTION

CCSS Standards R1–9: The standards do not specifically address the development and use of prior knowledge but it is essential for comprehension.

Comprehension requires knowledge. Consider the first grader who has never slept over at a friend's house grasping the subtlety of *Ira Sleeps Over* (Weber, 1975), the story of a boy who must abandon his favorite blanket for his first sleepover, or the second grader who knows nothing about labor strikes comprehending *Click, Clack, Moo: Cows That Type* (Cronin & Lewin, 2000). *Click, Clack, Moo* can be appreciated by some children as a funny story about cows that type but a deeper understanding, considering strikes and labor issues, requires more knowledge. The competent reader can link the ideas and sentences together to produce a rough approximation of text, but meaningful understanding of the stories occurs when that information is integrated with prior knowledge. In Chapter 1 we called the first step in the process *construction* and the second step *integration* (Kintsch, 1998). The more that is known, the better the comprehension.

The CCSS cautions against front-loading instruction and telling students information they can derive from reading. Many students, however, require knowledge that must be built before students read. The CCSS did not repeal the schema view of reading comprehension (R. C. Anderson & Pearson, 1984) nor make unnecessary the knowledge that drives the construction and integration process (Kintsch, 1998).

There are three general ways to develop prior knowledge and all overlap.

1. Construct units of instruction where each text provides the knowledge necessary to comprehend the next text. Instructional units can be constructed that build thematic or conceptual knowledge, genre knowledge, or text structure knowledge.
2. Develop knowledge by specifically explaining concepts and building knowledge before students read a particular text. Much can be done through discussion, read-alouds, and technology to activate and build prior knowledge.
3. Teach vocabulary. Words are labels for concepts and when you teach vocabulary, you build conceptual knowledge.

In this section we first describe how to build genre and thematic units for instruction. Then we explore how to develop knowledge for a single text. Finally, we discuss vocabulary instruction.

Building Genre Units

A unit of study might be as short as a week when the focus is very narrow, such as one biography—or as long as a month, when students are exploring rich, thematic topics such as justice or immigration.

Knowledge of genre allows the reader to set a purpose for reading and to knit together the many pieces of a text into a coherent whole. When reading a mystery like *Nate the Great* (Sharmat, 2002), a second grader needs to know that he or she will find a crime, a detective, clues, and a plot sequence that chronicles when and how these clues are discovered and interpreted until a solution is determined. In fiction the structural elements are not as clearly signaled as they are in an informational

CCSS Standard R10: Knowledge of genre will build students' understanding of text elements and structures.

textbook. The writer does not label the conflict with a bold heading "CON-FLICT." Thus genre knowledge guides the thinking of the reader and helps him or her infer the structural elements.

Narratives can be classified into subgroups, or subgenres, by their shared thematic and language characteristics. If a story contains a spaceship, an alien, and a robot, and takes place in the future, it is likely science fiction. In a strong curriculum children will read all of the major genres, learning the characteristics of each. Figure 5.2 lists the genres that students should know by the end of middle school.

Teachers can construct genre units that help students explore the characteristics of a particular genre or compare and contrast two different genres. It is not realistic to explore all of these genres in a school year; therefore, a school or a district should first consider its standards and then spread the study of the genres over several years. We believe that traditional fantasy and realistic fiction are the easiest for younger children to grasp with historical fiction, science fiction, and modern fantasy requiring more knowledge and experience.

A Second-Grade Genre Unit

At the beginning of the school year, Mr. Barden wants to start with a unit that will engage his second graders and build their desire to read. The CCSS call for students to be conversant with a range of genres and he decides that fantasy would be a good place to begin. He uses the resource book *A to Zoo: Subject Access to Children's Picture Books* (Lima & Lima, 2006) to locate book titles and then checks to make sure the school library has what he wants. Within *A to Zoo* are books about science, holidays, history, and geography, or themes like optimism, old age, feeling, or justice. He also consults *www. lexile.com* to determine the reading level of each book, plus he reads the plot summary on the website (see Chapter 2). Mr. Barden's fantasy unit includes the following titles[*]:

- *The Mysterious Tadpole* (Kellogg, 2004), Lexile 650; the story of a boy whose uncle sends him a strange tadpole from Scotland that grows up to be a very large and playful monster.
- *The Mysterious Giant of Barletta* (dePaola, 1988), Lexile 520; a mysterious giant saves a town through nonviolent means—trickery.
- *Dogzilla* (Pilkey, 1995), Lexile 340; this spoof of Godzilla is a fantasy where a town of mice save themselves from a giant marauding dog and her puppies.

[*]Note that when we denote reading levels, we use the Lexile system *(www.lexile.com)*.

Genre	Characteristics
Realistic fiction	Everything in a realistic story—plot, characters, and setting—is consistent with the lives of real people in our contemporary world. The story is not true, but it could have happened. Mystery and adventure are subgenres of realistic fiction.
Historical fiction	Historical fiction is realistic fiction set in a time remote enough from the present to be considered history. The setting, the time, and some characters must reflect historical facts.
Science fiction	Science fiction stories take place in the future, in time traveled past, involving scientific principles and mechanisms currently unknown or defying current scientific laws.
Fantasy— Traditional	
Folktales	They are timeless tales that tell the adventures of animal or human characters. They contain supernatural adversaries, supernatural helpers, tasks, and quests that reward good and punish evil.
Fables	Fables are brief tales in which animal characters that talk and act like humans indicate a moral lesson or satirize human conduct.
Fairytales	Fairytales are a type of folktale that contains elements of magic or enchantment in characters, plots, or setting. The well-known fairytales (Grimm, Anderson) are relatively recent translations of older folktales.
Myths	Myths are prose narratives that in the culture in which they are told are considered to be truthful accounts of what happened in the remote past.
Legends	Legends are prose narratives that, like myths, are regarded as true by the narrator and audience, but they are set in a period considered less remote, when the world was much as it is today. Legends are more secular than sacred and the principle characters are human.
Fantasy— Modern	Authors create modern fantasy by altering one or more characteristics of everyday reality. They may create whole new worlds *(The Hobbit)* or characters with supernatural powers *(Harry Potter)*.
Poetry	A composition often containing rhyme or rhythm that evokes images and gives special intensity to the expression of feelings and ideas.
Drama	A play, serious or comic, organized into scenes and acts with dialogue and directions for actors.

FIGURE 5.2. Narrative genres.

While reading and comprehending the stories, the students' understanding of fantasy grows as they compare and contrast the elements of the stories. Mr. Barden and his students enter the book titles on the class genre chart that lists the characteristics and purpose of each genre (see Figure 5.3). As new genres are studied, they are added to the chart; as new stories are read, they are added to the example column.

> **CCSS Standard R9:** Comparing and contrasting stories lead to a deeper understanding of theme.

Developing Knowledge of Narrative Elements

Children should dig deeper than the characteristics of genre by exploring the elements of narrative structure and then homing in on plot, character development, theme, and figurative language. Begin, as do most teachers, by studying narrative structure through story mapping. Many narratives, but not all, follow a predictable structure that is relatively easy to describe and explain. Knowledge of narrative structure acts as a scaffold allowing the readers to focus on the important ideas, to remember what has been read, and to recall it more completely. Knowledge of narrative structure guides the reader to focus on characters, setting, problems, events, and the resolution (Gordon & Pearson, 1983; Stein & Glenn, 1979).

Story mapping can be introduced as early as first grade through an oral read-aloud. Let's peak into Mr. Dillon's room as he introduces the concept to his first graders.

Genre	Characteristics	Purpose	Examples
Fantasy	Tales that contain the supernatural, fairies, or other strange elements	To entertain	• *The Mysterious Giant of Barletta* (dePaola, 1988) • *Dogzilla* (Pilkey, 1995) • *The Mysterious Tadpole* (Kellogg, 2004)
Realistic fiction	Real stories told in the here and now about real people and problems	To entertain, learn from life's experiences	• *Hatchet* (Paulsen, 1987) • *The View from Saturday* (Konigsburg, 1996)

FIGURE 5.3. Expanding genre chart.

MR. DILLON: Today we will read a story to enjoy it and discover how writers think. We want to know what goes into writing a story because after lunch we are going to write our own story. I am going to read you a story. Then we are going to discuss the parts of the story. Today's story is *The Bear's Toothache* by David McPhail [1988]. *(Reads the story through and stops occasionally to discuss what is happening and asks the students some questions. When finished, returns to the story.)* Now we are going to study the parts of the story; we are going to look for the characters, the people, or animals that the story is about. We will look at the setting, where the story takes place. Also we will look at the problems the characters face and how they try to solve their problems.

MR. DILLON: Who are the characters in the story?

TALIA: The little boy is a character, but I don't know his name.

ERICA: The bear is a character.

DANNY: I think the father is a character.

MR. DILLON: You have found all of the characters in the story. I am going to record them on our story map. Understanding the parts of a story will help us remember and retell them.

MR. DILLON: Where does the story take place?

TALIA: In a home, the boy's bedroom.

The explanation of story structure continues in this vein until the students have identified all of the elements in the story, as in Figure 5.4.

After lunch Mr. Dillon pulls out a blank story map and uses it to guide the students as they compose a class story. He links reading and writing as students use story maps to comprehend and compose. The students are asked to generate characters, setting, problem, and events; then, together, the class composes the story. The next day Mr. Dillon reads a new story and the students complete another story map with his assistance. He repeats the activity until the students can identify the story elements with little assistance. After three or four read-alouds he changes the procedure slightly and asks the students, "Before I read the story what story elements are we looking to discover?" He hopes the students have begun to internalize the concept of narrative

CCSS Standards R1, 2: Knowledge of text structure is key to locating information within a story and summarizing the story.

structure and respond with characters, setting, problem, events, and resolution.

As the instruction continues, Mr. Dillon releases the responsibility of mapping the stories to the students. First they complete the story map with partner support, later without partner support. Those who still need additional work can focus on story structure during small-group instruction. Once students can remember and recall stories well the activity should be discontinued and the students should move on to more advanced concepts (Singer & Donlan, 1982).

The study of narrative structure should change as students move through the grades, digging deeper into each element of the story. An event in a narrative can be divided into the initiating event, the internal response, the attempt, and the consequence. Consider the partial, but expanded, story map in Figure 5.5.

Focusing on stories at this deeper level leads the students to think about the causal chain of events within a story, what drives a character, and his or her inner emotional responses. Much of this must be inferred because writers often neglect to make these connections and motives explicit. Mr. Dillon keeps this structure in mind when he develops questions for a postreading discussion making sure that students understand the characters' inner feelings and the causes for their actions (Beck & McKeown, 1981).

Characters	The boy, the bear, and the father.
Setting Time Place	A home in a neighborhood, late at night.
Problem	The bear has a toothache and it hurts.
Goal(s)	The boy decides to help the bear.
Plot	
Event 1	The boy gives the bear a tough piece of steak to chew on, but it does not loosen the tooth.
Event 2	The boy hits the tooth with a pillow, but it does not come out.
Event 3	The boy ties a rope around the tooth, the bear jumps out of the window, and the tooth pops out.
Event 4	(Add more events as needed.)
Resolution	The bear gives the tooth to the boy to put under his pillow.

FIGURE 5.4. A story map for *The Bear's Toothache* (McPhail, 1988).

Element	Definition	Example
Initiating event	An action that sets up a problem or dilemma	The bear has a toothache.
Internal response	The characters' internal reaction	The bear is in pain and the boy wants to help.
Attempt	The action of the character	The boy hits the tooth with a pillow.
Consequence	The result of the action	The tooth does not come out, but the lamp breaks in the process.

FIGURE 5.5. A more complex story map for *The Bear's Toothache* (McPhail, 1988).

In the upper grades the understanding of narrative elements becomes more complex. The problem in the story is redefined as conflict and students learn about various forms of conflict: the individual versus the individual, the individual versus self, the individual versus nature, the individual versus society, and the individual versus technology. When studying plots students look for rising action or how the writer creates suspense, the climax or point of highest conflict, and other plot devices such as foreshadowing, hints about what will come, and flashbacks where the order of events is not chronological. Learning about these plotting devices improves the students' comprehension. Just as the story map improved the comprehension of young children, these concepts of plot help students focus on important ideas and remember what they read. A focus on story structure and other aspects of narrative structure promotes a close reading of the text.

Focusing on Character Development

Teachers can develop instructional units that help students understand any of the elements in a story: character development, setting, suspense, point of view, foreshadowing, and figurative language. To build such units the teacher needs to select texts that exemplify one of these literary elements. Mrs. Wilson, our focus sixth-grade teacher, wanted her students to study how an author goes about developing characters so they can draw inferences about character traits, emotions, and motives. She begins the unit with picture books, because these short texts help focus on the different ways an author can develop a character without wading through a long novel (Ivey & Broaddus, 2000). Mrs. Wilson selects the following books:

CCSS Standard R3: Work for in-depth knowledge of character development including traits, motives, and feelings.

- *Mirette on the High Wire* (McCully, 1992), Lexile 580; the story, told in the third person, of a young girl who yearns to walk on a high wire by studying with a retired and disaffected circus performer.
- *Brave Irene* (Steig, 1986), Lexile 630; the story of a very determined young girl who delivers the dress made by her mother, through a driving snowstorm to the palace.
- *Alexander and the Terrible, Horrible, No Good, Very Bad Day* (Viorst, 1972), Lexile 970; the story of a young boy's relentless, bad day and the desire to flee to Australia.

Mrs. Wilson first explains that the class will be studying how a writer creates characters. Sometimes the author simply describes physical and personality traits of each character. Sometimes we learn about the characters through their actions—a helping hand, a deft theft. Conversations take us to the comments and thoughts that one character has about another. Sometimes the author takes us into the minds of the characters and we are privileged to explore their inner thoughts. Mrs. Wilson and her students developed the chart in Figure 5.6 as they discuss the three books and their main characters.

As the students listen and discuss these three books their understanding of character development grows and they can apply what they have learned to understand and appreciate the characters in the books they choose to read.

	Mirette on the High Wire (McCully, 1992)	*Brave Irene* (Steig, 1986)	*Alexander and the Terrible . . .* (Viorst, 1972)
Main character	Mirette	Irene	Alexander
How the author describes the character	She is hardworking, good listener	She is small, strong, brave, loving	He really doesn't describe Alexander
The character's actions	She is willing to try dangerous things	She is resourceful, helpful	Many "bad" things happen to him
What we learn from other characters	She can take direction, criticism	She can be trusted	They don't talk to him, they push him, they call him names
Inside the mind of the character	She is determined, fearless	She is determined, concerned, scared	He feels unappreciated, angry, frustrated

FIGURE 5.6. Techniques used to develop characters.

Developing Knowledge through Thematic Units

Thematic units can consist of picture books, short stories, plays, novels, or poems that share a common theme or concept. The theme might be a historical period like the Holocaust, the Harlem Renaissance, or late 19th-century immigration. Some units might focus on a topic like ancestors, family life, or sports. Still other units might focus on behaviors, bullying or sharing or social issues, justice or the environment. The purpose of such units is to develop students' knowledge; something that a basal reading program rarely does (Dewitz, Leahy, Jones, & Sullivan, 2010). If at all possible, construct units that support the topics your students are studying in science and history.

> **CCSS Standard R2:** Creating thematic units help students understand the concept of theme.

Because of the wide range of reading levels within any classroom, a thematic unit should be differentiated. To create a unit, Mrs. Wilson does the following:

1. Develops a list of interesting topics by talking with students and using an interest inventory. Mrs. Wilson modifies this list by considering the topics covered in the science and social studies curriculum. She picked friendship and acceptance as the first unit because it will help build the social climate in the classroom. Some units work so well that they can be repeated year after year.
2. Defines the unit's goals in terms of developing knowledge, using strategies, and fostering metacognition and motivation.
3. Decides the unit's outcomes or products. Will students write a paper, create a report, write a play, create a video, or create a Power-Point presentation?
4. Develops a text set for the unit. Figure 5.7 is the text set that she developed for the unit on friendship and acceptance. She uses the Lexile website and *Amazon.com* to identify books for the unit and consults with her school librarian. She differentiates the unit by employing books of different reading levels.
5. Develops activities, identifies assignments, selects vocabulary, and writes out thought-provoking guided reading questions for each book.
6. Creates assessments that will measure students' knowledge, vocabulary, genre knowledge, and reading strategies.

The students read their books independently and use Post-it notes to record what they are learning about friendship. Mrs. Wilson meets daily with the low group to support their comprehension, helping them think

---

Friendship and Acceptance

The Other Side by Jacqueline Woodson (2001), Lexile 300; Clover's mom says it isn't safe to cross the fence that segregates their African American side of town from the Caucasian side where Anna lives. But the two girls strike up a friendship and get around the grown-ups' rules by sitting on top of the fence together. This read-aloud introduces the unit.

There's a Boy in the Girls' Bathroom by Louis Sachar (1987), Lexile 490; an unmanageable, but lovable, 11-year-old misfit learns to believe in himself when he gets to know the new school counselor, who is sort of a misfit too.

Because of Winn-Dixie by Kate DiCamillo (2000), Lexile 610; a coming-of-age story of a girl and her father who move to a small town and she works to make friends and find acceptance.

The Wanderer by Sharon Creech (2000), Lexile 830; on the way to visit their grandfather, 13-year-old Sophie and her cousin Cody record their transatlantic crossing aboard *The Wanderer*, a 45-foot sailboat that is en route to England.

FIGURE 5.7. Sample text set on friendship and acceptance.

strategically and read closely. She meets less frequently with the on- and above-grade-level students. At the end of each day, she reserves 5 minutes for students to share what they are learning about friendship. These insights are recorded on a chart. At the end of the unit, each group reports on the project they selected from Mrs. Wilson's list.

DEVELOPING PRIOR KNOWLEDGE FOR INDIVIDUAL TEXTS

Building prior knowledge before students read a passage has been a staple of reading instruction for the last 60 years and is reflected in many instructional approaches and theories of reading (R. C. Anderson & Pearson, 1984; Betts, 1946; Graves & Graves, 2003). The need for developing knowledge varies with the nature of the text and the background of the students. Teachers must distinguish knowledge students need to understand a text from knowledge they can develop by reading it. Third graders about to tackle *Freckle Juice* (Blume, 1984), a story about, well, freckles, need little additional knowledge, but the picture book *Pink and Say* (Polacco, 1994) requires some knowledge of the Civil War. Building knowledge must also be distinguished from activating prior knowledge. Some students approach a book without the knowledge necessary to comprehend it. Other students have that knowledge, but do not use it. Psychologists call this *inert knowledge* and the failure to use knowledge may underlie some of the difficulties students have making inferences (Renkl, Mandl, & Gruber, 1996).

Activating Prior Knowledge

Discussions, read-alouds, and technology are three ways of activating prior knowledge. Consider the unit on friendship we outlined above. All sixth graders have a concept of friendship but not all realize that friendship may require tolerance, forgiveness, and bravery. The picture book *The Other Side* (Woodson, 2001) can be used to stimulate thinking before students embark on their reading. Read the book, stop occasionally to pose thoughtful questions, and make comments. When you are done, you could have a discussion centered on the questions appearing at the top of Figure 5.8 (see the figure for students' responses). As children respond, they learn from each other, delve into their own experiences, and think more deeply about friendship.

Prior knowledge can be activated by a well-crafted discussion that does not require the reading of a picture book. Hansen (1981) developed a technique called the *weaving strategy*, which weaves text information with the students' prior knowledge. Imagine that Mrs. Wilson plans to introduce a book about a boy moving to a new neighborhood. She starts her discussion by asking the students two questions:

1. "What is it like to move to a new city or new neighborhood?"
2. "What is it like when new kids move into your neighborhood?"

Both of these questions are designed to elicit knowledge already known to students. They write their answers on gray strips of paper, with gray representing the gray matter of their brain. In the course of the discussion, the students who lack these experiences learn from those who share their experiences. Mrs. Wilson then ties the discussion closer to the book. She says, "In this story Jackie has just moved to a new house, and she meets

What is a good friend?	What sometimes makes friendship difficult?
Likes what you like.	Living far away from people.
Spends time with you.	Not being allowed to text friends.
Helps you when you have a problem.	If you are different.
Invites you to things—like parties.	

FIGURE 5.8. Discussion questions for *The Other Side* (Woodson, 2001).

three boys who look Jackie over with suspicion. What do you think Jackie will do to make friends?" The students share their answers, and then write their responses on colored pieces of paper representing ideas from the text. The colored strips and the gray strips are woven together as Mrs. Wilson makes the point that prior knowledge is integrated with text information to comprehend the story.

An instructional approach developed by Judith Langer (1981) called the *prereading plan* (PreP) helps the teacher activate prior knowledge, assess what students know, and then work to expand it. You begin the activity by writing a key word on the board and then asking the students what they know. In the case of the story about moving to a new neighborhood, you might begin with the word *friendship*. The teacher asks, "Tell me what comes to mind when you hear the word *friendship*?" You record the ideas on the board and then work to connect them, building a network of ideas. The teacher asks, "What made you think of kindness?" One student responds, "It is part of being a friend." The teacher is helping the students make connections and see that kindness is a characteristic of friendship, as are shared interests, trust, and fun. Finally, the teacher asks the students if they have thought of any new ideas about friendship. The PreP approach is more than just brainstorming because the teacher takes the students' responses and shapes them into a coherent structure. This can be illustrated on the board by creating a concept map.

Building Prior Knowledge

Even though fiction deals with common human events and experiences, successful comprehension requires prior knowledge. We should not assume that all students bring the same experiences to the page. For example, *The Voyage of the Frog* (Paulsen, 1989) requires knowledge of sailing. The author invites you to study sailing by placing a well-labeled diagram of a sailboat before the first chapter. Historical fiction is created around the premise that you know a bit about the historical era surrounding the events in the narrative. Science fiction writers, even while breaking the laws of science, require that you have some understanding of science so you can grasp the characters' peril.

In Mrs. Wilson's sixth-grade class a group of students have selected to read *Bud, Not Buddy* (Curtis, 1999), a novel set in the Great Depression and jazz era about a boy trying to find his musician father. Mrs. Wilson decided to give each member of the group the task of viewing a short video and then reporting back to the group. Some focused on how the Depression affected ordinary people *(www.youtube.com/watch?v=TpfY8kh5lUw)*; others examined the music and art of the era *(www.youtube.com/watch?v=h5tucwcS-_o&feature=related)*. After the students viewed the videos, they shared what they learned and developed a chart about the Great Depression.

Building and activating prior knowledge requires careful decision making. Provide too much knowledge and there is little left for the students to discover while reading the narrative. Provide too little and the students will not be able to make the inferences that fiction requires. A successful prereading lesson demands a careful assessment of the text and the students. In Chapter 6 we will delve deeper into this lesson planning process.

VOCABULARY INSTRUCTION AND LITERARY CONCEPTS

We teach vocabulary because it builds knowledge and makes reading comprehension possible (Stahl & Nagy, 2006). It is likely that at least 50–75% of our comprehension ability is explained by our word knowledge (R. C. Anderson & Freebody, 1981; F. B. Davis, 1944). Vocabulary knowledge and comprehension are linked in at least three ways (Stahl & Nagy, 2006). First, knowing more words makes you a better reader. Second, knowing words means that you also possess the knowledge or concepts that underlie the word. It is not just word knowledge that facilitates comprehension, but the conceptual knowledge words represent. Third, reading comprehension and vocabulary are both related to general underlying verbal ability. The ability to make inferences is critical to reading comprehension and vocabulary growth. We infer the meaning of many words during reading and making inferences is essential to comprehension (Sternberg & Powell, 1983). Thus, reading comprehension and vocabulary are reciprocal. Knowing more words enhances reading comprehension, and reading more builds vocabulary.

> **CCSS Standards L5, 6:** Vocabulary instruction is essential for building comprehension. The most difficult problem is deciding which academic vocabulary and domain-specific words to teach.

In the classroom, four comprehensive instructional experiences build vocabulary (Graves, 2006; Stahl & Nagy, 2006):

- Teach word meanings explicitly (Beck, McKeown, & Kucan, 2002).
- Provide students with rich language experiences by reading to them daily and showcasing new vocabulary. Students build much of their word knowledge by reading widely and deeply (Stahl & Nagy, 2006).
- Use word-learning strategies to build vocabulary: infer word meanings from context, use word parts (i.e., prefixes, suffixes, and word roots) to derive a word's meaning, and use the dictionary skillfully (Graves, 2006).
- Cultivate word consciousness, delighting in the idiosyncrasies and power of words. Children can play games with them, explore their origins, and study their idioms (Graves & Watts, 2002).

Our discussion of vocabulary straddles this chapter, Chapter 7 on inquiry, and Chapter 9 on basals. Here, we emphasize the teaching of individual words and devote attention to the importance of wide reading. We also focus on words common in literature, whereas in Chapter 7 we consider the teaching of content-area vocabulary. Unfortunately, an extensive discussion of word-learning strategies and developing word consciousness is beyond the scope of our book, so we suggest that you read Graves (2006) and Stahl and Nagy (2006).

Teaching Individual Words

CCSS Standard R4: A good reader can often determine the meaning of a word or idiom, but they sometimes need to be explicitly taught.

Two important questions drive the teaching of individual words: What words should I teach? How should I teach them? Selecting words to teach is complex and involves many different factors including the difficulty of the word, the richness of the context, and the experiences of the reader. We recommend that you select key words from the text students are reading, and not from some generic word list. We offer the following guidelines for selecting words to teach (Graves, 2006):

- Select words that are critical to the meaning of the story. The words must be central to understanding the characters, setting, plot, or theme.
- Select words that are likely to be used beyond the context of the story. In *The Voyage of the Frog* (Paulsen, 1989) the sailing terms *jib* and *boom* are important to the story but unlikely to be encountered in other texts. In contrast, the word *cremated* does have utility beyond the novel.
- Avoid words that students can easily figure out on their own, such as those with rich context clues or with familiar affixes and roots.

How you approach the teaching of individual words depends on the word and on the students. If the word represents a known concept, it will require much less explanation than one that represents a new concept. Returning to *The Voyage of the Frog* (Paulsen, 1989), the nautical words *pitch* and *roll* represent new concepts, whereas the words *resembling* and *compartment* represent known concepts. New concepts require more explanation and discussion than do known concepts. Some words represent neither new nor known concepts but require clarification of two closely associated words, such as *incredible* versus *astonished*. When explicitly teaching word meanings, consider the following guidelines derived from Graves (2006), Beck and her colleagues (2002), and Stahl and Nagy (2006):

- *Word learning requires both conceptual and contextual information.* Conceptual information means explaining the concepts that underlie the word and discussing the class into which a word fits. This is often followed with a formal definition. The students must experience how a word is used in a context. "Astonished is a feeling that leaves you speechless or amazed." *Feeling* is the word's class, *speechless* and *amazed* are concepts underlying the word.

- *Involve students in active discussion of the word's meaning.* Vocabulary instruction requires give and take. Urge students to think of examples of a word's use and then consider nonexamples of the word (A tiger is a *carnivore*, but a cow is not). Have students try out the word orally in a sentence and then provide corrective feedback.

- *Students must have multiple exposures to a word.* Students should discuss the word, read the word in context, use the word in writing, and compare the word to others. Once a word has been taught it should be reviewed multiple times over the next few weeks.

- *Involve students in deep processing of the word.* Deep processing means considering many facets of a word's meaning, comparing it to other words of similar meanings, discovering synonyms and antonyms, and considering subtlety of meaning. Filling in the blanks on a worksheet or matching words to a definition rarely requires the depth of thinking as does responding to the following questions: "Can you make an appointment for your accident? Why or why not?"

Teaching Figurative Language

Figurative language is a special case of vocabulary instruction. Literature, unlike science or technical language, abounds with words and phrases that give depth to writing. Writers frequently use language in a way that goes beyond the literal meaning of words to add layers

> **CCSS Standard L4:** Students should be taught academic and content vocabulary, figurative language, and nuances of word meaning. The CCSS do not tell us which words to teach.

of meaning and subtle connotations. When a writer employs similes, metaphors, hyperboles, and other modes of figurative language (see Figure 5.9), he or she is trying to express his or her thoughts or capture an image with greater power than the denotative meaning of the words. Thus, the sentence *Susie is like a giraffe* has more visual impact than saying *Susie is tall*. Figurative language is the playful, inventive part of the language—something children seem to enjoy early in the elementary grades. In some way, all forms of figurative language are metaphorical, describing something in terms of another.

Teaching figurative language requires some explicit instruction, continual comparison to other forms of figurative language, and regular discussion of these forms when they are encountered in text. Follow these steps to teach figurative language:

- Introduce two specific forms of figurative language with numerous examples. Stress the definition and characteristic of each form. Forms of figurative language are easier to learn if one can be compared with another.
- Write down on a whiteboard or smartboard many examples of each form and have students label them. Discuss why they used that label.
- Have students classify examples of different forms of figurative language and discuss their reasons for their groupings.
- Have students write a sentence that uses each form and share it with the class. Write these examples on a class chart. This is particularly useful for idioms that students might encounter.

Type	Definition and Examples
Simile	One object or person is compared to another using the word *like* or *as*. *She is as busy as a bee.*
Metaphor	One thing is described as another. *She is a cat.*
Personification	An object is described using human characteristics. *The house stared down on us from the hill.*
Hyperbole	The use of exaggeration or overstatement for emphasis. *He was so cheap that he knitted dryer lint back into sweaters.*
Onomatopoeia	Words that sound like what they mean. *Boom, snap, pop.*
Alliteration	The repetition of initial sounds when writing, most often in poetry. *The gardener grew gruesome green grapes.*
Idiom	A group of words that over time takes on a meaning totally independent of their original meanings. *A piece of cake, fuddy-duddy.*

FIGURE 5.9. Types of figurative language.

- Analyze everyday text, magazines, newspapers, Internet texts, and commercials for the use of figurative language. For homework, students should record examples that they can find.
- In your comprehension discussions, focus on how the use of figurative language can help writers achieve their purposes.

MOTIVATION AND INDEPENDENT READING

At the beginning of the chapter we posed two approaches for teaching literature. One was based on the teacher generally selecting the text and the other focused more on student selection, the reading workshop approach. The teacher needs to select the texts if the goal is to teach specific genres, text structures, or forms of figurative language. Student selection is critical when the goal is motivation and engaged reading. Student selection leads to wide reading, which is necessary to build knowledge and vocabulary (Stanovich, 1986). Let's return to Mrs. Wilson and take a closer look at how she promotes motivation and independent reading.

In Mrs. Wilson's room, knowledge and choice are key to motivation. Think about how you choose what to read next. You might listen to a friend talk up a book he just read. While driving home and listening to National Public Radio, you might catch an intriguing book review,

> **CCSS Standard R10:** To meet this standard teachers need to focus on complex texts and students need to choose them.

and jot down the title on a piece of scratch paper. You might go to the library or the bookstore and search for the newest work by Jodi Picoult, one of your favorite authors. You might read the bestsellers list in the *New York Times*. Knowledge underlies all of these book selection approaches. Deciding what to read next requires knowledge of books and authors. We need some assurance that the book we are considering will match our tastes, interests, and reading level. We need to trust those who guide us. Mrs. Wilson takes all of these insights into account as she creates her independent reading program. She plans to:

- Systematically build an extensive and interesting classroom library. She has over 200 books purchased from used bookstores, scoured from garage sales, and acquired from points earned from Scholastic Book Club sales. The classroom library is organized by level and genre and the books are rotated so that the ones buried in the back are moved to the front to stand out. The library is stocked with fiction, nonfiction, poetry, and periodicals. The classroom library is an inviting area where students can relax and read and may include a rug, beanbag chairs, a floor lamp, and colorful posters.

- Read regularly to her students and conduct author studies. She shares the work of prominent authors, letting the students know what they have written.

- Engage in book talks at least once a week. She shares personal favorites and new works just emerging on the scene.

- Provide an opportunity for students to talk about what they are reading. Frequently called "status of the class," every Friday she selects a number of students to discuss and evaluate what they are currently reading.

- Provide time for the students to read. Mrs. Wilson hopes that the habit of reading at school will encourage reading at home.

Giving students choice is not confined to independent reading. Mrs. Wilson allows for choice even in the more teacher-directed activities. When students are forming book clubs or literature circles, the groups form around a commonly chosen book. Mrs. Wilson does not provide unlimited choice but structures it so that her 25 students can choose from 10 different titles when forming their next literature circle.

Careful planning is critical to the success of Mrs. Wilson's reading program. She plans her instructional units carefully, as well as the books she intends to use within those units. She anticipates the prior knowledge that students will need to develop. She thoughtfully plans her vocabulary instruction, selecting words that matter in advance. Finally, she identifies a set of captivating books for independent reading because she realizes that students do not easily find books to read in this media-intense age.

LOOKING BACK, LOOKING FORWARD

In this chapter we explored some of the facets of teaching children to comprehend literature. We began with the premise that any act of comprehension requires knowledge, motivation, strategies, and metacognition. We then focused most of our discussion on the development of knowledge and motivation. The successful reader of literature brings an array of knowledge to comprehending fiction. He or she draws upon his or her personal experiences, knowledge of genre, and specific knowledge of text structure and literary conventions. Children's knowledge can be developed through carefully crafted units of instruction that focus on genre, text structure, and theme; it also depends upon preteaching specific concepts and vocabulary before reading. Finally, we looked at motivation and its importance in prompting independent reading.

In Chapter 6 we extend our study of narrative comprehension and examine how we can promote the strategic and metacognitive thinking of students. We explore how to lead a reading discussion that builds comprehension ability and how to help students lead their own discussions.

APPLICATIONS AND EXPLORATIONS

1. Work with your grade-level colleagues, your school's librarian, or classmates to develop units of instruction. Begin with the books you already own and then work with your principal to purchase new sets of novels. You can purchase relatively inexpensive novel sets through Scholastic and Follett; sometimes they can be found on eBay.

2. Build a text set for a genre or topical unit.

3. Select a short story, chapter book, or novel and, with your colleagues, work on the problem of selecting vocabulary. Pick one chapter and independently identify the vocabulary words that make the most sense to teach explicitly. Then discuss the words you selected and your reasons for selecting those words. This will help improve your skill in selecting vocabulary. You might also want to consult lists like the first 4,000 words *(www.sewardreadingresources.com/img/fourkw/4KW_ Teaching_List.pdf)* or the Marzano (2004) list. These lists can guide your thinking by helping you decide which are the most important words to teach.

4. Practice explaining and defining words with your colleagues to improve your vocabulary teaching skills. We have found that teachers often overestimate their word knowledge. Also, a good dictionary like the *Cobuild,* provides student-friendly definitions *(http://dictionary.reverso.net/english-cobuild).*

CHAPTER 6

Teaching Reading Comprehension
with Literature

It is traditional to think of reading comprehension instruction in terms of what we do before, during, and after reading a text. In Chapter 5, we considered the planning that is necessary for students to build knowledge, learn about genre and text structure, and develop word knowledge before reading. We also stressed building motivation through self-selected reading and exciting units of instruction. In Chapter 6, we also consider what to do before students read, but our focus shifts to during and after reading. We consider two important questions: What are the most valuable things a teacher can do to help students comprehend the text they are currently reading? and Which of the things that a teacher can do will build students' ability to comprehend new texts when reading independently (Tierney & Cunningham, 1984)?

Teaching comprehension is tricky because our interactions with students need to balance three critical factors. First, comprehension involves using strategies to understand the ideas in the text. But we don't want to push strategies at the expense of content and ideas (McKeown et al., 2009), nor do we want to ignore the strategies, especially since they can be valuable tools for unraveling and retaining a text's meaning (Palincsar & Schutz, 2011). Second, when reading fiction we want students to have an aesthetic or expressive response (Rosenblatt, 1937) to the text. Yet, we also feel compelled to talk about text structure and literary elements because this knowledge can heighten students' comprehension and appreciation. Focusing too much on one aspect of comprehension kills the other. Third, as we interact with students we assess their understanding, but our inquisitorial desires must be balanced against the need for "grand conversations" that allow freedom for alternative interpretations and personal response (Eeds & Wells, 1989).

Let's look again into the classroom of Mrs. Wilson and observe how she balances these elements while the students are discussing a short story. The on-grade-level students have been reading "Papa's Parrot," a short story from the collection *Every Living Thing* (Rylant, 1988). Papa, Mr. Tillian, owns a small candy and nut shop. As his son, Harry, grows from a young boy to a teenager, he spends less time at his father's store, preferring to hang with his friends. Mr. Tillian is lonely, misses his son, and acquires a parrot, Rocky, for companionship. Sometime later the father suffers a heart attack, and Harry has to go to the store to manage things. While sorting the new boxes of candy, Harry learns a vital truth about his father.

> **CCSS Standard R1:** Although it is important for students to cite explicitly from a text, each reader has a unique experience and response to a poem or a novel.

Harry opened the new boxes his father hadn't gotten to. Peppermints. Jawbreakers. Toffee creams. Strawberry kisses. Harry traveled from bin to bin, putting the candies where they belonged.

"Hello!"

Harry jumped, spilling a box of jawbreakers.

"Hello, Rocky!"

Harry stared at the parrot. He had forgotten it was there. The bird had been so quiet, and Harry had been thinking only of the candy.

"Hello," Harry said.

"Hello, Rocky!" answered the parrot.

Harry walked slowly over to the cage. The parrot's food cup was empty. Its water was dirty. The bottom of the cage was a mess.

Harry carried the cage into the back room.

"Hello, Rocky!"

"Is that all you can say, you dumb bird?" Harry mumbled. The bird said nothing else.

Harry cleaned the bottom of the cage, refilled the food and water cups, then put the cage back in its place and resumed sorting the candy.

"Where's Harry?"

Harry looked up.

"Where's Harry?"

Harry stared at the parrot.

"Where's Harry?"

Chills ran down Harry's back. What could the bird mean? It was like something from *The Twilight Zone.*

"Where's Harry?"

Harry swallowed and said, "I'm here. I'm here, you stupid bird."

"You stupid bird!" said the parrot.

Well, at least he's got one thing straight, thought Harry.

"Miss him! Miss him! Where's Harry? You stupid bird!"

Harry stood with a handful of peppermints.

"What?" he asked.

"Where's Harry?" said the parrot.

"I'm here, you stupid bird! I'm here!" Harry yelled. He threw the peppermints at the cage, and the bird screamed and clung to its perch.

Harry sobbed, "I'm here." The tears were coming.

Harry leaned over the glass counter.

"Papa." Harry buried his face in his arms.

"Where's Harry?" repeated the bird.

Harry sighed and wiped his face on his sleeve.

He watched the parrot. He understood now: someone had been saying for a long time, "Where's Harry? Miss him."

Harry finished his unpacking, then swept the floor of the shop. He checked the furnace so the bird wouldn't get cold. Then he left to go visit his papa. (pp. 24–25)

Mrs. Wilson made several decisions to preserve the aesthetic quality of the experience, engage students in some strategic thinking, and guide the discussion away from a gentle interrogation to a grand conversation. She had the students read the story in two different ways. The bulk of the story was read silently, stopping only twice to discuss the problem and the events. The last part of the story, the part reproduced above, was read as a readers' theater with one student reading the role of Harry, another the parrot, and a third, the narrator. This role taking helped the students appreciate the comic undertones of the story. After reading the text, Mrs. Wilson asked a few higher-order questions designed to promote some strategic thinking and to help the students make connections to other stories.

MRS. WILSON: What did we learn at the end of the story? Can someone summarize what the author revealed to us? Nice parrot talk, by the way, Jonas!

TORI: Harry was very upset about things, and was crying, like his father was in the hospital and his father missed him.

MRS. WILSON: That is true, Tori, but how did Harry figure that out, what inference did he need to make and what inference should we make?

LIZ: Well, Harry was talking to the parrot and figured out that the parrot was repeating what his father had been saying.

MEGAN: This is just like the other story where the mean aunt and the boy became closer because of the hermit crabs.

MRS. WILSON: That's great, Megan, you figured out the common theme of the two stories.

The most optimal time to shape the thinking of young readers is during the act of reading; stopping, modeling, guiding, and coaching them to make the connections and use strategies that will help them construct a full and useful model of the text.

GOALS FOR THIS CHAPTER

✓ Identify the strategies most critical to comprehending narratives.

✓ Demonstrate how to introduce strategies, specifically how to make inferences.

✓ Discuss the role of metacognition and how to develop it in children.

✓ Demonstrate how to help students comprehend and use strategies while reading short fiction, novels, and poetry.

✓ Consider how teacher- and student-directed discussions boost an aesthetic appreciation of literature.

Comprehending narratives means building understanding at several levels with the reader determining the depth of understanding. At the simplest level the reader is building a mental model of the text. By connecting elements within the text and then making additional connections to prior knowledge, we grasp the essential characters, problem, plot, and resolution of the story. Going deeper we can explore the motivation of the characters, their traits and states, how the setting influenced the characters, and explore the theme. At a still deeper level, we can consider how the author's writing created a tone and mood that facilitated his or her purpose. Much of these understandings are voluntary and depend on the reader's purpose and the context. It is unlikely that at the beach you will focus on the author's craft while gripped by *The Hunger Games* (Collins, 2010), but in a reading class your students are much more likely to focus on these literary elements.

STRATEGIES ESSENTIAL FOR LITERATURE

A few strategies are critical to comprehending narratives and they include predicting, self-questioning, using narrative structure, summarizing, visualizing, and making inferences. Making inferences may be the key strategy. When we ask a reader to determine a character's motive or traits, uncover the themes of a story, or discern the author's purpose, inferential thinking is required. It is best to think of making inferences as a collection of strategies and not one single strategy. First, the reader must link different parts of the text, connecting one word or sentence to another. This is essential to develop a cohesive model of the text. Second, the reader must supply ideas because writers do not spell out everything. The writer counts on a shared experience with the reader who fills in what the author only implied, thereby making a connection to prior knowledge, personal experiences, or other texts. The currently popular approach of making connections (text to text, text to world, text to self) can be thought of as the building block of inferential thinking (Harvey & Goudvis, 2007).

> **CCSS Standards R1, 2, 3:** Guiding students to use inferential strategies is key to helping them make interpretations about theme and character development.

Inferences That Build Links

The reader builds cohesion and forges connections or links between one idea, and one sentence and another. Figure 6.1 lists examples of the links necessary for the comprehension of literature. In example 1 the reader must recognize that the pronoun *he* stands for *John*, and the adjective *some* stands for *chocolate chip cookies*. These are anaphoric links or cohesive devices. Whenever a reader has to relate a pronoun (*he, she, it, we, they, you*) to a noun or an adjective (*few, some, many, others*) to a noun, he or she is constructing a link within or between sentences. Children with comprehension

Types of Inferences	Examples
Anaphoric links (connecting pronouns and nouns)	1. John made chocolate chip cookies. *He* gave *some* to Helen.
Lexical links (connecting synonyms or words of similar meaning)	2. The *horses* stand alert. . . . The *stallion* snorts and nudges the others forward.
Conjunctive links (making logical connections)	3. Dillon *and* Dusty went to the circus, *but* Montana had to stay home.
Causal links (inferring cause and effect)	4. Juan gave his umbrella to Melanie *because* she did not want to ruin her dress. 5. Soon the horses are charging across the open range, their hooves churning up clouds of dirt. The helicopter has roared within a few feet, forcing the horses into a tight group.

FIGURE 6.1. Inferences that build links between ideas.

difficulties, compared to same-age children without comprehension problems, have more difficulty answering questions that demand an understanding of these cohesive devices (Oakhill & Yuill, 1986; Yuill & Oakhill, 1991).

The reader also builds cohesion by recognizing lexical connections and realizes that one word is a semantic substitute for another. In example 2 the reader has to connect the concept of a *stallion* to the *horses*. Stallion is not a new idea, but part of the original idea. Making this inference requires both vocabulary knowledge and recognizing the semantic equivalence between the two words.

The third type of cohesive processing is recognizing the connections between sentences by processing the conjunctions, as in example 3. Some words connect ideas (e.g., *and*), some words negate ideas (e.g., *but*), and some words modify ideas (e.g., *although*). Strictly speaking these are not inferences but they are essential to building a complete model or understanding of the text. Should the author omit the conjunction, to shorten the sentence length, the reader has to infer it. The revised example 3—*Dillon and Dusty went to the circus. Montana stayed home.*—requires the reader to infer the contrast, whereas in the original the contrast is stated more directly.

The fourth type of cohesive processing is constructing causal links between ideas or actions. Causality is key in reading any narrative. Sometimes these causal connections are very clear as in example 4 where the word *because* signals the causal relationship that Juan wanted to help Melanie. In example 5 the causal relationship is less clear and the reader has to work harder to understand that the helicopter overhead scared the horses, forcing them into a tight group.

Inferences That Fill Gaps

We often speak of reading between the lines, and what we mean is figuring out what the author implied or simply omitted. Figure 6.2 presents examples of these so-called, gap-filling inferences because there is unstated information in the text that requires knowledge and insight from the reader. When the author writes *Juan got a cup of coffee. It was very hot. Now there is a big mess on the rug*, the first two sentences are linked through an anaphoric connection. The third sentence is linked to the first two through a gap-filling inference. Juan dropped or spilled the coffee because he could not stand the heat of the cup.

First, the reader can infer motive. In example 6 we can infer that Mary's motive is economy, while John is motivated by love. In example 7 we can infer that Clyde embodies the trait of industry, and in example 8 Janice expresses the emotion of embarrassment because of the over-the-top

Types of Inferences	Examples
Inferring character motives	6. Mary looked at the menu trying to find the cheapest entrée while John gazed lovingly in her eyes.
Inferring character traits, emotions	7. Clyde mowed the lawn, planted the three new trees, cleaned the deck, and readied the barbecue, all before 10:00. 8. When her teacher praised her for a good job, Janice lowered her eyes and blushed. When her teacher continued to praise her, Janice got even redder in the face.
Inferring states or setting	9. The street was covered with glass and scraps of twisted metal. The smell of gasoline and burning rubber made my stomach turn.
Inferring causality	10. Fears about radicals led to new limits on immigration into the United States. There were other reasons as well. Many Americans had long worried that the mainstream culture of the United States was being overwhelmed by immigrants from southern and eastern Europe. In addition, U.S. workers were often concerned that newcomers would compete for their jobs.

FIGURE 6.2. Gap-filling inferences.

attention. In example 9 we can infer a state, an accident occurred. Finally, in example 10 we can infer that there are multiple causes of America's desire to limit immigration.

The inferences we described work within the construction–integration model (Kintsch, 1998) presented in Chapter 1. Inferences that build links take place during the construction phase of comprehension. Inferences that fill gaps take place during the integration phase. In both cases readers make these inferences to build a coherent understanding of the text. Most of these same linking and gap filling inferences are also necessary for the comprehension of informational text.

The research is quite clear that poor comprehenders have difficulty making inferences and that answering inferential questions is more difficult than responding to literal questions in both reading and listening (Oakhill, 1984; Dewitz & Dewitz, 2003). The source of this difficulty is complex. To make an inference the reader has to have the necessary prior knowledge. A reader who had never been in a restaurant would have difficulty placing John and Mary in one when given the clues *menu* and *entrée* (example 6). Certainly, some of the difficulties that children encounter in reading also stem from a mismatch between their cultural experiences and the knowledge demands of the text. Second, the reader has to bring his or her knowledge to the text. When poor comprehenders encounter sentences like *The boy was chasing the girl. The girl ran into the playground,* they are much less likely to infer that the boy too ran into the playground, even though the necessary knowledge is present in the text. These readers have a lower standard of coherence. They are satisfied with a level of comprehension that lacks deeper insights (Oakhill & Cain, 2007). Finally, even when prior knowledge is controlled and both good and poor readers have similar prior knowledge, poor readers are still challenged to make the necessary inferences. In one study, good and poor readers were taught about an imaginary planet, Gan, and then tested on their knowledge of that planet (Cain, Oakhill, Barnes, & Bryant, 2001). After the researchers were sure that both groups knew the same amount, the students listened to a story and then orally answered literal and inferential questions. The poor comprehenders performed less well on the inferential questions even though they had the knowledge needed. It is likely that their lack of metacognitive thinking and lower standards of coherence inhibited the ability to generate inferences.

METACOGNITION

As we mentioned in a previous chapter, strategies can play more than one role. Sometimes they are used to build meaning and sometimes they are used for monitoring and problem-solving purposes. Metacognitive strategies are essential, and important ones are predicting-confirming, self-questioning, and summarizing. When readers make predictions, they anticipate the course of the story. A prediction is an inference that anticipates what might happen, drawing upon text information and prior knowledge. The prediction keeps the reader grounded to the text, monitoring what happens. When a prediction is not confirmed, the reader must problem solve to reconsider the meaning he or she has constructed. If the prediction is confirmed, the reader knows he or she is on the right track. He or she experiences the click of comprehension, not the clunk of misunderstanding (Klingner, Vaughn, Arguelles, Hughes, & Leftwich, 2004).

> **CCSS Standards R1, 2, 6:** Metacognition is only implied in the standards, but standards like making inferences, comparing and contrasting, and considering the author's point of view requires metacognitive and cognitive strategies. The reader must initiate these thoughtful mental activities.

Self-questioning is another strategy that fosters metacognition; the reader engages in an internal discussion with the text and its author. Through self-questioning, the reader challenges his or her understanding ("Does the story make sense at this point?"), considers alternative interpretations ("Why did that happen to the character?"), or critiques and evaluates the author's decisions ("Was it necessary for the story to take that turn?"). As the reader poses and answers questions, he or she is evaluating and challenging the developing meaning. Self-questioning is a strategy that can be taught and it will facilitate comprehension (Rosenshine, Meister, & Chapman, 1996).

Summarizing plays a dual role in the comprehension process. At one level the cognitive act of producing a paraphrase or a summary promotes understanding and at another level a summary serves to check or evaluate understanding. When we teach children to summarize we are actually teaching a small collection of strategies. To summarize, a reader must focus on important text elements and sort the wheat from the chaff, categorizing small facts into larger ideas (blocks, balls, cards, dolls = toys), and restating what is left as a paraphrase (A. L. Brown & Day, 1983). This act of summarizing helps the reader to develop an integrated understanding of the text (Kletzien, 2009).

The act of summarizing also promotes metacognition. When in the midst of a difficult passage, a reader might generate a summary to check understanding. If you can restate in your own words what you just read, you can have more confidence that you grasped the gist. An inability to construct a coherent representation of the story clues a good comprehender to reread to clarify meaning. Teaching summarization can begin in the primary grades by having students complete story maps and then using those scaffolds to guide retelling. Facility differentiating interesting from important details and stating the gist likely appears to develop over time (A. L. Brown & Smiley, 1977).

CCSS Standard R2: Students need to employ specific strategies to construct a summary of the text.

INTRODUCING STRATEGIES

All comprehension and metacognitive strategies require some introduction as part of the GRRM-C. There is a phase in the development of comprehension where the teacher, as the expert, does most of the thinking, modeling it for the students and gradually turning over the responsibility to the students. Strategies require some explicit explanation, but not a lot. It is important for students to understand what is the strategy (declarative knowledge), how to perform the strategy (procedural knowledge), and when and why to use it (conditional knowledge). It is also important to note that our best explanations are incomplete. We cannot fully explain how to make an inference or summarize, nor can we explain all of the particulars of why a strategy is important and when to use it. At best we can generate an "instructional approximation" of real strategic thinking and hope that the reader can reconstruct what we model and explain (Resnick, 1987). As Ed Koch, the former mayor of New York, said, "I can explain it to you, but I can't comprehend it for you" (Madden, 2013). Most effective strategy instruction happens while students are constructing meaning—during guided reading (Rosenshine & Meister, 1994) and not in isolation from real text.

Anaphora: Building Local Comprehension

One of the earliest books devoted to teaching comprehension (Pearson & Johnson, 1978) paid considerable attention to comprehension of sentences and anticipated some of the issues developed in the construction–integration model. Some students have difficulty linking pronouns (*he, she, it*) and indefinite adjectives (*some, few, many*) to their nouns. It is important to specifically teach these relationships to the students who struggle with comprehension including word callers (Cartwright, 2010) and English language learners.

> **CCSS Standard R1:** An explicit understanding of the text does require constructing a coherent text base. Do not avoid teaching and discussing the connections that hold ideas together.

Begin by introducing a chart (see Figures 6.3 and 6.4) of the most prominent pronouns and indefinite and demonstrative adjectives, and discuss their use (Baumann, 1984). Review with students which are plural or singular, which refer to men, women, both, or neither. Next, display sentences or short paragraphs and have the students match the antecedents with the appropriate pronouns. The students will need a text of their own to write on.

Tim and Kathy are good friends. <u>He</u> sometimes gets angry with <u>her</u>, but most of the time <u>they</u> play together well.

One person	*I* *she* *he*	*me* *her* *him*	Boys or girls Girls only Boys only
One person or more	*you*		*Boys or girls*
More than one person	*we* *they*	*us* *them*	Boys or girls

FIGURE 6.3. Common pronouns essential for making connections.

| Demonstrative adjectives | this, that, these | If I hear that parrot again, I will call the cops. |
| Indefinite adjectives | no, any, many, few, several | People say there are no deer in Scottsville, yet several were seen last week. |

FIGURE 6.4. Adjectives that make connections.

Have the students draw lines from the pronouns to their antecedents and discuss their relationships. Repeat this activity with several short pieces of text until the students are reasonably proficient. Next, discuss demonstrative adjectives and indefinite adjectives and repeat the same process so that students come to understand that the word *several* in the example in Figure 6.4 stands for *deer*. Follow up these activities by focusing some of your text discussions at the sentence and pronoun level. When students have difficulty retelling a story, probe their understanding of key pronoun–noun connections to see if they are having difficulty, for example, ask "Who is the author referring to when he uses the word *they*?"

Text-Processing Strategies

Good readers use a few comprehension strategies as tools to construct meaning. For the youngest students and for some older readers who are not yet strategic readers, it is important to spend time introducing or reviewing these strategies. For some students, it may be necessary to take a step back and explain just what is a strategy. Mrs. Wilson explains by way of an analogy. She draws the following chart on the board (see Figure 6.5) and begins a discussion about goals and strategies. (Note, this is how the chart looks at the end of the lesson.)

In the discussion Mrs. Wilson first asks students what toy or video game product they would most like to have. This elicits easy and quick responses. Next she asks, "What could you do to get a Wii system?" The students generate many responses reflecting their ingenuity. Mrs. Wilson explains that the former are goals and the latter are strategies. She next switches the discussion to reading and asks, "What are your goals when you read?" This is a more difficult question because some students have never considered their goals; they have not thought metacognitively. Initial answers are vague and hesitant including "To finish the book" and "To read quickly." Eventually through discussion, the students realize that understanding, enjoyment, and learning are goals.

	Goals	Strategies
Toys and games	Wii PlayStation Xbox	Get a part-time job and earn the money. Ask for it as a birthday or Christmas present. Beg.
Reading	To finish the book. To understand. To enjoy. To learn.	Predicting Summarizing Making inferences Self-questioning

FIGURE 6.5. Discussing the goals and strategies of reading.

Mrs. Wilson then draws an analogy for the students that video games require goals and strategies and so does reading. She and the students then discuss the strategies employed by successful readers. She lists them in the final quadrant of the chart. For some students, this activity needs to be repeated regularly. They need to be reminded of goals and strategies whenever they are engaged in a guided comprehension lesson.

Mrs. Wilson's next task is to introduce the strategies. Because many of her students are strong readers, she moves the strategy introduction to a small-group lesson, meeting with just those students she feels might benefit from the instruction. She uses an approach called *guided discovery*, where the teacher helps the students discover the process and

> **CCSS Standard R1, 2, 3, 4, 9:** All of these standards require inferential thinking, so teaching students to make inferences requires clear explanations and support for a long time through classroom dialogue.

purpose of the strategy (Dewitz & Wolskee, 2012). In the example in Figure 6.6, Mrs. Wilson helps her students understand the process of making inferences. She begins by assembling a series of short texts that require the reader to generate an inference. As each text is read, the students are led to make four discoveries: (1) identify the strategy, (2) discuss why it is important, (3) uncover the process, and (4) determine when to use it.

Strategies are used to solve problems (Duffy, 2009). Sometimes asking a question gets us back on the right track; a summary confirms that we get it, and an inference is necessary to complete what the author implied. Not all readers, however, feel the need to solve these problems. Some read with a lower standard of coherence; they do not infer a character's feelings or determine his or her underlying traits. Our job is helping students achieve a higher level of comprehension and adopt a higher standard of coherence.

| Define the Strategy

Why are inferences important? | Mrs. Wilson reveals the first sentence on the SMART Board.

John waited in line for two hours, and just as he reached the ticket window the clerk put up the "sold out" sign.

She then asks the students "What did the author not tell us? What can you figure out?" Through discussion, students should be able to infer that John was waiting for some movie, theater, or sports tickets, and that he must have experienced some disappointment. She points out that inferences are ideas, information that the reader adds to the story. The author counts on us to bring shared knowledge to the text by supplying what he or she didn't say overtly.

Mrs. Wilson also helps the students keep track of what they have inferred. In this simple passage, the students have inferred the character's goal, buying tickets, and his feelings, disappointment.

Mrs. Wilson continues to reveal new examples to illustrate what readers can infer. She believes in treating inferences as a series of specific types, avoiding the general question, "Can anyone make an inference?"

Jesse was sitting in the van and was ready to go. He checked and rechecked his sunscreen, towel, surfboard, extra water, and emergency radio. Jesse wanted to make sure that nothing bad happened.

What we can infer:
- Character goals
- Character feelings
- Character traits
- Setting

From this example, Mrs. Wilson leads the students to infer that Jesse is very careful, a bit obsessive—this is his nature, a character trait. She adds traits to the class inference chart. She also adds the setting, the beach, to the chart. |
| Discover the Process | Mrs. Wilson then puts up a new example so she can model the process of making an inference.

As they pulled up to the drive-in window, Joshua slouched in his seat. He wouldn't look up; he wouldn't talk to his dad. It just wasn't fair that his sister again got her pick for lunch. Even though his stomach grumbled he would not talk to his dad.

Mrs. Wilson began to think aloud. "Let's see; if I slouched in my seat, I would not talk or even look at my father. I must be pretty mad. Plus my sister probably got to pick the lunch place again. That means I was feeling mad and jealous. The author never really tells me how the character feels, but some clues in the text and my own experiences helped me to make that inference. So the steps to making an inference are:

1. Realizing that the author has left something out.
2. Looking for text clues or important words that imply what is missing.
3. Think about what I already know.
4. Combine text information and what I know to make the inference.
5. Ask, 'Does that inference make sense?'" |

(continued)

FIGURE 6.6. A lesson for introducing the strategy of making inferences.

Determine When to Make an Inference	Mrs. Wilson explains "We must be alert to where we can add what the author has omitted. The chart above reminds us to be on the lookout for opportunities to infer settings, problems, character traits, feelings, and motives. Let's read another text and spot places where inferences are desirable."
	She tried to talk all of the way, but I hadn't answered. I slumped in my seat, feet up on the glove compartment, wearing an A&S baseball hat with the brim yanked low over my forehead. If someone looks into your eyes, I read in a book one time, he'll see into your soul.
	I didn't want anyone to see into my soul.
	I knew she was dying to tell me to get my sneakers off her dashboard, but she didn't. She was waiting to deliver her speech.
	I could hear her getting ready for it with a puff of breath. "This can be a new start, Hollis, A new place." She licked her finger and scratched at the mustard stain. "No one knows you. You can be different, you can be good, know what I mean?"
	Maybe she gave that speech to every foster kid in every driveway as she dumped them off like the UPS guy dumping off packages on a busy day, but I didn't think so. I had looked into her eyes once, just the quickest look, and I had seen that she felt sorry for me, that she didn't know what to do with me. (Giff, 2002, p. 4)
	"In the first paragraph the author gives a vivid description of Hollis's behavior. Sometimes we can infer how a person is feeling by studying actions and attitude, so I infer that Hollis is angry and he doesn't want the person in the car to know too much about him. I also infer that the woman must be a social worker who is placing Hollis with a new family. Since she says he can make a new start, his past must have been bad."

FIGURE 6.6. *(continued)*

The introduction and modeling of strategies alone will not do this. However, well-facilitated discussion can prompt students to dig deeper into a text and glean more from it.

TEACHER-DIRECTED COMPREHENSION DISCUSSIONS

Over 25 years ago Durkin (1978–1979) criticized the whole enterprise of comprehension instruction for failing to show students how to comprehend. Most recently researchers have begun to discuss whether the focus on a teacher-guided discussion should be on the content or the strategies (McKeown et al., 2009; Wilkinson & Son, 2011). We believe you can and should focus on both. Small-group instruction is the most effective venue for guiding the development of students' reading comprehension (Taylor et al., 2000). In this venue the teacher can provide guidance to students who need it and fashion less structured discussions for students who do not.

Reading Short Stories and Poems

In history, Mrs. Wilson's sixth graders have been studying World War II and its aftermath. In English, they have been exploring science fiction. The short story "There Will Come Soft Rains" (Bradbury, 1950b) provides an excellent link between the two subject areas. The short story tells the tale of an automated house that has survived a nuclear war even though the family that lived there did not. Mrs. Wilson used the history period to develop prior knowledge, especially knowledge of Hiroshima, Nagasaki, and the destructive power of nuclear weapons. To prepare for the small-group discussion with seven struggling comprehenders, she reads the short story twice— first, for her own enjoyment, and second, to discover what aspects of the story might present a problem for the students. She considers the following (Dewitz & Wolskee, 2012):

- "What big ideas or themes do I want my students to take away from this short story?"
- "What vocabulary words will they need to know?"
- "What knowledge do they need to bring to the text?"
- "What text-processing problems are they likely to encounter?"
  - ♦ Complex pronoun–noun relationships students might not connect.
  - ♦ Complex sentences that obscure cause and effect.
  - ♦ Ideas or sentences that must be linked to others.
  - ♦ Inferences required for understanding the text.

Based on her study of the text, she plans her questions, prompts, and opportunities to model strategic thinking. Let's look at bits of her lesson. The story begins:

> In the living room the voice-clock sang, **Tick-tock, seven o'clock, time to get up, time to get up, seven o'clock!** as if it were afraid that nobody would. The morning house lay empty. The clock ticked on, repeating and repeating its sounds into the emptiness. **Seven-nine, breakfast time, seven-nine!**
>
> In the kitchen the breakfast stove gave a hissing sigh and ejected from its warm interior eight pieces of perfectly browned toast, eight eggs sunnyside up, sixteen slices of bacon, two coffees, and two cool glasses of milk.
>
> "Today is August 4, 2026," said a second voice from the kitchen ceiling, "in the city of Allendale, California." It repeated the date three times for memory's sake. "Today is Mr. Featherstone's birthday. Today is the anniversary of Tilita's marriage. Insurance is payable, as are the water, gas, and light bills."

Somewhere in the walls, relays clicked, memory tapes glided under electric eyes.

Eight-one, tick-tock, eight-one o'clock, off to school, off to work, run, run, eight-one! But no doors slammed, no carpets took the soft tread of rubber heels. It was raining outside. The weather box on the front door sang quietly: "Rain, rain, go away; rubbers, raincoats for today. . . . " And the rain tapped on the empty house, echoing. . . .

Ten-fifteen. The garden sprinklers whirled up in golden founts, filling the soft morning air with scatterings of brightness. The water pelted windowpanes, running down the charred west side where the house had been burned evenly free of its white paint. The entire west face of the house was black, save for five places. Here the silhouette in paint of a man mowing a lawn. Here, as in a photograph, a woman bent to pick flowers. Still farther over, their images burned on wood in one titanic instant, a small boy, hands flung into the air; higher up, the image of a thrown ball, and opposite him a girl, hands raised to catch a ball which never came down. The five spots of paint—the man, the woman, the children, the ball—remained. The rest was a thin-charcoaled layer. (p. 71)

Mrs. Wilson plans to stop after the problem has been revealed.

MRS. WILSON: Can someone summarize what we have read? What is going on in the story?

> **CCSS Standards R1, 2, 3, 4, 9:** All of these standards can be addressed in the context of a rich teacher-led discussion.

IRENE: Well, the house is going about its business. It is being run by a bunch of robots and things.

RODNEY: The house or the robots are fixing breakfast and like an alarm is getting people off to school and work.

MRS. WILSON: That appears to be the case. The house is functioning as if people were living in it, but what has happened to the people? Can someone infer what happened to the inhabitants of the house?

IRENE: They were killed in a war?

MRS. WILSON: Can someone expand on what Irene said? What kind of war? How were they killed?

JUAN: I think it was a nuclear war because toward the end of the first page it says, "the ruined city gave off a radioactive glow," and we learned in history that the atom bomb made the cities in Japan radioactive. Many people died.

MRS. WILSON: Very good, Juan, you read the text closely and used what you know to understand. Now how exactly did the people in the house die? What did the author show us?

STUDENTS: They were killed; blown up?

MRS. WILSON: Let me show you how I thought about how the people died. Close to the end of the page the author paints a vivid picture. I see the charred or blackened side of the house, except for silhouettes in the paint. The father was mowing the lawn, the mother was picking flowers, and the two children were playing ball. In an instant the bomb went off and the heat and explosion burned their images into the wall. I remember the same thing happened when we read about the atom bomb dropped on Hiroshima in Japan.
Do any of you have questions about the story?

IRENE: Why did the house keep working when everything else was destroyed?

Our ideas for leading a discussion borrow from questioning the author (QtA; Beck et al., 1997) and transactional strategies instruction (TSI; R. Brown et al., 1996). The former approach focuses on the content, the ideas in the text, and the latter focuses more on the use of strategies and knowledge to build interpretations. This discussion exemplifies a close reading of the text, especially for students struggling with comprehension. A good teacher-led discussion would:

1. Begin by asking students to retell or paraphrase what has happened in the story. This allows the teacher insight into what the students understand and what they are thinking.
2. Ask follow-up questions to clarify ideas that are difficult for students to comprehend.
3. Focus on making inferences, especially those that require the reader to build connections between ideas in the text and supply information from prior knowledge.
4. Use strategy words in forming questions (i.e., *summarize, infer, predict*). These words remind students of the thinking processes they should use.
5. Encourage students to ask their own questions.
6. Model the teacher's thinking when the students are stuck on something in the text.

After reading and discussing the story, Mrs. Wilson returns the students to the story for a second reading so she can focus students' attention on the language and structure of the literature, a goal of close reading. In this story, she wants the students to explore how the author developed the main character, which is the house. She poses the following questions:

MRS. WILSON: We have been studying narrative structure and we realized writers do not use the same structure for all their stories. In "There Will Come Soft Rains," who are the characters?

IRENE: I think that the house is the main character because the story is really about the house.

JUAN: But, but there is also a family that died, a father, mother, and two kids.

IRENE: I think they are just part of the house, but the house is the character.

MRS. WILSON: I agree with all of you, but how does the author help us see that the house is a character?

DAVID: On the first page Bradbury writes that the house has a throat and it digests stuff, just like a human.

ALICIA: On page two the house inquires and it seeks protection. It is like the house is alive.

MRS. WILSON: What literary device is that called?

STUDENTS: Personification.

Short stories and poems can be approached in a similar fashion. Mrs. Wilson picked the Bradbury short story because its title derives from a poem by Sara Tisdale (1920). In effect, the poem is contained within the story. She has the students read the poem several times to work out the proper phrasing, stressing that each line does not function like a sentence. She then has the students read the poem aloud, almost competing for the best interpretative reading. This builds some fluency. As they improve their expression or prosody, their understanding grows.

> **CCSS Standards R4, L4, 5:** A rich classroom discussion can be used to review word-learning strategies and figurative language. Do so only after grappling with the meaning of the text.

There will come soft rains and the smell of the ground,
And the swallows circling with their shimmering sound;

And frogs in the pools singing at night,
And wild plum trees in tremulous white;

> Robins will wear their feathery fire,
> Whistling their whims on a low fence-wire;
>
> And not one will know of the war, not one
> Will care at last when it is done.
>
> No one would mind, neither bird nor tree,
> if mankind perished utterly;
>
> And Spring herself, when she woke at dawn
> Would scarcely know that we were gone. (p. 2)

MRS. WILSON: This would be an excellent time to use our visualizing strategy. I am going to read the first sentence again. I want you to then tell me what you are seeing. (*Reads the sentence.*)

IRENE: I see a beautiful meadow with birds singing, flowering trees, and frogs singing.

RODNEY: But the last part was about war.

ALICIA: I suppose it means that animals and trees have nothing to do with war. They don't care about war.

DAVID: But wars affect them; they can get killed and their environment destroyed.

MRS. WILSON: Let me read the last four lines of the poem and see how that might enlarge our understanding of it. (*Reads the last lines of the poem.*)

ALICIA: Maybe it means that after all the killing, nature will eventually cover it all up.

Mrs. Wilson moves to wrap up the discussion so she can meet with her next group. She asks the students to think about what they have been studying in history, especially the atomic bomb and the other technologies that are part of war. She asks the students to describe in a short response what the authors, Bradbury and Teasdale, believe about technology. Do you agree with them? This sets the stage for collaborative reasoning, which we discuss in Chapter 10.

Reading Novels

The principles of teacher-guided discussion apply to teaching and reading novels, but with one caveat. You do not want to conduct a page-by-page discussion of a novel. It would take weeks, fostering boredom and impatience.

Plan for moments of interpretative discussion when you feel that text is difficult or a key idea or theme must be emphasized. The rest of the time the students are on their own, but with guidance from you and from graphic organizers. Let's look in as Mrs. Wilson's colleague, Mr. Williams, works with his third graders who are reading *Ramona Forever* (Cleary, 1984), the story of an 8-year-old girl, Ramona; her older sister, Beezus; their parents; and extended family and friends.

Ramona Forever is not a traditionally structured novel with one or two clear problems or goals; rather, Ramona has a series of encounters with friends and family as she learns about life and others. In this book Ramona and Beezus enjoy their freedom from the after-school sitter and deal with the responsibilities of staying alone. They also must cope with a beloved cat that has passed away, a pregnant mother, serving as bridesmaids in a favorite aunt's wedding, and a father who is trying to find his first teaching job.

> **CCSS Standard R10:** It is only through the reading and discussion of complex texts that students will be challenged to make a range of important interpretations.

Mr. Williams structures the reading of the novel so that the students do much of their work on their own or with a partner and three times a week meet for an in-depth, small-group discussion. At this point in the book Ramona and Beezus are staying by themselves after school. Let's look into part of the discussion:

> By Wednesday Ramona began to dread being good because being good was boring, so she was happy to see Howie coming down the street, wheeling his bicycle with his unicycle balanced across the seat and the handlebars. She was even happier when he laid both on her driveway. Ramona met him at the door.
>
> "Come on out, Ramona," said Howie. "Uncle Hobart helped me learn to ride my unicycle, so now you can ride my bicycle."
>
> Ramona's wish had come true. "Hey, Beezus," she shouted, "I'm going out and ride Howie's bike."
>
> "You're suppose to ask first," said Beezus. "You can't go out unless I say so."
>
> Ramona felt that Beezus was showing off in front of Howie. "How come you're so bossy all of a sudden?" she demanded.
>
> "You talk the way you and Mary Jane used to talk when you played house and made me be the baby. Well, I'm not a baby now." Ramona grew more determined and contrary. "Mom always lets me go out and play with Howie."
>
> "Just the same, if you get hurt, I'm responsible," said Beezus. (Cleary, 1984, p. 37)

MR. WILLIAMS: Last time we talked, Ramona and her sister no longer had to go to Mrs. Kemp's house after school and they stayed by themselves until their mom got home from work. So how are things going for Ramona? What has Ramona learned about staying with Beezus?

TIFFANY: She doesn't like it because her older sister bosses her around.

MR. WILLIAMS: Do you all agree? Does the writer give us some clues about how she feels?

MARK: Well, Ramona thinks she is being treated like a baby and then. . . . Actually there are two words that I think we need to talk about—*determined* and *countrary* [sic].

MR. WILLIAMS: I am glad you asked that question. Let's see if we can figure out what those words mean.

JOEL: I think *determined* means that you want something very much and you will work hard to get it. But *contrary*, I am not sure.

GLORIA: Ramona is not obeying Beezus, so maybe *contrary* has something to do with not obeying.

MR. WILLIAMS: That is a very good inference. Yes, *contrary* means that you are acting like you won't get along or go along with the others. I also have a question. What does the author mean when she writes that Ramona "began to dread being good because being good was boring"?

After Mr. Williams and the group wind up the discussion for the day, he gives them some directions, tells them to read the next two chapters, about 30 pages, and asks them to complete the response sheet. They will meet again in 2 days. There is no reason to make predictions because the next incident in the book can't be predicted from what went before it. While the students are reading, they are to complete their notes on the response form shown in Figure 6.7.

This assignment will keep the students engaged with the text while they are reading independently and it will also be fodder for the discussion. The students will be prepared to summarize the story, ask questions, and clarify words that are new to them.

STUDENT-DIRECTED COMPREHENSION INSTRUCTION

As students' reading ability grows they are better able to manage their own group discussions. Student-led discussion groups *can* produce as much growth in reading comprehension as occurs with teacher-led groups

Name: _____	Chapters read: _____	Date: _____
Words We Need to Discuss	**Summary of the Chapters**	**Questions I Want to Ask**

FIGURE 6.7. Preparing for a small-group discussion.

(Almasi, 1995). To promote this result, the teacher begins with modeling the process, coaching the students as they begin to discuss on their own, and helping them to evaluate the success of their discussions. It is safe to say that the teacher is never far from a student-led discussion group, scaffolding their success.

> **CCSS Standards 1, 2, 3, 4, 5, 6, 7, 9:** Student-led discussions, book clubs, and literature circles provide the opportunity to review and reinforce important interpretations. Both discussion formats encourage comparisons between texts.

Book Clubs

Book clubs promote independent reading, comprehension, and writing through structured discussions and sharing. Book clubs have both a direct and an indirect effect on comprehension. They contribute directly because the discussions build metacognitive understanding, strategy use, and vocabulary (Murphy et al., 2009; Wilkinson & Son, 2011). They contribute indirectly because the social aspect encourages students to select and read more books. As students read more, their fluency, vocabulary, and knowledge grows, resulting in improved comprehension. Book club members need to read books that match their reading level. From among those books, they are free to select whatever title they want to read and discuss. The students in a book club can all read the same book or the group can focus on a particular author. For example, Patricia Polacco and Jack Gantos are two authors who write for a number of reading levels, with each group member reading a different book by that author. Another approach is to find books that all share a common theme (e.g., trust, tolerance, survival) and have students discuss across books (Block, Parris, Reed, Whiteley, & Cleveland, 2009).

Book clubs include these four related activities that might be spread out over several days:

1. Read a self-selected book for 10 to 20 minutes.
2. Write a teacher-assigned journal response or a student-selected response.
3. Discuss the student response to the book with the other members of the club. This meeting is peer led; the goal is for students to learn how to discuss a book in depth.
4. Participate in teacher-led, whole-class shares. If sharing takes place before the students begin reading, you can use that time to build background knowledge and teach strategies, such as story structure or summarizing. After the text is read, students share their responses to their book, discuss parts that were confusing, and recommend, or not, the book to others.

Much of the time is spent reading, reflecting, and writing. Only then do the book club members come together to share and discuss.

Literature Circles

In a literature circle, a small group of students have a discussion on the same student-selected book (Daniels, 1996). The teacher provides three or four books (ideally related to the current topic, genre, or author) and the students choose the one that appeals to the majority. The teacher always keeps reading levels in mind when selecting books. Each student assumes one of the following roles in the literature circle:

- The *discussion director/questioner*, who leads the discussion and asks questions.
- The text *connector*, who makes connections between the text being read and previously read texts.

- The *vocabulary enricher,* who discusses new and unclear words and phrases.
- The *literary luminary,* who identifies passages that are funny, interesting, difficult to understand, or exciting. He or she can also focus on figurative language.
- The *character cartographer,* who keeps track of the comings and goings of each character, especially changes in his or her fortunes.
- The *summarizer,* who summarizes the content of what has been read.

The roles change each time the group meets, so it's very important to model and practice each role several times before letting the students fly on their own.

1. The students in each group select their book and determine how much of the text they will read before they meet for the discussion. They also select a role for the first meeting.

2. The students read a chapter or more of the text independently, develop the responses they will share during the discussion, and record these responses on their role sheet (for copies of these role sheets, see Daniels, 1996). The discussion director develops questions, the vocabulary enricher lists words he or she found, the literary luminary marks book passages and makes evaluative statements, and the summarizer writes a summary.

3. The group discusses the text. (Because the discussion director keeps the literature circle going, you may initially want to assign this role to a particularly strong, verbal student.)

4. During the discussion, the teacher acts a facilitator, not a participant. He or she helps the students complete their roles. For example, if the vocabulary enricher has missed any new words, point them out; if the literary luminary failed to discuss a rich phrase, bring it to the group's attention.

5. At the end of the meeting, the students determine how much to read before the next meeting. Each student also assumes a new role. (At first they are going to need some guidance.)

With younger and less competent readers, you can begin literature circles using the role sheets since they provide the structure and guidance some students need. As the students develop reading ability and gain experience you can dispense with them. In fact, a more recent incarnation of literature circles calls for dispensing entirely with the roles. Research on literature circles indicates that the procedure improves students' general reading performance, their ability to discuss literature, and their motivation for reading (B. H. Davis et al., 2001).

LOOKING BACK, LOOKING FORWARD

In this chapter we walked you through a series of instructional approaches designed to help students improve their ability to read literature. We began by discussing the strategies that are essential for reading literature with the most important being the ability to make a wide variety of inferences. We also stressed the importance of metacognition. A good comprehender must monitor reading, predict when necessary, ask questions, and summarize to ensure that most everything makes sense. To help students read in this thoughtful and insightful way, we recommend that you begin with small-group teacher-guided instruction using short stories or poems, and then move into novels. At some point, especially when students have achieved reasonable expertise, they are ready to begin to discuss books on their own. Peer-led, small-group discussions, with the teacher hovering close by, can lead to improved independence, strategy use, metacognition, and literal and inferential comprehension. And don't forget—comprehension is as much about knowledge and motivation as it is about strategies.

APPLICATIONS AND EXPLORATIONS

1. Learn as much as your time allows about children's literature. The more you know, the better you will be at selecting texts and matching students to books. Spend some time with your school's librarian and discuss what is new, good, and hot. Read *The Reading Teacher*, which regularly reviews books and makes recommendations. In particular, pay close attention to the issue published every November, which includes yearly recommendations.

2. Work with your colleagues to develop lesson plans for introducing comprehension strategies. Use as a guide, either our model lesson on page 138 or the book *Explaining Reading* by Gerald Duffy (2009).

3. Sit with your colleagues or classmates and read a short story together. Then plan together the places where you would stop and discuss. As you plan, write down the questions you would ask and the places where you need to model strategic thinking.

CHAPTER 7

Planning Comprehension Instruction in an Inquiry Framework

Does this sound like a classroom you know?

It's time for science or social studies instruction. The teacher tells the students to whip out a textbook and turn to a designated page. Briefly, the teacher introduces the topic and begins to read the selection aloud. Sometimes, the students read the material silently or take turns reading it aloud. The teacher stops periodically to ask a few fact-checking questions, to highlight a point or two, or to have someone paraphrase the content. When finished with reading, the teacher distributes a practice or homework worksheet and informs students that the covered material will be tested on a short-answer quiz on Friday.

There is an alternative to this teacher-centered approach and it's called inquiry learning. An inquiry framework prepares students to gain understanding through participation in the types of actual literacy practices that real historians or scientists undertake when performing tasks in their fields. It accounts for the type of motivated learning that occurs when individuals, in their homes and communities, inquire into topics of interest or importance to them (Moje et al., 2011). In this chapter we explain the instructional framework of inquiry-based instruction using informational texts and describe how it supports comprehension development.

GOALS FOR THIS CHAPTER

✓ Explore inquiry-based literacy instruction.

✓ Consider two frameworks for teaching inquiry.

✓ Connect the good comprehender model to reading as inquiry.

✓ Discuss connections to the CCSS.

✓ Describe planning for curriculum-guided inquiry.

EXPLORING INQUIRY-BASED LITERACY INSTRUCTION

Inquiry-based instruction involves several interdependent parts, which are depicted in Figure 7.1. This approach fosters prolonged interaction with a meaningful topic as students deepen understanding and consolidate learning. Over time, students learn and refine their use of an array of strategies needed to become self-reliant, critical thinkers.

Inquiry-based instruction offers several advantages (Harvey & Daniels, 2009):

1. The approach requires active participation on the part of the student, and such deep engagement promotes better comprehension and knowledge retention.
2. Inquiry promotes problem-solving, research, and teamwork skills.
3. Exposure to diverse texts exposes students to multiple viewpoints.
4. Students learn that similar content can be framed differently in nonfiction trade books, textbooks, historical fiction, Internet texts, and magazine articles.

Past Practices in Teaching Content

Traditionally, teachers have used content-area textbooks to teach science and social studies in the upper elementary grades and beyond. However, some very specific limitations and challenges have been observed over time. First, these one-size-fits-all texts pose challenges for some readers (Moss, 1991), causing teachers to come up with makeshift solutions. For instance, Rachel observed on more than one occasion a teacher hastily reading a textbook aloud to keep pace with curriculum demands. A barrage of quick-fired literal comprehension questions usually followed such reading. She also witnessed teachers restating in simpler terms the text they had

WHAT HAPPENS IN EACH PART OF THE CYCLE?	
Asking and Activating	• *Explaining the inquiry process* • *Determining what students know; providing context* • *Fostering curiosity and excitement* • *Generating questions and narrowing the focus*
Experiencing and Investigating	• *Locating resources and gathering information* • *Evaluating quality, utility, trustworthiness, and currency* • *Conducting an experiment; participating in hands-on learning* • *Keeping track of and recording data*
Organizing and Analyzing	• *Disregarding useless or irrelevant information* • *Sorting, comparing, and contrasting data* • *Drawing conclusions and explanations based on evidence* • *Gleaning big ideas; looking for patterns across sources*
Consolidating and Reflecting	• *Reflecting on what was learned and on self as a learner* • *Developing new insights* • *Evaluating overall inquiry performance* • *Formulating more questions*
Applying and Communicating	• *Sharing findings with others; celebrating success* • *Defending conclusions* • *Transferring learning to new contexts/tasks, in and out of school* • *Taking action based on findings*

FIGURE 7.1. A model for inquiry-based literacy instruction.

just read to students. A repetitive cycle of rapid reading or paraphrasing continued, with little student input, as teachers zipped through a requisite number of pages.

Second, the material presented in a textbook may be outdated, misleading, or even wrong. Such was the case in Virginia where a history textbook incorrectly noted that the Confederate army included companies of African American soldiers (Sieff, 2010). After the mistake was found, a commissioned group of historians reviewed the textbook. They produced a 31-page report detailing a remarkable number of errors (Chen, 2011).

Textbooks, like all books, reflect a writer's personal interests, interpretation, and biases. An author's or editor's knowledge, motivation, and sociocultural perspective influences what he or she writes. Every print and digital text represents a particular rendering of the "truth." Teachers need to know this and direct students to multiple resources to expose students to multiple perspectives. When a class reads multiple books on a topic they also can bring more knowledge to the discussion. By consulting an array of resources, we are more likely to learn that Abraham Lincoln had several reasons for fighting the Civil War and that the brontosaurus never existed.

A Growing Need for Nonfiction

In recent years, a persistent appeal has gone out to teachers to expose students to more nonfiction texts in primary school and beyond (Duke, 2000; Duke & Bennett-Armistead, 2003; Pappas, 2006). Several myths about children's reading of nonfiction texts have been debunked, paving the way for greater use of informational texts: (1) that youngsters can't cope with informational material, (2) that they don't enjoy reading about those topics, and (3) that they first need to read fiction before wrestling with nonfiction (Duke, 2000).

There are multiple reasons for having students read nonfiction right from the start (Duke & Bennett-Armistead, 2003; Moss, 2004):

- Students build knowledge and learn conceptual vocabulary, which both support comprehension.
- Students who prefer informational texts are more likely to read if these texts are in the classroom—and increased reading means enhanced comprehension.
- Students can roam a broad range of topics or dig deep within a single area.
- Students can use informational texts more skillfully in later years when introduced to them in the primary grades.

Teaching children to comprehend nonfiction texts complements and supports subject-area instruction (Saul & Dieckman, 2005). Several large projects have merged the learning of science or social studies with the development of reading comprehension. For example, *concept-oriented reading instruction* (CORI; Guthrie, Wigfield, & Perencevich, 2004) is a research-based approach that promotes scientific learning through the integrated teaching of science, comprehension strategies, and inquiry skills in a setting that fosters peer collaboration, student engagement, and motivation to read. John Guthrie and his colleagues have found that students learn comprehension strategies more effectively when the strategies are a tool for studying science than when they are taught for their own sake.

> **CCSS Standards R1, 2:** Students in the primary grades need to hear and read a greater diversity and quantity of informational text.

Another approach, *Seeds of Science, Roots of Reading* (Cervetti & Barber, 2009; Duke et al., 2011) is a comprehensive program that promotes the development of scientific knowledge, literacy, and know-how. The published curriculum for second through fifth graders integrates reading, writing, and discussion with firsthand science investigations. Students engage in protracted study of scientific topics in grade-level units. Knitted into this instruction is explicit instruction in reading comprehension and inquiry strategies.

TWO FRAMEWORKS FOR TEACHING INQUIRY

Inquiry-based instruction means different things to different educators (Harvey & Daniels, 2009). In some classrooms, inquiry learning begins with an existing, prescribed curriculum, whereas in other classrooms it arises from student interest. The teacher or the students can pose inquiry questions. Inquiry units can span a week to several months; they can target a single subject or cut across content domains.

Curriculum-Guided Inquiry

In curriculum-guided inquiry students research a topic within a prescribed curriculum. The teacher ensures that district-mandated learning objectives are met while channeling students' interests, promoting self-reliance, fostering purposeful learning, and nudging students beyond superficial understandings. Because almost all states have detailed science and social studies curricula, this curriculum-based approach is observed frequently, especially in public schools. Private and charter schools are not obliged to follow these state standards. We elaborate on this inquiry approach in the latter part of this chapter when we explore a second-grade inquiry unit.

Student-Centered Inquiry

In this open-ended approach, students' curiosities fuel the learning process. Instruction evolves from students' choice rather than from a fixed curriculum. Topics for inquiry emerge by canvassing students' interests or letting individuals pursue their own interests. This approach requires significant preparation and a huge leap of faith for teachers, as considerable decision making is turned over to students. Lessons are not fleshed out in advance, but instead unfold. It takes a flexible and confident instructor to teach on the fly and to provide responsive support in the moment with a wide range of materials.

Sometimes teachers attempt to work instruction backward and match the topics the students select to their district standards, a practice called "backmapping" (Harvey & Daniels, 2009). However, this attempt at alignment is questionable because those who know their subject well believe that there is a logic and sequence to studying a branch of history or science. It would not be possible to consider the causes of World War II without understanding World War I, nor is it easy to understand the destruction of the rain forest without first understanding how one species supports another. For this reason, we intentionally focus in Chapters 7 and 8 on the curriculum-based approach to inquiry.

THE GOOD COMPREHENDER MODEL AND READING AS INQUIRY

A curriculum-based approach to inquiry builds comprehension with informational texts. Instruction aligns with the good comprehender model (see Chapter 1, Figure 1.2, p. 14).

Good comprehenders in any discipline are thinkers! They use comprehension strategies to build nuanced understandings, to explore complex concepts, and to respond critically to ideas. They possess much knowledge in their areas of expertise, and rely upon reading to continually update and deepen that base. They mindfully regulate their learning. No one needs to convince them of the benefits of collaborating with others—they readily discuss their ideas to sharpen thinking and defend interpretations. What's more, no one has to beg them to read or to prod them to inquire. They display formidable motivation for what they do.

Despite these similarities, historians, scientists, and other academic experts interact quite differently with texts (Shanahan, Shanahan, & Misischia, 2011). The texts they read, the text structures they encounter, the interpretive and analytic strategies they employ, and the ways they evaluate credibility can all vary (Alexander & Jetton, 2000). Take texts, for instance. Historians tend to work with original artifacts, visuals, and documents as well as secondary sources written by experts who interpret primary sources. In contrast, scientists typically read scientific journals that deal with theoretical issues, describe natural phenomena, or summarize experiments (Juel, Hebard, Haubner, & Moran, 2010; Moje et al., 2011; Shanahan et al., 2011).

Wineburg (1991a, 1991b) studied historians as they thought aloud and found that they rely on four cognitive strategies when reading: (1) sourcing, (2) corroboration, (3) contextualization, and (4) credibility. When *sourcing* a document, historians think about what they know about the author as well as that author's biases and purposes for writing. *Corroboration* involves seeking confirmation of facts and interpretations by comparing events across multiple texts. Historians regularly synthesize an enormous amount of information while working with primary and secondary sources. In *contextualization* events are understood relative to the particular instances in the time and place in which they occurred. Finally, *credibility* refers to assessing the reasonableness of an author's interpretations and arguments. These four disciplinary strategies indicate that historians adopt a questioning and evaluative stance when reading in their fields.

In contrast, scientists use texts to support investigations about the wonders of the natural world. They use texts to provide background knowledge and to inform thinking prior to initiating scientific inquiry. They are highly evaluative and critical (Bazerman, 1985; Pressley & Afflerbach, 1995; Shanahan et al., 2011; Shanahan, 2009). They question the veracity of information found in the journals they read and the soundness of the research design and the procedures used for data collection and analysis. They also read for proof of scientific claims. They seek sufficient detail to replicate a study, if desired, and scrutinize summaries of data presented in charts and graphics.

Nobody expects students in the elementary years to read like these disciplinary experts. However, young children can learn that literacy is situated in particular contexts. They can learn that reading and thinking like a scientist or a historian means accessing and gaining specialized subject knowledge, understanding conceptual vocabulary, comprehending content materials, and performing text-based tasks for particular purposes. Furthermore, it is realistic for a third grader, like a historian, to interrogate a history text, using questions such as the ones below (derived from the work of Wineburg, 1991a, 1991b):

- What do I know about this author or this text? Is it historical fiction or nonfiction? (*sourcing*)
- Do I know anything about when this was written? Does it matter? (*contextualizing*)
- Do other authors say the same things in their books on the same topic? Does what this author says make sense based on my experiences? (*corroborating*)
- Do I believe what this author says? Where's the proof? (*credibility*)

In most schools, students in the elementary grades never learn to interact with texts like disciplinary experts. However, just as educators can learn about comprehension from watching proficient readers, our understanding of subject-area reading can be enhanced by understanding how experts in various fields work with texts in their areas of expertise.

> **CCSS Standard R6:** The point of view adopted by an author shapes the content and style of a text.

THE COMMON CORE STANDARDS

The intensive focus on nonfiction is evident in the CCSS due, in part, to the fact that the majority of texts encountered in college and careers are expository in nature (see Figure 7.2). Over time, students are expected to internalize the literacy practices of disciplinary experts, professionals, and other specialists. Therefore, there is a push to prepare students to comprehend informational texts from the primary grades onward.

To bring about the CCSS's vision for working with informational texts, several practices need to be enacted:

- Encourage or require extensive reading in social science and science.
- Develop content or disciplinary knowledge via sustained research and study with traditional print and digital texts.
- Allocate time for students to articulate and defend their views by citing evidence.
- Provide opportunities for students to critically evaluate overt and hidden messages.
- Ask students to judge the credibility, validity, and utility of stated information.

In this chapter, we focus on the reading of informational texts in an inquiry framework. Although literature is totally suitable as a supplement for inclusion in inquiry units, students find answers to their social studies and science questions in materials that convey factual information. To

COMMON CORE STATE STANDARDS

Key Ideas and Details

1. Read closely to determine what the text says explicitly and to make logical inferences.
2. Determine the central ideas of a text or themes of a text and analyze their development; summarize the key supporting details and ideas.
3. Analyze how individuals, events, and ideas develop and interact over the course of a text.

Craft and Structure

4. Interpret words and phrases as they are used in a text, including determining technical language, connotative and figurative meanings, and analyze how specific word choices shape meaning or tone.
5. Analyze the structure of texts, including how specific sentences, paragraphs, and larger portions of texts (section or chapter) relate to each other and the whole.
6. Assess how point of view or purpose shapes the content and the style of a text.

Integration of Knowledge and Ideas

7. Integrate and evaluate content presented in diverse media and formats, including illustrations with a text.
8. Delineate and evaluate the argument and specific claims in a text, including the validity of the reasoning, as well as the relevance and sufficiency of the evidence.
9. Analyze how two or more texts address similar themes or topics in order to build knowledge or to compare the approaches the authors take.
10. Read and comprehend complex literary texts independently and proficiently.

FIGURE 7.2. CCSS for informational texts.

begin our exploration of teaching comprehension with informational texts, we observe how our representative teacher, Mr. Rodriguez, prepares for inquiry instruction. Mr. Rodriguez is a second-grade teacher in a small rural school. His 25 students have a wide range of reading abilities, including students who are reading well above grade level and those still struggling with decoding and fluency. Mr. Rodriguez uses a comprehension instructional approach known as transactional strategies instruction (TSI; Pressley et al., 1992; R. Brown, 2008) in his inquiry unit. TSI exemplifies the CCSS's notion of close reading because the students use their cognitive and metacognitive strategies to construct interpretations of meaning that are grounded in the text. During discussions they share and defend their interpretations with direct evidence, citing specific words and phrases, details in picture clues, and knowledge already gained from reading to support and justify their predictions, inferences, visualizations, identification of important information, and summarization. Looking back, asking questions, rereading, and re-examining texts closely are critical elements in developing deeper understanding, engaging in interpretive discussion, and building knowledge.

PLANNING FOR INQUIRY

Mr. Rodriguez's vision represents one depiction of inquiry instruction that can be tweaked based on your unique curriculum and pacing mandates, your instructional know-how, and your students' needs. We describe our planning for inquiry-based instruction in terms of five basic steps, displayed in Figure 7.3.

Step 1: Specify Subject-Area Standards and Content Goals

Mr. Rodriguez designs an integrated inquiry unit on community and weather and targets the following second-grade subject-area state standards for his students:

- Social studies: Understand the differences among urban, rural, and suburban communities.
- Science: Understand basic weather concepts, including different types of weather, how weather is measured, and extreme weather conditions.
- Social studies and science: Understand that regular and extreme weather have effects on communities.

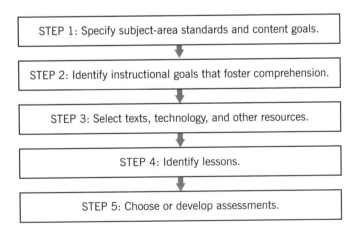

STEP 1: Specify subject-area standards and content goals.

STEP 2: Identify instructional goals that foster comprehension.

STEP 3: Select texts, technology, and other resources.

STEP 4: Identify lessons.

STEP 5: Choose or develop assessments.

FIGURE 7.3. Five basic steps of planning for inquiry instruction.

These standards help to identify the overarching content goals for the unit. They guide the selection of texts the students will read, the instructional activities, the student products, and the assessment tools. The learning goals also influence the selection and teaching of comprehension-fostering strategies the students will need to complete the unit. Comprehension and metacognitive strategies are at the service of these content learning goals. Mr. Rodriguez must ensure that his planning helps students meet subject-area goals as well as demonstrate proficiency on state assessments.

Step 2: Identify Instructional Goals That Foster Comprehension

Mr. Rodriguez knows that strong comprehension instruction is necessary to promote subject-area learning. Each aspect of the good comprehender model—knowledge, metacognition, strategies, and motivation—is essential within each phase of inquiry learning. Motivation is necessary to sustain question asking and topic development, reading and observing, working with data, reflection, and reporting the results. In a similar way comprehension strategies and metacognition are needed throughout the process as students build knowledge and understanding.

It goes without saying that foundational skills like word recognition and fluency are essential for comprehension and need to be taught during literacy instruction. Although these topics go beyond the scope of this book, it bears reminding that the teaching of comprehension entails much more than what we cover here (Block, Gambrell, & Pressley, 2002; Duke et al., 2011).

Building Motivation

One important way to prepare students to read like disciplinary experts is to ignite a sense of wonder for the world around them. Students need to transition from a fleeting or situational interest in a particular topic or task to an abiding and intrinsic motivation for learning (Alexander, 2005). Mr. Rodriguez intends to address motivation by:

- Identifying topics and questions of interest that relate to the curricular focus and allow students some choice.
- Discussing how curiosity is a powerful motivator that induces readers to tackle challenging materials and to persevere when the going gets tough.
- Tapping students' existing knowledge about the local geography and environment.

- Selecting a range of texts at varied levels of complexity so that all students can participate in the inquiry process regardless of background and abilities.
- Arranging tasks so that students experience success in order to foster positive beliefs about self-competence.
- Encouraging students to share their stories of successful strategies use during inquiry.

Building Knowledge

Knowledge building is a cornerstone of subject-matter instruction. Mr. Rodriguez knows that there is a reciprocal relationship between reading and knowledge building. That is, "if you don't know content you will have a difficult time understanding the texts, and if you don't understand the texts you are unlikely to learn content" (Lee & Spratley, 2010, p. 3). Nowadays, students come across a range of print and digital texts both in and out of school that contain unfamiliar vocabulary or complex sentence structure. Essentially, the text, for whatever reason, may depart radically from students' everyday language. As such, Mr. Rodriguez considers how his instruction can promote conceptual, word, and text structure knowledge.

DEVELOPING CONCEPTUAL KNOWLEDGE

Mr. Rodriguez plans to use an array of texts to build students' knowledge about communities and weather (see Figure 7.4). Activating and building prior knowledge will play a significant role in the first phase of the inquiry process, and it will remain an indispensable instructional focus in the other phases as well.

Mr. Rodriguez knows the importance of finding out what students already know about a topic before he begins to teach. He wants to make the most of students' personal experiences and funds of knowledge (Moll et al., 1992). For example, the school district is located in a rural setting where many individuals hold agricultural jobs. With the close proximity to several towns and a city, a percentage of residents commute to work in neighboring areas. Thus, students possess everyday knowledge of various communities and can relate to farming and other suburban and urban occupations and pursuits. Students on or near farms know of the critical role of weather for planting, cultivating, and harvesting. Other children know that weather can play havoc with their parents' commute. Drawing on such funds of knowledge situates their learning in a meaningful context that values their out-of-school experiences.

Social Studies	Science
Laying the Foundation	
What is a community? • Definition of community • Introduction to key concepts/vocabulary • Characteristics of a community	What is weather? • Definition of weather • Introduction to key concepts/vocabulary • Characteristics of weather and climate
What are the different types of communities?	What are different types of ordinary and wild weather?
What do we know about our community?	What do we know about our weather and climate?
⇩	
Posing Inquiry Questions	

FIGURE 7.4. Building conceptual knowledge in the subject areas.

Mr. Rodriguez plans to systematically develop his students' knowledge and the class will track what they learn from their readings, observations, and experiments. For this task, Mr. Rodriguez plans to use a large concept map, tacked to the wall; it will enlarge as students read and develop knowledge. The word *weather* will appear in the center circle. Related ideas will be added throughout the unit to create a network of interrelated ideas. Constructing this concept map will be a joint venture with students; the visual will trace where the class has gone and foreshadow where it is heading. This unit lends itself to the making of comparisons and Mr. Rodriguez will structure the concept map so that students can compare and contrast rural, urban, and suburban communities.

> **CCSS Standard R9:** The use of a concept map will allow students to compare and contrast ideas from multiple texts while they are learning.

DEVELOPING VOCABULARY

No coverage of informational texts would be complete without a discussion of academic vocabulary, or the words that students learn to demonstrate knowledge in specific subject areas. These words differ considerably from conversational English, which are the words of their oral language or new labels for old concepts. Words like *hide* or *hug* are part of most students' oral vocabulary; words like *conceal* or *embrace* are new labels for these old concepts. Academic vocabulary is the label for new concepts. These words are the language of school and subject-area instruction and play a very significant role in school achievement (Townsend, Filippini, Collins, & Biancarosa, 2012). In effect, they are the garbs that concepts, structures, and processes wear. Academic vocabulary is the most difficult to teach because these words represent new concepts.

Figure 7.5 contains examples of second-grade academic vocabulary for Mr. Rodriguez's integrated unit on community and weather.

Discipline-specific vocabulary, one part of academic vocabulary, stands for concepts associated with specific subject areas—*suburban, rural, evaporation,* and *precipitation.* In comparison, cross-disciplinary vocabulary includes words that are found in multiple subject areas—*pattern, inquiry,* and *infer.* They also relate to comprehension and inquiry processes, providing a shared language for discussions about thinking, doing, and learning. As part of his planning, how does Mr. Rodriguez decide which vocabulary to teach explicitly (Graves, 2006; Stahl & Nagy, 2006)?

1. Before teaching, he will probe students' knowledge of terms for the upcoming topic.
2. He will identify words that cut across subject areas—the cross-disciplinary words. These are the "high-octane" words that frequently appear in spoken and written language in the classroom.

Discipline-Specific Words		Cross-Disciplinary Words	
Social Studies	**Science**	**Nouns**	**Verbs**
region	atmosphere	pattern	compare–contrast
community	melting	relationship	classify
city	evaporation	visual	measure
continent	water cycle	fact	sort
country	precipitation	symbol	observe
rural	weather	type	study
urban	Fahrenheit	proof	report
suburban	scientist	clues	explain
state	meteorologist	research	predict
map	temperature	inquiry/inquirer	infer
climate	data	genre	evaluate
location	thermometer	text feature	summarize

FIGURE 7.5. Examples of academic vocabulary.

3. He will disregard words that can be deciphered through analysis of word parts or context.
4. He will select words that capture the core concepts of a topic without which students' comprehension would be hampered (Beck et al., 2002; Baumann & Graves, 2010).

Learning academic vocabulary requires delving into the concepts that underlie the word (Graves, 2006). First, students must explore an example of the concept—rain, hail, and snow are examples of precipitation. Then they consider nonexamples—wind is not precipitation. Next they consider characteristics of the concept—precipitation is wet and cold. They then work to develop a definition—*precipitation* is many forms of water that fall from the sky as part of the water cycle. Eventually, students apply the word on their own in written and spoken language.

> **CCSS Standards R4, L5, 6:** Students need opportunities to develop academic vocabulary to gain access to concepts in text and to build conceptual knowledge.

DEVELOPING TEXTUAL KNOWLEDGE OF GENRE AND STRUCTURE

Students run into many kinds of texts in content instruction. These include books, magazine and newspaper articles, technical directions, television and magazine ads, movie trailers, public service announcements, Internet sites, and other social media. To be successful in school and in everyday life, students need to comprehend, learn from, and evaluate a wide assortment of texts.

GENRE KNOWLEDGE

In preparing for this chapter, we read broadly about teaching nonfiction. We found a confusing use of terminology and conflicting ways to classify its subtypes. We divide the overarching term, *nonfiction*, into four genres: (1) *informational texts* that tell and explain—textbooks, trade books, Internet sites; (2) *literary nonfiction* that employs literary language and conventions to provide factual information about a particular person, event, issue, or phenomenon—biography and autobiography; (3) *persuasive texts* that sway someone to think or act in a certain way—editorials; and (4) *functional texts* that provide language and graphics to accomplish particular purposes or tasks—how to program your TV remote.

> **CCSS Standard R5:** It is beneficial for students to examine and understand the purpose of different text structures and their text features.

In Figure 7.6, these nonfiction genres and their associated types, structures, and some common features are described.

In this unit, Mr. Rodriguez plans to expose students to various nonfiction genres, although they will primarily research answers to inquiry questions with informational text. More about text selection is presented later in this chapter.

TEXT STRUCTURE

Informational texts use familiar and specific text structures to organize content. Authors present information in texts with organizational schemes such as *description, numerical order, chronological sequence, compare–contrast, cause–effect,* and *problem–solution.* (Refer back to Chapter 2 for a refresher on each of these.) Mr. Rodriguez will collect "mentor texts" or samples to provide examples of how authors organize their printed or digital materials. Mentor texts can be books, magazine articles, commercials, or websites used to illustrate a concept of text structure or to model a specific reading skill or strategy (Harvey & Goudvis, 2007).

CCSS Standard R10: Students need to read widely across a range of informational print and digital text to learn to comprehend increasingly complex texts.

In this unit, Mr. Rodriguez plans to highlight the text structure patterns of description, cause–effect, and compare–contrast text. As students understand these text structure patterns they are better able to discern and remember important information (Meyer, Brandt, & Bluth, 1980; Williams, 2008). They then can organize and store their facts in graphic organizers that parallel the way authors structure their ideas in writing. For example, Mr. Rodriguez will point out an author's use of a compare–contrast text structure and then will model how to use a graphic organizer to record important similarities and differences among urban, rural, and suburban communities using the same text.

TEXT FEATURES

In addition to text structure, authors signal readers with specific text features. These include titles, headings and subheadings, print styles (e.g., font sizes, bullets, italicizing), organizational supports (e.g., index, table of contents) and assorted visuals (e.g., charts, photographs, drawings; see Figure 7.6). To use websites well, students need to learn even more features, such as URLs, links, interactive visuals, icons, cursor-activated definitions and annotations, definitions, logos, symbols, emoticons, and pull-down menus.

Genre	Text Type	Text Structure	Text Features	Unit Example
Informational	Picture/ trade books; magazines; brochures; pamphlets; websites; other printed, visual, electronic, and digital resources	Description, explanation (i.e., chronological order, numerical order, problem–solution, cause–effect, compare–contrast)	• Bold or italicized print • Bullets or numbering • Titles and headings • Labels and captions • Diagrams and charts • Maps • Index and glossary • Photos, pictures, and drawings	**Trade books:** *What Will the Weather Be?* (DeWitt & Croll, 1991) *Living in Suburban Communities* (Sterling, 2008b) **Websites:** Sky Diary Kidstorm *http://skydiary.com/kids* Web Weather for Kids *http://eo.ucar.edu/webweather* **Magazine article:** *Lightning Chasers* (2013)
Functional	Picture/ trade how-to books; forms; reference materials; technical manuals; directions	Description, numerical order, listing, alphabetical order	• Bold or italicized print • Bullets or numbering • Alphabetized • Titles and headings • Labels and captions • Diagrams and charts • Table of contents • Index and glossary • Photos, pictures, and drawings • Maps	**Reference books:** *Wind and Weather* (Time-Life, 1989) *Weather Words and What They Mean* (Gibbons, 1992) **Websites:** Google Maps Google Images **Magazine article:** *TIME for Kids www.timeforkids.com/news/green-tips/10961*

(continued)

FIGURE 7.6. Characteristics of nonfiction text.

Genre	Text Type	Text Structure	Text Features	Unit Example
Persuasive	Opinion pieces in magazines or newspapers; speeches; editorials; essays; websites; advertisements	Argument: position with supporting reasons that invokes the writer's character and/or appeals to logic (i.e., *ethos, pathos, logos*; *http://courses. durhamtech.edu/ perkins/aris.html*) Discussion/debate: position with listed reasons for and against viewpoint	• Highly visual, gut-wrenching, or captivating lead/conclusion that draws one in, such as a scenario, question, quote, joke, anecdote, cautionary example, or heading • Statement of topic and point of view/supportive evidence or reasons/concluding statement • Enticing visual with overt or underlying message	**Magazines or brochures:** Travel advertisements from brochures or magazines for beach and ski destinations
Literary Nonfiction	Picture/trade books; magazine articles; autobiography; biography; memoir; essay; travel writing; food writing; other printed, visual, electronic, and digital resources; Internet texts	Hybrid form, blending narrative, descriptive, and informative elements and/or structures	• Uses features, figurative language, and other literary elements (such as dialogue, themes, descriptive settings in the writing of factually accurate, high-interest nonfiction writing • Tells story of a true person, place, event, issue, or phenomenon in science or history • Uses less technical or academic vocabulary • Uses frequently chronological sequencing, first-person narration	**Picture books:** *Desert Town* (Geisert & Geisert, 2001) *Snowflake Bentley* (Martin, 1999)

FIGURE 7.6. (*continued*)

Because Mr. Rodriguez plans to bookmark appropriate websites for students in advance, he will teach a relevant subset of these features.

Keeping track of the text features students encounter in the unit is easy. Mr. Rodriguez will use a chart to capture this information as discussed in Chapter 5 with genres of literature. At the close of each day's inquiry workshop, he will encourage students to share the different nonfiction features they encountered. Students will explain how a particular feature helped them better understand or find information.

Building Strategy Knowledge and Use

There is a dynamic relationship between disciplinary knowledge and strategies use (Alexander, Kulikowich, & Jetton, 1994; Pressley et al., 1989). When reading in their fields, experts rely upon strategies to understand and acquire knowledge from conceptually dense texts (Alexander, 2005). The more knowledge readers have, the more strategic their reading becomes. Knowledge allows them to infer, interpret, critique, and evaluate what they read.

When we shift to teaching students, Duke, Pearson, Strachan, and Billman (2011) state that the learning of comprehension strategies complements the learning of inquiry strategies—and vice versa. You may be asking, "What is the difference between an inquiry and a comprehension strategy?" Comprehension strategies are the conscious tactics that readers enlist to construct meaning when reading (Duke et al., 2011).

For inquiry, it's all about the "doing" of science or history. That is, inquiry strategies are the conscious tactics that scientists and historians use to make meaning when working in their fields (i.e., a scientist conducts an experiment; a historian reads primary source material, newspapers of the era, diaries, and speeches). When translated to schools that means students learn to ask questions whether they are reading *The Story of Salt* (Kurlansky & Schindler, 2006) or whether they conduct an experiment about why an egg, which normally sinks to the bottom of a glass filled with water, floats when salt is added to liquid. In Figure 7.7, we provide a list of some basic comprehension and inquiry strategies for comparison. If you look closely, you will notice how the two lists overlap and yet contrast.

Mr. Rodriguez explicitly will draw upon what students can learn from the reading of disciplinary experts. Although second-grade students are too young to make the fine distinctions that professionals do when reading, Mr. Rodriguez will lay the foundation for future work in the area. At some point in the inquiry unit, he will invite a local meteorologist to speak to his class to demonstrate that people with jobs in different fields rely on reading to

Comprehension strategies	Inquiry strategies
• Setting goal(s) for reading • Making connections • Predicting • Making inferences • Monitoring, clarifying, and fixing • Self-questioning • Visualizing content • Determining importance • Summarizing and integrating ideas within and across texts • Evaluating (both aesthetic and efferent) ideas, content, quality, and features • Reflecting on what you learned from reading	• Considering what you know to inform your inquiry and choice of question • Developing a hypothesis • Setting goals for and planning the search • Making sense of data/evidence by making connections to previous sources and prior knowledge • Monitoring progress of inquiry and troubleshooting problems • Determining importance by deciding whether the data/evidence obtained from reading supports or advances your case • Inferring to draw conclusions • Questioning whether your conclusions make sense • Integrating and summarizing data and ideas; finding patterns and constructing visual representations • Reflecting on the inquiry process

FIGURE 7.7. A comparison of cognitive and metacognitive comprehension and inquiry strategies.

carry out important tasks. To answer their questions, they have to conduct research, just like the students during inquiry.

Given the compatibility of comprehension and inquiry strategies, Mr. Rodriguez will teach them as two sides of the same coin. Although a variety of cognitive strategies will be mentioned, modeled, and prompted during instruction, Mr. Rodriguez will use focus lessons to deepen knowledge of a specific strategy that is exceptionally well matched to a text, purpose, or phase of the inquiry cycle. For example, the strategies of self-questioning and making connections lend themselves naturally to more detailed instruction in the asking and activating phase of the inquiry process. Students will make connections to what they know about their own communities when reading information about the city or farming and seasonal fluctuations in the weather (e.g., *Living in Rural Communities*, Sterling, 2008a; *A Year in the City*, Henderson & Howard, 1996; *Four Seasons Make*

> **CCSS Standards R1, 2, 3:** Students need to use comprehension strategies such as making inferences, determining importance, and summarizing to integrate, interpret, and critically analyze the content in texts.

a Year, Rockwell & Halsey, 2004; *The Reasons for Seasons,* Gibbons, 1996). In terms of inquiry, the budding scientists will draw upon these same strategies to make connections between what they read and their charted weather observations throughout the unit.

As students read during the inquiry cycle they will need to draw on their existing knowledge of the content while employing many cognitive and metacognitive strategies. The content, the projects, and the success that the students experience will drive their reading and learning. The readers as they interact with informational text will deploy the strategies we outlined in Chapter 3. For example, making inferences with informational text is just as vital for comprehension as making them for narrative fiction. Graesser, León, and Otero (2002) have identified a specific set of inferences that are necessary to understand informational text and we present these in Figure 7.8.

Inference types	Explanations	Examples
Anaphoric reference	A noun (he, it, they) or indefinite adjective (few, some, many) that refers to a noun or noun phrase previously introduced in the text.	Have you seen ocean waves? The water looks as if it is moving across the ocean ridges. But it is not.
Bridging inference	Any inference that is necessary to connect one sentence or idea to another.	Gorillas have adapted to living in high, cool mountains. They have thicker hair, shorter arms and legs, and a bigger chest than lowland gorillas.
Explanation inference	The current event or process is explained by a causal change or list of other attributes.	The bottom of the waves slows more than at the top. This causes the wave to fall over, or break.
Predictive inference	The reader predicts or forecasts what event will follow the event described.	As the farmers in Brazil cleared the forest to plant more corn, the ecology changed and so did the climate.
Goal inference	The reader infers that someone or something has a goal or motive to explain its actions.	The remora fish likes sharks. When the shark eats its dinner, the remora likes to hang around.
Process inference	The reader must keep track of the detailed steps and dynamics within a natural process.	As the seeds float down to the ground they become embedded in the soil. Next . . .

FIGURE 7.8. Classes of inferences necessary for reading science text. Based on Graesser, León, and Otero (2002).

Building Metacognition

Experts in the disciplines are highly metacognitive. They have specific goals or purposes for reading, they monitor understanding during the course of reading, they take corrective action when they encounter a glitch, and they evaluate text use in relation to their goals. Students, too, can plan more carefully, identify appropriate materials for their purposes, stick to their goals, and keep track of information from multiple texts.

Metacognition plays a significant role in reading digital texts (Coiro, 2011; Afflerbach & Cho, 2009):

- Reading online is more difficult because students, as they grow more comfortable with print, now need to gain familiarity with features of digital texts and how to navigate them.
- Working with websites presents more challenges because they often contain more distractions—advertisements, cluttered pages, flashing icons, interactive features—and other bells and whistles that compete for the reader's attention.
- It is easy to get lost in nonlinear texts with their many links and tantalizing options.
- Since anyone can upload to the Internet, little quality control exists. It is often hard for students to locate current, just right, "considerate," and unbiased texts, particularly for younger students or those with knowledge, language, or reading challenges.

CCSS Standard R7: Students need to read more than print found in conventional texts; they need to learn how to read digital and other multimedia texts as well.

As Mr. Rodriguez plans he needs to decide how and when to embed metacognition into learning science and social studies. He has two goals when teaching metacognition. First he stresses the importance of metacognition to experts in any field. Historians and social scientists monitor their reading to ensure that they do not accept a particular viewpoint because of an impassioned plea rather than an evidence-based argument. Second, Mr. Rodriguez aims to demonstrate the benefits of metacognitive strategies for both reading and inquiry. For example, students need to draw upon problem-solving strategies when comprehension breaks down, as well as when their search efforts prove unproductive. Whenever students discuss what they read Mr. Rodriguez will stress metacognition, asking questions like "Does that make sense?," "How could you confirm your idea?," "How did you figure that out?," and "What made you think that was an important idea?"

Aligning Comprehension Instructional Goals with CCSS

Now that Mr. Rodriguez has thought through what he wants to cover, he creates an alignment chart to ensure that his comprehension goals map onto his state's ELA standards. In Figure 7.9 we show how Mr. Rodriguez does this with one example for each component of the good comprehender model. This chart is a work in progress because he may modify his instruction because all planning is tentative. For example, Mr. Rodriguez may change or add rows as needed. Right now for the sake of clarity, we focus solely on the CCSS for reading informational texts—and not on the standards for science, social studies, or information and communication technology (ICT). In actual practice, a teacher needs to consider all these standards during planning.

We have described Mr. Rodriguez's planning through Step 1, the identification of broad goals, and Step 2, an explanation of how Mr. Rodriguez will foster comprehension throughout his inquiry unit by building conceptual, word, and text structure knowledge. He will also develop comprehension by helping students use cognitive and metacognitive strategies. Now we shift to the remaining steps in the planning process—selecting texts, identifying lessons, and determining assessments.

Step 3: Select Texts, Technology, and Other Resources

During all inquiry-cycle phases, students rely on texts, along with direct observation and experiments, to gather them with information. In the *asking and activating* phase, Mr. Rodriguez uses texts to provide context, generate curiosity, and build background knowledge. When actively engaged in the *experiencing and investigating* phase, students draw upon an array of printed and Internet texts to locate and gather information. Mr. Rodriguez uses mentor texts to model the use of comprehension strategies. When students are *organizing and analyzing*, they need to attend to text structure and text features to locate important information. Students must return to these texts to justify what they have learned. In terms of *applying and communicating*, students write their own texts, emulating the genres and text structures they have read.

Nowadays, teachers have access to an abundance of high-quality trade books and magazines. There are numerous resources to aid teachers in finding excellent nonfiction. Several Internet search engines have been very helpful to us. *Lexile.com* allows you to search for books by topic and by reading level. The advanced search function on *Amazon.com* allows you to

Component of the Good Comprehender Model	Instructional Goal	CCSS for Reading Informational Texts
Knowledge Conceptual Text: Text Features Vocabulary	Teach that illustrations, including maps, graphs, and charts, contain text features that enhance comprehension and employ a visual format to summarize important information.	CCSS—*Craft and Structure, 5* Know various text features (e.g., captions, bold print, subheadings, glossaries, indexes, electronic menus, icons) to locate key facts or information in a text efficiently. CCSS—*Integration of Knowledge and Ideas, 7* Explain how specific images (e.g., a diagram showing how a machine works) contribute to and clarify a text.
Strategies: **Knowledge and Use** Predicting/Inferring Questioning Making Connections Visualizing Determining Importance Summarizing Evaluating	Teach students to use the strategy of asking questions to support their understanding.	CCSS—*Key Ideas and Details, 1* Ask and answer questions as *who*, *what*, *where*, *when*, *why*, and *how* to demonstrate understanding of key details in a text (as well as important ideas).
Metacognition: Knowledge and Use Self-Awareness Planning Monitoring Problem Solving: "Fix-Up" Strategies Evaluating progress/ performance	Teach students to apply a set of clarifying and problem-solving strategies to fix something when it doesn't make sense.	CCSS—*Craft and Structure, 4* Determine the meaning of words and phrases in a text relevant to a grade 2 topic or subject area.
Motivation Feeling Competent Social Support and Sharing Curiosity Persistence Challenging Self	Teach students that nothing builds feelings of competence and confidence more than experiencing success— so picking a just-right book is essential.	CCSS—*Range of Reading and Level of Complexity, 10* Read and comprehend complex informational texts independently and proficiently (by considering reader variables, such as motivation).

FIGURE 7.9. Matching comprehension instructional goals to the CCSS.

search for book by author, subject, key words, and age appropriateness of the reader. Finally, the book *A to Zoo* (Lima & Lima, 2006) provides a good way to search for picture books by topic or by author. We also recommend consulting these children's literature awards for books:

- The National Council of Teachers of English's Orbis Pictus Award (*www.ncte.org/awards/orbispictus*).
- The International Reading Association's Children's Book Awards for primary, intermediate, and young adult nonfiction (*www.reading.org*).
- The *Boston Globe's* Horn Book Award for Outstanding Nonfiction (*www.hbook.com*).
- The American Library Association's Coretta Scott King Award (*www.ala.org/emiert/cskbookawards*).
- The American Library Association's Robert F. Sibert Informational Book Award (*www.ala.org/alsc/awardsgrants/bookmedia/sibertmedal*).
- *Kirkus Reviews'* Best Children's Nonfiction Books (*www.kirkusreviews. com/book-reviews/childrens-books*).

Mr. Rodriguez first needs to think about the types of books to include in his unit. He wants to expose students to diverse and increasingly complex informational texts on weather and communities, in keeping with the CCSS. To do this, he needs to have some notion of students' reading levels so he can gradually expand the types of genres and text types they read. That means selecting texts that possess clear expository text structures, particularly the ones he will teach—comparison–contrast and cause–effect. Mr. Rodriguez also aims to include differentiated texts to accommodate a wide range of students in terms of language experience, reading ability, interest, and knowledge. He will address this need by creating text sets, a procedure previously outlined in Chapter 5. (Some of the principles we address here also are covered in Chapter 5 so it might make sense to review that information to compare the selection of literature to informational texts.)

Second, Mr. Rodriguez evaluates each potential text for inclusion in the unit. The criteria for selection fall into three broad areas (Saul & Dieckman, 2005, p. 505):

1. The *content*—evaluating accuracy, credibility, and bias.
2. The *writing*—judging the degree of "artistry" and "passion" along with "coherence" and "unity."
3. The *design*—considering appearance, organization, text features, and visuals.

Third, Mr. Rodriguez carefully considers the purpose of each text in the inquiry process. He decides which books to use for various phases of the inquiry process. An example of how Mr. Rodriguez takes the first phase of the inquiry cycle into account when selecting texts appears in Figure 7.10. He thinks about materials that will accomplish his instructional goals for asking and activating. As he does so, he asks himself two questions relevant to both comprehension and inquiry: "Which texts will work well for motivating and fostering curiosity, and prompting solid inquiry questions?" and "Which ones are most effective for activating and building students' knowledge?"

In Figure 7.10, we see some of the texts Mr. Rodriguez plans to use, including print (fiction and nonfiction books), visuals (photographs, maps), and digital resources (websites). These materials represent a range of complexity, reflecting multiple levels of difficulty—as evident by the Lexile ratings.

Finally, Mr. Rodriguez examines each text's instructional function, or how it will be used specifically in the inquiry workshop. Once again, he asks himself several questions: "Will this book be good to use during a read-aloud for activating or building background knowledge?" "Should I employ this text during small-group instruction as a mentor text to teach or reinforce a comprehension or inquiry strategy? Or maybe it is better for independent reading? Perhaps I should reserve this book for pairs or small groups of students for shared reading during inquiry?" and "Which texts might serve multiple purposes in the inquiry cycle?" This decision-making process is important because such planning will make Mr. Rodriguez's teaching purposeful and reasoned. Plus, he can allude to this real-life example when it comes time to talk with students about how they will select texts to match their inquiry goals.

Step 4: Identify Lessons

The next step in planning is designing lessons for each part of the inquiry cycle. In the asking and activating phase, Mr. Rodriguez needs to teach a lesson that activates knowledge and curiosity (inquiry goals) and a lesson on self-questioning and previewing (comprehension goals). In Figure 7.11, we provide an example of one lesson that is associated with each of the four components of the good comprehender model.

Mr. Rodriguez certainly will not teach something new about every component of the good comprehender model each day. Instead, he will repeat and deepen knowledge of content and strategies throughout the unit. He will aim for depth of learning, rather than breadth. By revisiting topics, he will reteach and extend students' knowledge, as well as give them more time for practice.

INQUIRY PHASE 1: ASKING AND ACTIVATING	
Social studies text	Science text
What is a community?	**What is weather?**
What Is a Community? From A to Z (Kalman, 2000; 680L)	Travel advertisements
Living in Urban Communities (Sterling, 2008c; 300L)	*How's the Weather?* (Berger & Berger, 1993; 300L)
Living in Rural Communities (Sterling, 2008a; 360L)	*Animals in Winter* (Bancroft & Van Gelder, 1997; Adult-directed, 380L)
	Weather Wiz Kids:
	www.weatherwizkids.com
	Weather Encyclopaedia:
	www.theweatherchannelkids.com/ weather-ed/weather-encyclopedia
What are different types of communities?	**What are different types of severe weather?**
Google Images: urban, rural, and suburban communities	*Cloudy with a Chance of Meatballs* (Barrett, 1978; 730L)
Town Mouse, Country Mouse (Brett, 2003; 530L)	Google Images on types of severe weather
The Little House (Burton, 1978; 890L)	*Web Weather for Kids:*
	http://eo.ucar.edu/webweather
	Weather Words and What They Mean (Gibbons, 1992; 450L)
	Wild Weather: Blizzards! (Hopping, 1999; 610L)
What do we know about our community?	**What do we know about our weather and climate?**
Google Images of local community	National Weather Service:
Selected pages from local newspaper and advertisements	*www.nws.noaa.gov/om/reachout/kidspage. shtml*

FIGURE 7.10. Some selected texts for the inquiry unit.

Of course, the choice of how many lessons to teach is influenced by the length of the inquiry unit and the learning skills of the students. If they pick up ideas and comprehension strategies quickly, then fewer lessons will be needed. If they struggle Mr. Rodriguez will have to review and reteach. It makes intuitive sense that fewer key topics can be taught in a unit lasting 2 weeks than

> **CCSS Standard R8:** When students analyze and organize what they read within the inquiry cycle they must reason to support the points they are making.

Inquiry Cycle Phase	Sample Lessons That Map onto the Good Comprehender Model
Asking and Activating	**Knowledge** (*conceptual knowledge*): We need to think about what we already know about a topic when we begin to learn more about it. **Strategy** (*self-questioning*): Asking oneself questions is important for both comprehension and inquiry. **Motivation** (*curiosity*): Good readers like to read to answer their questions about the world in which they live. **Metacognition** (*planning*): Good inquirers make plans before they start their research.
Exploring and Investigating	**Knowledge** (*text types and genres*): Reading for information on the Internet is the same but also different than reading printed books and magazines. **Strategy** (*text features*): Good readers know that authors use certain text features in both print and websites. **Metacognition** (*monitoring*): *Stop and ask*: Am I paying attention or am I distracted by information or visuals that are not important? Do I understand what I am reading? **Motivation** (*perseverance*): Sometimes I can't find the information I need right away when I am reading. How do I keep going and not give up? Why shouldn't I give up?
Organizing and Analyzing	**Knowledge** (*text structure*): Authors group similar facts and ideas together using some kind of pattern. **Strategy** (*determining importance*): An author uses these patterns to help us find the big ideas. **Metacognition** (*monitoring and problem solving*): *Stop and ask*: Do I understand how this author uses a chart to organize information? If not, will looking back in the book and rereading the words or thinking more about what I already know about this topic help me to better understand it?

(continued)

FIGURE 7.11. Inquiry-phase lessons aligned with the good comprehender model.

Inquiry Cycle Phase	Sample Lessons That Map onto the Good Comprehender Model
Organizing and Analyzing *(continued)*	**Motivation** *(social support)* Sometimes just trying to explain something that isn't clear to a classmate can help you.
Consolidating and Reflecting	**Knowledge** *(conceptual)*: When you study something, sometimes your understanding about it changes over time. What new thoughts have you had about your topic since you started answering your question? **Strategy** *(self-questioning)*: When you learn about a concept/topic, it raises new questions for inquiry. **Metacognition** *(evaluating)*: After an inquiry, you should think about how things went. What did you learn about yourself as a learner during this inquiry? What did you do really well? What could you do better next time? **Motivation** *(challenge, self-efficacy)*: Completing an inquiry is hard work. What did you do to stay interested and keep working even when things became challenging? Do you think you'd like to work on another inquiry again? Why or why not?
Applying and Communicating	**Knowledge** *(conceptual knowledge)*: When presenting to classmates, you need to think about what is important to share about your topic; you also need to think about how to share that information so your classmates will learn about the topic. **Strategy** *(good readers)*: As we learned, good readers use all kinds of strategies. For example, good readers have to figure out what's important when they read. Good inquirers also need powerful strategies for writing. They have to decide what facts are important to share with others. **Metacognition** *(evaluating)*: Because you care about your audience, you can proofread your PowerPoint presentations, include important facts, choose visuals that support your ideas, and rehearse your presentation. **Motivation** *(social support)*: It feels good to share your ideas and what you learned with others. It feels good when others can see how hard you worked and how much you learned. Plus, they can learn something from you that they didn't know before.

FIGURE 7.11. *(continued)*

in one that spans 2 months. Given the fact that Mr. Rodriguez plans on a 6-week unit, he will winnow down his more comprehensive list of lessons to a manageable subset.

Step 5: Choose or Develop Assessments

In our steps for planning inquiry instruction (see Figure 7.3), the last task is selecting and designing assessments. But in reality, Mr. Rodriguez starts to think about assessment tools as he considers his goals. He needs to track students' growth in content knowledge and their use of comprehension and inquiry strategies throughout the 6 weeks of instruction. The students need to know how they are doing because feedback guides their efforts. At the end of the unit he wants to assess their growth in content knowledge, their understanding of the inquiry process, and their growth as strategic readers. For each subject-area, inquiry, and comprehension goal he identifies at least one way to assess it.

To assess content, Mr. Rodriguez will have groups of students brainstorm what they already know about weather and communities, using vocabulary words associated with those topics. Later, when students record notes on their graphic organizers, he will judge how well they perceive interrelated ideas. Finally, through inquiry projects, like a poster or a simple PowerPoint presentation, he will learn whether students understand key concepts.

Mr. Rodriguez also will have process goals related to strategies use, metacognition, inquiry, and motivation. To capture this information, he will record anecdotal records of observations, use checklists, and confer one-on-one with students. Because he wants students to take more responsibility for their own learning over time, Mr. Rodriguez will ask students to complete short self-assessments of motivation and performance using a simple rating scale or response in a learning log (see Chapter 4). To learn more about students' thinking processes, he will conduct conferences, eavesdrop on their conversations, analyze completed think sheets, and listen to student think-alouds during small-group instruction. Finally, he will have students assemble a portfolio that contains their final project, their notes, rough draft, and records of experiments and observations. He will confer with each student and ask him or her to reflect on what he or she learned.

LOOKING BACK, LOOKING FORWARD

Disciplinary experts know full well the importance of stockpiling knowledge in their areas of specialization. For one, experts in each field use knowledge better than those who are not familiar with the domain (Pressley & Afflerbach, 1995). So, building conceptual, textual, and vocabulary knowledge always makes sense, whether for novices or experts. Teachers perform a huge service by preparing students from an early age to understand how knowledge in different fields is generated, how it is judged and communicated, and how it is applied (Juel et al., 2010). What's more, the immense role that strategies and metacognition play in comprehension and inquiry cannot be downplayed. They serve both inquiring experts and students. Last but not least are motivation and interest. Inquiry acts as an antidote to boredom because it arises from students' curiosity. However, putting fun and interests first should not come at the expense of a robust learning experience.

In this chapter, we demonstrated planning for inquiry-based instruction with informational texts. In the next chapter, we take these assorted plans and see how they are put into action in accordance with the gradual release of responsibility model.

APPLICATIONS AND EXTENSIONS

1. Do an audit of some nonfiction texts you know or are currently using with students. Are they diverse enough? Is the range broad enough so that all students can find books they want to and can read? Can students with different reading abilities and cultural and linguistic backgrounds gain access to content?

2. If you are not teaching, try developing a text set of your own. Use the information here and in Chapter 5 to develop a text set in a particular subject area.

3. There are many systems for selecting academic vocabulary (see Baumann & Graves, 2010). Choose their system or another, and generate a list of core vocabulary words for teaching one subject-area unit.

CHAPTER 8

Teaching Reading Comprehension with Informational Texts

Mr. Rodriguez, the second-grade teacher we've been following, completed his preliminary unit planning as we outlined in Chapter 7. He identified the relevant science, social studies, and reading standards for his integrated unit on weather and communities. His goals are to develop his students' subject-area knowledge, their cognitive and metacognitive strategies, and their motivation. He selected nonfiction books for whole-class instruction, readied his classroom library for small-group and independent reading, bookmarked websites for research, and prepared text sets so that students, regardless of reading ability, could access content. He mapped out topics for his focus lessons following the five phases of the inquiry workshop. Finally, he decided that students would complete a culminating project of their choice to demonstrate what they learned. At this point, Mr. Rodriguez sketches out his daily lessons and begins to teach. He knows that he will need to adapt these plans in response to the instruction, students' needs, and their progress.

In Chapter 3, we introduced a modified version of the Gradual Release of Responsibility Model (GRRM; Pearson & Gallagher, 1983), which describes how students develop comprehension strategies and build knowledge. The adapted GRRM proposes that young or inexperienced students learn by first interacting with skillful others who walk them through a desired process before they internalize and apply the new strategies and knowledge by themselves. The teacher begins the unit with considerable content knowledge; but gradually, the students' knowledge builds as they take charge of their own learning. To facilitate this transfer of responsibility, students receive just enough support to achieve their objectives independently. As learners gain proficiency, the supports are withdrawn, little by little. The GRRM-C applies to the development and use of cognitive and metacognitive strategies, as well as to the building of knowledge and motivation to read.

In the following sections, we describe how Mr. Rodriguez teaches inquiry lessons that focus on knowledge building, metacognition, strategies use, and motivation. We begin by describing the way Mr. Rodriguez organizes his daily literacy block. Then we explore how he manages comprehension instruction in each phase of the inquiry cycle, consistent with the GRRM-C.

GOALS FOR THIS CHAPTER

✓ Discuss the structure of inquiry-based instruction during the literacy block and the subject-area block.

✓ Learn how to embed comprehension instruction in the asking and activating phase of the inquiry cycle.

✓ Learn how to embed comprehension instruction in the experiencing and investigating phase of the inquiry process.

✓ Learn how to embed comprehension instruction in the organizing and analyzing phase of the inquiry process.

✓ Learn how to embed comprehension instruction in the consolidating and reflecting phase of the inquiry process.

✓ Learn how to embed speaking and writing instruction in the communicating and applying phase of the inquiry process.

INQUIRY-BASED INSTRUCTION DURING THE LITERACY BLOCK

Figure 8.1 shows how the thematic, integrated unit maps onto the phases of the inquiry cycle. Mr. Rodriguez and the students begin by considering what they know and pondering what they want to learn. Then they move into the 3 weeks of reading, observing, and experimenting. In the final 2 weeks of the unit they organize, consolidate, and share what they have learned.

Mr. Rodriguez combines science, social studies, and literacy in his themed unit. To do so, he allocates instructional time from his morning literacy block, as well as from his afternoon science and social studies instruction. The unit takes 6 weeks because of subject-area instruction in both science and social studies. Figure 8.2 describes how Mr. Rodriguez structures his daily second-grade literacy block.

Week 1
Phase 1: Asking and Activating
The teacher develops knowledge and a sense of wonder in the students. The students' curiosity grows as they set learning goals.

Weeks 2, 3, and 4
Phase 2: Experiencing and Investigating
The students with the teacher's guidance read, observe, experiment, and take notes. The teacher helps the students use strategies to accomplish their goals.

Week 5
Phase 3: Organizing and Analyzing
The students organize and analyze what they have learned, focusing on big ideas.

Week 6
Phase 4: Reflecting and Consolidating
The students integrate their learning throughout the inquiry unit, discuss insights, and reflect upon their performance and what they discovered about themselves as learners and collaborators.
Phase 5: Sharing and Communicating
The students bring together what they learned in a final project, reflecting on the process and the content. They share their learning with others.

FIGURE 8.1. Inquiry unit overview.

Literacy Block	Time	Parts of the Literacy Program
Whole-class reading	20–45 minutes	Teacher instruction and guided practice with teacher-selected text
Small-group, teacher-guided reading and partner reading/work time	45–60 minutes	Shared practice with teacher- and/or student-selected text(s)
Independent reading	10–15 minutes	Self-guided reading with student-selected text

FIGURE 8.2. Organization of inquiry instruction: The literacy block.

Whole-Class Reading

Mr. Rodriguez's whole-class reading instruction varies from 20 to 45 minutes depending upon his instructional objectives each day. He selects either one or two books related to a thematic unit for whole-class instruction each week. First, the featured text is presented in a read-aloud; then, it is revisited several times throughout the week. A common text enables Mr. Rodriguez to expose children to topical material that otherwise would be too hard for some to read. While reading these texts Mr. Rodriguez can model fluent reading, build vocabulary, and explain and model cognitive and metacognitive strategies. The shared text also allows him to demonstrate important points about the craft of writing (Ray, 2002). Finally, these teacher read-alouds and discussions provide opportunities to scaffold students' comprehension.

Teacher-Guided Small-Group Reading

As some students work with a partner, Mr. Rodriguez pulls other small groups of students together for various purposes. For one, he meets regularly with his group of struggling readers, devoting 5 to 15 minutes each day to the explicit teaching of word-recognition skills and strategies in the literacy block. This word-level instruction enhances students' fluency, which directly impacts their strategies-based, interpretive discussions of text. Research studies indicate that low-achieving readers in kindergarten through third-grade benefit from longer and more frequent decoding and word-recognition instruction, and so, the literacy block is utilized, in part, for that purpose (Connor, Morrison, & Underwood, 2007).

Mr. Rodriguez also meets with specific groups of students according to their needs to review progress with comprehension and inquiry. Sometimes he earmarks small-group time to reteach and reinforce comprehension strategies introduced during whole-class instruction. Or, for example, when four students with little Internet experience work on similar inquiry questions, Mr. Rodriguez gathers them for additional instruction on how to navigate websites to search for relevant information. As another example, he meets with those students who are creating a digital, PowerPoint "book" for an inquiry project to familiarize them with the needed features of the software. When Mr. Rodriguez is not meeting with groups of students, he circulates informally to assess their progress, or he confers with students, stopping to provide support as they read, take notes, organize, and work on their projects.

Independent Reading

Students read by themselves for 10 to 15 minutes each day. The classroom library is structured so that students can easily access books. Texts on communities and weather are sorted according to genre and complexity in labeled baskets. The books that Mr. Rodriguez uses for whole-class reading are available to students for rereading once they have been introduced in class. Students also have access to laminated copies of articles clipped from children's magazines, as well as digital picture books created by students in past years that have been printed and lovingly added to the classroom library.

To facilitate independent reading and responding, Mr. Rodriguez sometimes asks all students to respond to the main text by writing in reading logs. To develop fluency, students orally reread copies of the main text with a partner, or quietly practice the book alone. From time to time, he conducts a fluency check to assess progress (Stahl & Huebach, 2005). During this period, children often can continue to make progress on their inquiry projects, which they typically work on in the afternoon.

INQUIRY-BASED INSTRUCTION
DURING THE SUBJECT-AREA BLOCK

Mr. Rodriguez continues to teach about weather and communities in the afternoon during his subject-area time. Whereas the literacy block often emphasizes comprehension and metacognitive strategies to enhance understanding of literature and informational texts, the afternoon block focuses on inquiry strategies and the application of comprehension strategies to research and learning from informational texts.

The inquiry format presented in Figure 8.3 shares commonalities with other workshop formats (Reading Workshop, Atwell, 1998; Writing

Subject-Area Block	Time	Parts of the Inquiry Workshop
Whole-class instruction	15–20 minutes	Teacher instruction and guided practice with teacher-selected text or resource
Independent work time	20–30 minutes	Small-group and/or independent practice with student-selected text
Debriefing	5–10 minutes	Workshop wrap-up

FIGURE 8.3. Organization of the inquiry workshop: The subject-area block.

Workshop, Calkins, 1994; Internet Workshop, Leu, Leu, & Coiro, 2004). These approaches generally adopt a three-part structure: (1) whole-class instruction, (2) independent student work time, and (3) whole-class sharing and debriefing.

Whole-Class Instruction

Each inquiry workshop session begins with a focus lesson that lasts between 10 and 15 minutes that covers specific concepts, strategies, or processes. Often, instruction centers on explaining and modeling a cognitive or metacognitive strategy that supports the inquiry process. At other times the class discusses what they have learned about weather and communities and they consider their next steps. Occasionally, Mr. Rodriguez takes time to explain or review the process of completing inquiry projects. Before this period ends, Mr. Rodriguez allots approximately 5 minutes to make sure that the students know what they will work on next.

Independent Work Time

Students spend 20 to 30 minutes reading, observing, measuring, and conducting experiments set up by the teacher. They apply the inquiry strategies taught during the whole-class focus lessons. Mr. Rodriguez creates text sets so that all students can access the same content regardless of reading level. He minimizes frustration and maximizes success by previewing and bookmarking websites in advance that are appropriate for a range of second-grade readers. He provides the materials they need to conduct observations and record their results. Students then read, search for information, take notes, complete graphic organizers, and summarize what they have learned. In effect, they work through the inquiry cycle.

During independent work, students meet in variably sized groups depending on the task and their reading proficiency. For example, Mr. Rodriguez organizes groups around common or related topics, such as all those interested in learning about winter weather's impact on their community. Sometimes the students work without teacher support; at other times, Mr. Rodriguez directly assists them with some aspect of the inquiry cycle. As students work together, Mr. Rodriguez watches so he knows who needs additional support.

Whole-Class Debriefing

The 5- to 10-minute debriefing occurs at the end of the workshop. This time is used for several purposes:

- Mr. Rodriguez reviews important points raised in the whole-class focus lesson.
- Students describe any top-notch resources they have located.
- Students share what they have learned about weather and communities.
- Students troubleshoot problems.
- Mr. Rodriguez asks students to explain how a particular strategy fostered understanding, solved problems, or gained insight.
- Mr. Rodriguez prompts students to evaluate their learning and participation during the inquiry session.

COMPREHENSION INSTRUCTION
DURING THE INQUIRY CYCLE

Inquiry Cycle Phase 1: Asking and Activating

The first phase of the inquiry cycle lays the foundation for the unit. During the first week of instruction knowledge is developed, comprehension strategies are introduced, and culminating projects are outlined. First, each lesson presents baseline information upon which the remainder of the unit will be built. Second, the lessons are interconnected. Although new information is presented each day, it builds on the previous day's learning. Importantly, there is no "skill-and-drill" during small-group work; students do not practice skills or strategies in isolation from pertinent content on the weather or communities. Each lesson provides opportunities for review, integration, and consolidation of comprehension strategies even as Mr. Rodriguez "ups the ante" in terms of deepening students' knowledge. Third, each lesson addresses, albeit to different degrees on different days, the four components we've focused on in this book—knowledge building, metacognition, strategies use, and motivation.

As we proceed, we describe the instruction in the morning literacy block, the afternoon subject-area block, and explain how the two blocks are interrelated. We devote more attention to the first two phases of the inquiry cycle because it is here that students will do more of their reading.

Morning Literacy Block

Mr. Rodriguez lays the groundwork for his integrated unit in this phase. He introduces two books that will be used for whole-class instruction in the literacy block. One selection, *Town Mouse, Country Mouse* (Brett, 2003), is a variation on the well-loved fable of mice that swap homes, only to learn that everyone contends with their share of troubles—and that there is no such thing as a perfect community. A second text, *Wind and Weather* (Time-Life, 1989), is used to introduce students to important weather concepts and reading strategies. In Figure 8.4 we briefly describe the lessons that Mr. Rodriguez plans to teach during the first week of whole-class instruction.

During whole-class reading, Mr. Rodriguez builds students' knowledge about communities by teaching the necessary academic vocabulary and developing the students' prior knowledge related to *Town Mouse, Country Mouse* (Brett, 2003). He conducts a read-aloud lesson that includes before, during, and after reading instruction. Before reading, Mr. Rodriguez asks students to describe their community. Because they live in a rural community, he then shares photographs of a nearby city to discuss the differences. The students comment on the size of buildings, the traffic, and the number of people on the streets. From this, Mr. Rodriguez and the students record some of the differences between a city and rural area on a two-column comparison chart that also includes some academic vocabulary related to communities.

Next, Mr. Rodriguez reads the story, pausing to model comprehension strategies and to ask students questions. He prompts them to note the differences between living in a city and in the country. He wants the students to think about what would be difficult if you lived in the city and then moved to the country and vice versa. The students continue their study of communities as they read from a selection of leveled texts during their small-group and independent reading time.

> **CCSS Standards R4, L6:** Inquiry instruction provides an excellent opportunity to build students' academic vocabulary, both specific to a particular subject area and across subject areas.

At the end of the read-aloud Mr. Rodriguez returns to the photographs and to *Town Mouse, Country Mouse* (Brett, 2003) to introduce the strategy of self-questioning. Self-questioning is part of a suite of strategies known as transactional strategies instruction (TSI) (R. Brown, 2008; R. Brown et al., 1996), which Mr. Rodriguez and the students will use throughout the unit. Students use comprehension strategies to construct understandings of literature and informational texts through rich, interpretive discussions initially led by the teacher. For the most part, Mr. Rodriguez's students take an efferent stance because they read primarily informational text with a goal of learning from text. Yet excitement builds as they learn more about weather, especially severe weather. Equally important, Mr. Rodriguez emphasizes the signifi-

> **CCSS Standards R6, 7, 8:** Students are taught to make judgments, questioning trustworthiness of information in informational texts, considering the quality of evidence, and questioning the author's intentions and assumptions.

	Day 1	Day 2	Day 3	Day 4	Day 5
Whole-Class Instruction	Introduce the unit; discuss what the class will be studying, describe options, and present sample unit projects. Activate knowledge about communities and in the process build academic vocabulary. Teach that good learners are thinkers and strategy users with the text to model these ideas. Text: *Town Mouse, Country Mouse* (Brett, 2003)	Develop knowledge of rural, urban, and suburban communities, and activate in the context of knowledge about students' community. Continue to practice self-questioning in relation to read-aloud text (see Figure 8.6, Day 1 in subject-area block). Build academic vocabulary related to communities. Texts: *Town Mouse, Country Mouse* (Brett, 2003) PowerPoint on different kinds of communities	Understand text features that signal important information (bold, italics, heading, caption, label). Build academic vocabulary about weather. Continue to practice self-questioning in relation to read-aloud text. Text: *Wind and Weather* (Time-Life, 1989)	Self-questioning with information presented visually. Text: Aerial view photo of New York City skyline	Ask "thick versus thin" questions (Harvey & Goudvis, 2007). Review all "I wonder" questions collected throughout week about weather in the local community.
Small-Group Instruction	*Teacher:* Conduct small-group instruction focusing on decoding, fluency, and/or comprehension. *Students:* Compare and contrast different versions of *Town Mouse, Country Mouse* (Brett, 2003).	*Teacher:* Conduct small-group instruction focusing on decoding, fluency, and/or comprehension. *Students:* Compare and contrast rural, urban, and suburban communities in picture books.	*Teacher:* Conduct small-group instruction focusing on decoding, fluency, and/or comprehension. *Students:* Compare and contrast informational text features in several books about communities.	*Teacher:* Conduct small-group instruction focusing on decoding, fluency, and/or comprehension. *Students:* Sort Google photos by community and generate questions about information presented in visual format.	*Teacher:* Conduct small-group instruction focusing on decoding, fluency, and/or comprehension. *Students:* Explore informational books on weather and community to generate more inquiry questions.

FIGURE 8.4. Gist of literacy block lessons for the first phase of the inquiry cycle.

cance of critical evaluation during reading. This will become more important as they begin to read on the Internet.

The following instructional episode features Mr. Rodriguez as he initially explains and models how to ask questions when reading text and "reading" visual aids such as photographs (see day 4 in Figure 8.4). He begins the lesson by stating that good learners use multiple sources of information when learning something new. Previously, the class identified important facts about communities based on observations of their community, personal knowledge, and a PowerPoint presentation. Today students will be introduced to another source of information—looking at photographs to learn more about communities.

> **CCSS Standard R7:** Students need to think about content provided via different types of media and formats, including those presented visually, as in photographs.

Mr. Rodriguez explains that self-questioning is one of several strategies that good readers use to help them comprehend what they read. He wants the students to understand the strategy (declarative knowledge), gain insight into the mental processes involved in using the strategy (procedural knowledge), and know why and when to use it (conditional knowledge). Mr. Rodriguez starts to model self-questioning after he projects an enlarged black-and-white photograph of New York City on a SMART Board (see Figure 8.5).

Students then move into partner and independent reading. During paired reading, students share their questions orally; when reading alone, they write down a few questions on Post-it notes. As students read and practice asking questions, Mr. Rodriguez meets with small groups of students and later observes students' progress with asking questions.

Afternoon Subject-Area Block

In the afternoon Mr. Rodriguez continues the unit on communities and weather. The content covered in the afternoon block complements and supplements lessons taught in the morning literacy block. Mr. Rodriguez structures the lessons so the students employ the same vocabulary and build a common set of knowledge. He expands on some of the concepts he introduced in the morning, helps students apply the self-questioning strategy, and gives them time to read and learn. The outline for the first week of instruction is presented in Figure 8.6 (on pages 194–195).

Mr. Rodriguez's read-aloud text for the week is *Weather Words and What They Mean* (Gibbons, 1992), which introduces students to academic vocabulary and the concept that underlies this term. As he reads Gibbons's book, he records the new words on a chart. Then after reading, he and the students classify them—types of clouds, precipitation, severe weather, and degree of wind. As each word is entered on the chart (see Figure 8.6, Day 1)

Define the Strategy	Mr. Rodriguez begins by defining the strategy and explaining its importance. He is both explaining and thinking aloud.
Why is the asking of questions important?	"We already know that good learners use strategies to help them understand and learn. A strategy is a way of thinking, something you do inside your head when you read. Today we are going to learn about asking ourselves questions while we are reading because we are curious about the world around us and sometimes when we read we want to know more.
	"We also know that scientists and historians ask lots of questions. They want to know where the rain comes from, what makes a snowflake, and why people crowd together to live in cities. So to become better readers and learners, just like scientists and historians, we need to ask ourselves good questions.
	"I'm going to start by showing you how I ask myself a question."
Discover the Process of Asking Questions	Mr. Rodriguez continues to think aloud to model his use of the self-questioning strategy. As he models, he integrates additional direct explanations.
	"I'm looking carefully at this photo of New York City. I know it is New York City because I lived there when I was younger. So, this photo reminds me of lots of things I do know about this city. But, looking closely at this photo, I see lots of tall buildings that look like giant rectangles with lots of windows. I know from my experience that most of the buildings are shaped that way. But what I don't know is why these buildings share the same shape. I wonder by looking at the photo why I don't seem to see any circle- or diamond-shaped buildings. And why do these buildings have to be so close together? Who made that decision in the first place?
	"So you see, I just showed you how I came up with some questions. First, I found a clue in the photo that was interesting. Then I thought about what I already knew about that detail. That made me think about other things that I didn't already know about that detail—and so I asked a question about what I wanted to find out.
	"In this photo, I also see that the sky looks dark, as if it's going to storm any minute. I've been in New York City during some terrible storms and I know from my experiences that the buildings somehow all come through those storms all right. But, I don't understand why they remain standing. So I ask myself these questions: 'How is it that buildings like those in the photo stay up when the wind blows so hard?' and 'Why don't the buildings fall down when lots of heavy snow covers their rooftops?'
	"What questions would you like to ask about this picture?
	"What did I learn from looking at this picture? That's a really important question, because good readers and learners always ask themselves what they learned. This is what I learned today: There are times when looking at a photo or reading a book will make me ask lots

(continued)

FIGURE 8.5. A sample TSI lesson focusing on the self-questioning strategy.

Discover the Process of Asking Questions *(continued)*	of questions to which I don't know the answer—'I wonder' questions. But sometimes you can look at a photo and it is a good source of information right then and there. So, I'm looking at this photo and I can say that people really use their roofs. Look at how many buildings have water towers, gardens, playgrounds, artwork, and even pools on the roofs. And even though most of the buildings are rectangular, I can see in this photo how really different they are from one another—the incredible number of textures and styles I see. I always thought that rural places, like ours, are beautiful, with all our trees, and hills, and flowers. But now I can see from this photo that an urban skyline can be beautiful too. Wow!"
Determine When to Ask a Question	Mr. Rodriguez wraps up his modeling by providing conditional information about when it makes sense to use the self-questioning strategy. "We ask questions all of the time. Sometimes we ask a question before we start to read or inquire because we are curious; we ask 'I wonder' questions. Sometimes we ask 'I wonder' questions while we are reading because something surprises us. And sometimes we ask 'I wonder' questions when we are finished because what we learned makes us ask even more questions—and we want to keep on reading to find the answers."

FIGURE 8.5. *(continued)*

he explains the most important terms using the Frayer model (Frayer, Frederick, & Klausmeier, 1969; Graves, 2006). Blank forms and completed examples can be found by inserting the words "Frayer model" in Google Search and then selecting the Images option. In the Frayer model, the teacher defines the word, presents students with examples and nonexamples of the word, distinguishes the concept from similar concepts, and then asks students for further examples of the concept. For example, Mr. Rodriguez says the following:

- "Precipitation is water or snow or anything made of water that falls from clouds."
- "Precipitation is not the same as a storm, like a thunderstorm or blizzard. Big storms might include rain or snow, but we can have a rainy or snowy day that is not part of a big storm."
- "Hail or sleet are both frozen kinds of water that fall from the clouds."
- "Leaves that fall from trees are not precipitation; they are not made of water."
- "Can you think of other kinds of precipitation that we should include on our chart and make part of our weather unit?"

	Day 1	Day 2	Day 3	Day 4	Day 5
Whole-Class Instruction	Introduce the process of inquiry; relate to asking and answering questions. Build academic vocabulary related to weather. Activate knowledge about weather. Discuss how the strategies are important to inquiry learning—like self-questioning. Text: *Weather Words and What They Mean* (Gibbons, 1992)	Examine different sources for finding answers to questions, including making connections to knowledge and observing closely. Continue working on the strategy of asking questions, applying it to generating questions about weather in the local community. Text: *Weather Words and What They Mean* (Gibbons, 1992)	Introduce students to conducting weather observations outside. Understand that text visual aids help students to understand informational texts. Review text features (see Figure 8.4, Day 3 in literacy block), and examine visual aids (photo, illustration, diagram, map). Text: *Weather Words and What They Mean* (Gibbons, 1992)	Review the role of asking a question in the inquiry process. Conduct weather observations outdoors. Review instruments and procedures.	Review asking "thick versus thin" questions. Decide if questions reviewed in literacy block in preparation for selection of inquiry questions are "thick" or "thin" and lend themselves to sustained inquiry.

(continued)

FIGURE 8.6. Gist of subject-area block lessons for the first phase of the inquiry cycle.

	Day 1	Day 2	Day 3	Day 4	Day 5
Small-Group Instruction/Independent Work Time	*Teacher:* Meet with small groups as needed, watch students, and confer with them. *Students:* Read informational books to review vocabulary, concepts, and types of weather.	*Teacher:* Prepare students to make weather observations. *Students:* Read informational books to review vocabulary and concepts and make connections between what they observe and what they are learning about weather.	*Teacher:* Assist students with conducting weather observations. *Students:* Conduct weather observations, and practice recording data, including temperature, using illustration and words in groups. Read informational books on weather.	*Teacher:* Continue to assist students with weather observations. *Students:* Conduct weather observations and record data, including temperature, in pairs.	*Students:* Conduct weather observations and collect data, including temperature, independently. Review data and discuss what happened during our observations throughout the week, making comparisons.

FIGURE 8.6. *(continued)*

One of Mr. Rodriguez's objectives is to demonstrate that the strategies taught in the literacy block have relevance in the afternoon subject-area workshop. He reminds students that good learners apply their thinking tools whenever they read—and not just in the morning. He also reminds students about the importance of self-questioning and helps them to understand that asking good questions, wondering, is the first step in learning more about weather and communities. The strategy of self-questioning also links to Mr. Rodriguez's motivation plan. He not only promotes situational interest through his thoughtful choice of texts, topics, and tasks, but he also cultivates a sense of wonder by leading his students to ask good questions.

> **CCSS Standards R1, 2, 3, 5, 7, L4:** A core tenet of the CCSS Standards involves developing conceptual subject area and disciplinary knowledge through reading. Strategies are the tools that support students in accomplishing that aim, by supporting the construction of meaning and also providing a variety of approaches to clarify meanings of unknown words.

During the first phase of the inquiry cycle, the whole class generates questions that form the basis for their independent inquiries and projects. Mr. Rodriguez keeps a record of the questions on a chart:

What is the worst weather we've ever had?

What happens to the cows in a hurricane?

What is the biggest hail we ever got?

What happens if it doesn't stop raining for days?

Why do we get so much snow?

Why do snowflakes have different shapes?

What causes tornados?

Did kids ever make up snow days in the summer?

Do the fish freeze in the lake?

How do we know if it is okay to walk on the ice?

How do the birds know when it is time to fly away?

What can we do to be safe in really bad weather?

Is the weather really getting warmer here?

After discussing these and other questions, the students, assisted by Mr. Rodriguez, identify ones that they would like to study. During this process, some questions are combined, some elaborated, and some are dropped. For example, the questions about the cows, birds, and fish are combined into one question: How do animals deal with winter weather? Some questions have a more scientific bent; others integrate content across science and social studies. All this work sets the stage for the next phase of the inquiry workshop—reading, observing, and conducting experiments.

Phase 2: Experiencing and Investigating

Literacy Block

Mr. Rodriguez continues to use his whole-class time during the morning literacy block to build students' knowledge through read-alouds. As the GRRM indicates, the students become more responsible for building their knowledge, maintaining their motivation, and using strategies to do so. He selects at least two texts each week for developing students' knowledge and modeling of comprehension strategies.

The main text for the second week of the inquiry cycle is an informational picture book, *What Will the Weather Be?* (DeWitt & Croll, 1991). This text continues to build new discipline-specific vocabulary and also refers to weather forecasting as a type of prediction. In the following week, one text, *Tornado!: A Meteorologist and Her Prediction* (Curley, 2011), enriches students' understanding of scientific inquiry by informing students about the tools and practices specialists use to study and forecast the weather, which picks up where *What Will the Weather Be?* left off. This book also demonstrates the wonder and dedication that drives expert practitioners' investigations. Small-group work, independent reading and responding, and teacher conferences continue as usual.

Although many of the examples we provide in this chapter focus on science instruction, we need to bear in mind that Mr. Rodriguez continues to integrate learning about communities in both the morning and afternoon blocks. To that end, Mr. Rodriguez uses other books during whole-class instruction to introduce students to communities far different from their own (*Prairie Town*, Geisert & Geisert, 1998; *Mountain Town*, Geisert & Geisert, 2000; *River Town*, Geisert & Geisert, 1999; *Desert Town*, Geisert & Geisert, 2001). These texts enable Mr. Rodriguez to demonstrate how students can transfer their use of strategies from one subject area to another as well as make comparisons across texts.

> **CCSS Standards R3, 9:** The use of texts that cover similar topics (as in picture books that form part of a series and are written by the same authors) enables students to make connections and comparisons that support the building of knowledge.

Subject-Area Block

On the first afternoon of the second inquiry phase, Mr. Rodriguez states that students will select an inquiry question from the ones generated earlier by the class. A teaching point of this whole-class lesson is that good learners set goals for their inquiries and then plan how to achieve them. The answers will come from reading, studying the weather, and conducting experiments in and out of the classroom. Each step will inform the other. He reviews what resources they can read to answer their question, touching on the classroom library, the school library, and the Internet. Mr. Rodriguez also lists the types of observations that the class will conduct over the next 3 weeks.

As the children search for answers, they will need a way to record and keep track of the important information. Throughout the week, Mr. Rodriguez models how to record important facts on large Post-it notes during the whole-class read-alouds. For temporary storage, he shows students how to affix these notes in a folder. (Students will organize these notes later during Phase 3.)

During small-group and independent reading, students tackle other informational texts practicing their strategies and building knowledge. Sometimes during small-group time, Mr. Rodriguez gathers flexible needs-based groups for more comprehension support. On this day, he selects *Flash,*

Crash, Rumble, and Roll (Branley, 1985) for guided instruction. Mr. Rodriguez pulls out Brody, a low-achieving reader we met earlier in this book, along with a few other students. What follows is an instructional episode from that lesson, which is a depiction of TSI in action.

Mr. Rodriguez explains that the group is going to learn more about the weather by using their reading strategies. With Mr. Rodriguez's support, students briefly name and describe several comprehension and metacognitive strategies, including self-questioning, connecting what they know to what they are reading, and using various fix-up strategies (e.g., skipping, decoding, and rereading identifying word parts, and using context clues) to repair comprehension when encountering unknown words. Students also refer to using nonfiction text features—headings, labels, and visual aids—and deciding if presented information is important or interesting, which both help students to evaluate importance. They also mention making predictions.

As students talk about predicting, Mr. Rodriguez reminds them that weather forecasting is similar to making predictions—when making predictions you pay attention to the pictures and the words to make your best guess—and when forecasting weather you pay attention to your observations and make your best guess.

> MR. RODRIGUEZ: What else do we know about making predictions? Are they always right?
>
> ELIANA: Sometimes predictions are right. But sometimes they are wrong.
>
> BRODY: Yeah, and that's okay.
>
> MR. RODRIGUEZ: Why?
>
> MAX: Because you don't have all the information you need.
>
> BRODY: Things can change and your prediction can be wrong.
>
> MAX: Yes, but then you can make another prediction. And another. So it doesn't matter.
>
> BRODY: Yeah, but I don't agree. Like, remember this morning, with the weather forecast? In that book, they predicted only a few inches of snow but the prediction was wrong. They got eight inches.
>
> ELIANA: Yeah. If you get the weather forecast wrong, it could be bad because people could get stuck in the snow.
>
> BRODY: And if you don't forecast a tornado and there is one, then people and houses could get blown away.
>
> MR. RODRIGUEZ: So I guess some of you are saying that there is a difference between making a prediction when reading and forecasting

the weather. And you told us why there is a difference. What do the rest of you think? Do you want to keep your original thought or change your mind?

The students collectively decide that making predictions and forecasting are not exactly the same. Then, Mr. Rodriguez continues: "So today, with the book we are going to read, I want you to use all your strategies in your thinking tool kit to help you understand. You choose the strategy to understand and learn something important. Do you think you can do that?" The students nod in agreement. "And though I want us to use all of our strategies today, I want you to really focus on making predictions and finding important information."

Mr. Rodriguez asks the class to look at the cover and reads the title aloud. To cue thinking aloud, he asks the group, "So what do you think?"

BRODY: I want to make a prediction. I think this is going to be about thunderstorms.

MR. RODRIGUEZ: Why do you say that?

BRODY: Well, I see rain and lightning in the picture, and thunder sounds makes loud noises like a crash.

The other students agree and Brody volunteers to read the first page. As he stumbles over some unknown words, Mr. Rodriguez reminds Brody to use his fix-up kit. With this bit of guidance, he continues. When Brody finishes reading, Mr. Rodriguez asks: "So what are you thinking?"

BRODY: Well, it looks like a nice day so far in the pictures and I don't see a thunderstorm yet.

MR. RODRIGUEZ: So what do you want to do? Do you want to change your prediction?

BRODY: No. I want to keep reading.

MAX: (*turning the page*) Oh, look.

MR. RODRIGUEZ: Why did you say that?

MAX: Well, in the picture, there are really black clouds. So I agree with Brody—I think it is going to be a thunderstorm.

The group continues to alternate reading with thinking aloud and discussion. In this lesson, Mr. Rodriguez intentionally has these students read the text aloud so he can observe how well they apply fix-up strategies to deal with the difficult words in this book. However, sometimes students read aloud in pairs, read softly in unison, or read silently followed by oral rereading. His choice for student reading during TSI varies based on the particular students he teaches, the text he selects for instruction, and even the difficulty of specific pages. At one point, Mr. Rodriguez stops the class. "We are learning lots of good information about thunderstorms. Perhaps we should write down some of our important facts on Post-it notes." The students dictate ideas, Mr. Rodriguez records them on the Post-it notes, and then he sticks them to the chart paper.

The next few pages are dense with information about how thunderstorms form. Together, students begin to piece together what causes thunderstorms. In the process they encounter words such as *clouds, liquid, gas,* and *water vapor.*

Shayna haltingly reads a page that describes the formation of a rain cloud. The text states, "Warm air near the earth is rising into the clouds. . . . It may go all the way to the top and spill over." Mr. Rodriguez asks Shayna to summarize to check her understanding.

SHAYNA: Well, the water is going up into the cloud and then spills over as rain.

BRODY: I don't think that. See the picture, Shayna. That's not rain going into the clouds; it's arrows.

SHAYNA: But you can see the cloud is right over the lake and the arrow goes from the lake to the cloud.

BRODY: But look—the arrows don't just go from the water. And that word there is *air*. So the arrows show the air going up to the cloud—and not water.

SHAYNA: I still think that water is going up.

MR. RODRIGUEZ: Well, there seems to be two different ideas here. Let's keep those ideas in mind as we keep reading. Maybe as we continue to read, we'll get more information to make things clearer.

The students, together with Mr. Rodriguez, read the next page in unison. Shayna then raises her hand.

SHAYNA: See it said, "The rising air carries water." We were both right.

MR. RODRIGUEZ: So, we saw that it was a good idea to keep reading. We need to remember this—when something isn't clear, sometimes the best thing to do is to just keep reading. It may not work every time, but that strategy is at least worth trying when something you read doesn't make sense.

In this example of TSI, students used all types of strategies—fix up, predicting, making text-to-text connections, determining importance, stating gist to check comprehension—within a short span of reading. Students also confirmed their initial prediction—that the book, indeed, is about thunderstorms. And they used all of these strategies in the service of learning content and constructing a clearer understanding of the text, together.

CCSS Standard R1: Interpretive and critical discussions, which are features of transactional strategies instruction (TSI), provide students with opportunities to cite evidence from texts to support and defend thinking, reading, and learning. This is a key objective of "close reading."

Eliana volunteers to read next. The page states that the rapid air movement in thunderclouds can turn over a plane and rip off its wings. Since the class has been learning to distinguish interesting from important details, Mr. Rodriguez asks the group: "What do you think?" "Is that information important?" "Is it interesting?" and "Should I write anything down on a Post-it note?" The students discuss it, citing their reasons for why they think those facts are important or interesting. The group concludes that the two facts are really, really interesting—but not so important to remember about thunderstorms. A few pages later, the topic of interesting versus important details arises again when students read about the distance that lightning can travel.

BRODY: I think it is awesome that lightning can go so far. The book says it can hit another cloud, or a building, or a tree. And it can be a mile long. That's big.

SHAYNA: I know that lightning sometimes hits people standing under a tree and kills them.

ELIANA: I heard that someone was in a boat and lightning hit him and he died.

MR. RODRIGUEZ: So you know from your reading, knowledge, and experiences that lightning can travel far—and can be dangerous. Good job making connections. Now, is there anything here we want to add on a Post-it note?

BRODY: I think we should put down that lightning can hit clouds, buildings, and trees.

SHAYNA: I think that we should write down that lightning can be longer than a mile.

MR. RODRIGUEZ: Should we write down all of that information? Of all those facts, which ones are interesting and which are important?

Students discuss the merits and ultimately decide to have Mr. Rodriguez note that the lightning can be a mile long—because that fact is both interesting and important, and it is in the book.

The scenario above illustrates an important aspect of TSI. In addition to the explicit teaching of a coordinated set of strategies, TSI features interpretive discussions of texts during which students jointly construct meaning as they apply strategies. The emphasis on discussion as a tool for constructing meaning is apparent in several ways (R. Brown, 2008):

- The students work together to construct meaning.
- Discussion, rather than recitation, is encouraged and the teacher and the students control the topic and the turn taking.
- Students use strategies to support their claims, citing evidence from the text.
- The teacher facilitates the discussion rather than funneling students toward one "correct" interpretation.

In the experiencing and investigating phase, students continue to build knowledge and vocabulary about weather and communities. They also conduct observations outdoors, engage in small experiments, and research their inquiry questions in books and online. Figure 8.7 describes inquiry lessons that are covered in this phase.

Students gather information from books, magazines, newspapers, and the Internet. In today's world, it is inconceivable for students not to grapple with information found in nonlinear texts that anyone can post to the Internet (Leu et al., 2011). Yet, reading texts on the Internet poses its own set of

Lessons Related to Reading Informational Texts	Lessons Related to Observations and Experiments
• How to find print and Internet resources in the classroom to research inquiry question. • How to evaluate good sources of information. • How to identify important ideas in a source. • How to take notes from a source of information and store them. • How to sort important from interesting facts. • How to use multiple sources of information to confirm facts and gather more information.	• How to make predictions from weather forecasting and experiments. • How to observe closely and check understanding. • How to use tools to collect evidence (e.g., thermometer, barometer, wind sock, rain gauge). • How to record observations from nature and classroom experiments.
• How to compare and integrate information from observations, experiments, and readings.	

FIGURE 8.7. Different kinds of inquiry lessons.

challenges: overabundant choices, confusing stylistic/display features, and seductive links that can lure students away. All this means that students have to be even more metacognitive than when reading conventional print (Coiro, 2003; Coiro & Dobler, 2007).

On this day, Mr. Rodriguez teaches a lesson on evaluating websites to help students to decide whether particular websites are useful for answering their questions. He selects one of the questions posed by a student: "Is the weather really getting warmer here?" He explains that it is important to evaluate websites to gather useful and trustworthy informa-

> **CCSS Standards R7, 9, 10:** We need to prepare students for the high-level functioning expected of them in college and careers to read and apply information in varying, complex texts, especially given the explosion of information at the ready on the Internet.

tion. He introduces students to a tip sheet (see Figure 8.8) that will aid them in evaluating websites. Then, he projects the website (*http://tiki.oneworld.net/ globalwarming/climate _home.html*) on the SMART Board.

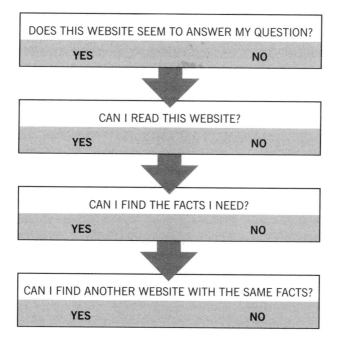

HOW GOOD IS THIS WEBSITE?

DOES THIS WEBSITE SEEM TO ANSWER MY QUESTION?
YES   NO

CAN I READ THIS WEBSITE?
YES   NO

CAN I FIND THE FACTS I NEED?
YES   NO

CAN I FIND ANOTHER WEBSITE WITH THE SAME FACTS?
YES   NO

FIGURE 8.8. Tip sheet for evaluating usefulness of a website.

Mr. Rodriguez models how he reviews this website, using the tip sheet to guide his thinking. As he thinks aloud, he clarifies what each question means and the decisions he makes at each point of the evaluation process. His first task is to decide whether the website even relates to his inquiry question. Next he checks to see whether he can comprehend the page's content without difficulty. If he answers *yes* to the first two questions, then he considers how easily he can find the needed information: Is the layout too cluttered or confusing? Are there too many distractions? Is there a clear link to follow to find some relevant facts? Once he finds some solid information, then he still needs to ask one more question: "Can I find another website with the same information to confirm my facts?"

> **CCSS Standards R6, 7, 8:** Learning to evaluate websites for accuracy, relevance, and adequacy is essential to integrating knowledge and ideas within and across texts.

As Mr. Rodriguez thinks aloud, he invites students to join in the decision-making process. He prompts them until they can take over the reins themselves. Here is an example in the context of a TSI lesson:

MR. RODRIGUEZ: Okay, so let us think more about the answer to this question: "Can I read this webpage?" See if you can read something on this page to someone next to you. Does what you read make sense? (*Gives students time to read and share their reactions with each other. Mr. Rodriguez observes students struggling significantly with pronunciation of these words. Also there is little to no fluency—even for the strongest readers.*) Now, let's share, what do you think?

BRODY: Well, it's hard to see the words. The size is too small.

MR. RODRIGUEZ: Why does that matter?

BRODY: It's too difficult to read.

MR. RODRIGUEZ: Can anyone add something to what Brody said?

RAYNA: When the words are too small, I sometimes skip over a sentence.

MR. RODRIGUEZ: I can see that happening. So, what can we do? We've been talking about different fix-up tools we can use when something we read doesn't make sense. Any ideas?

Students contribute several suggestions, such as using an index card when reading books or finding another website with bigger print. Mr. Rodriguez points out that by using the zoom function they can make the print bigger. He then asks another question to keep this exchange going:

MR. RODRIGUEZ: Did anyone else find something difficult to understand on this webpage?

MAX: I don't know lots of the words.

MR. RODRIGUEZ: What do you mean? Can you give us an example?

MAX: I don't know that word, *moster*. (*He substitutes the attempt* moster *for* moisture.)

LUKE: And what does *condense* mean?

MR. RODRIGUEZ: So we've been talking a lot about what you can do when you see a word you don't know. What do we already have in our fix-up kit that might help?

With some assistance, students mention different fix-up strategies: see if the word is made up of recognizable, smaller parts (*break it*), ask someone (*ask it*), or infer based on pictures or other words (*guess it*).

Mr. Rodriguez asks Max, "So, you are at a word you don't know. What fix-up strategy can you try?" Max skips over the word and reads to the end of the sentence but is still confused. Since the term is key to the topic, as is often the case with academic vocabulary, he can't ignore it. So Mr. Rodriguez pronounces the word correctly, gives a basic definition, and suggests that Max should write it down for later discussion. The class will return to this word during the final sharing time.

Mr. Rodriguez asks Luke, "Now what about the word *condense*? What fix-up strategy can you try?" Luke makes several attempts, with no success. Mr. Rodriguez asks if anyone else has an idea.

DORA: Well, I see that the word is in a different color. Maybe you can click it and that will help. Sometimes when something is in a different color or is underlined you can click it and it tells you something.

MR. RODRIGUEZ: What do the rest of you think? Shall we try this?

They select the word and it takes them to a definition. Mr. Rodriguez asks students if they think that *click it* might be another tool to add to their fix-up kit.

BRODY: Well, I like clicking links because it helps me sometimes, but this time it didn't.

MR. RODRIGUEZ: That's true, Brody, sometimes the fix-up strategies we pick at first don't help us. But, maybe another one will. So, when one strategy doesn't work, that's a good time to try another one to solve a problem.

Then another student, Kim, a student who reads above grade-level, raises a new issue: "On this page, I know what a *machine* is but I don't get what this means—*the climate machine*. They explain it, but I still don't understand."

It's true that Mr. Rodriguez could just intervene at this point and help this student out of the jam. But he deliberately resists. He wants students to persist in problem solving if there is a chance they can figure out a solution either together or by themselves. This builds students' confidence that they possess the strategic knowledge to get themselves out of difficulty. So, instead he says, "I can see what you mean. Hmm, another problem here, folks, what can we do?"

JOE: There's a video right near it. That might help. Can we listen to it?

MR. RODRIGUEZ: Sure.

The class listens to the video clip, but finds it makes things even more confusing.

Mr. Rodriguez says, "Okay, so we see that this page is difficult for many reasons. The words were too small, we couldn't figure out some important words we needed to know, and even when there was a link and a video provided to help us, they didn't. So what do you think? Based on all this, should we stick with this webpage?"

The students collectively decide that this website is too hard. Even when they used their fix-up kit, including some strategies unique to Internet texts, they still couldn't comprehend the content. So, when Mr. Rodriguez asked what they could do instead, one student suggested "find another website." Another quickly followed with "find a book that's easier to read."

Following the whole-class discussion, pairs of students practice the tip sheet with another website (*http://eo.ucar.edu/webweather*) along with finding the answer to the following question: What causes hail? Brody teams up with a stronger reader, Sasha, to accomplish this task. Brody has difficulty staying on task; he wants to check out some extraneous links, such as *Games, Stories, and Activities*. Instead Sasha helps Brody think about where to locate information about hail on the website. The partners infer that the topic might be found under *Blizzards/Winter Storms*. They click that link and successfully find a small section on hail.

CCSS Standard R10: Teachers need to scaffold students toward independence. One way teachers can do this is by adjusting the complexity of texts based on students' needs and the type and amount of social support provided to students so they can accomplish with assistance what they can't do by themselves (Almasi & Fullerton, 2012).

Shortly thereafter, Mr. Rodriguez convenes the wrap-up session. The students debrief the task of website evaluation. Mr. Rodriguez builds some knowledge around the concept of *moisture,* one word that came up during the lesson. Students also are encouraged to share amazing facts they encountered that day, which allows Mr. Rodriguez to reinforce the notion that curiosity motivates inquiry. At the end of this session, he briefly re-explains why evaluating websites during the inquiry process makes sense.

Mr. Rodriguez applied many scaffolding techniques to support students' thinking (Almasi & Fullerton, 2012) in this instructional sequence:

- Mr. Rodriguez reduced complexity by bookmarking sites and limiting options so that students didn't have to search for sites and become overwhelmed by choices.
- He reduced the complexity of reviewing websites by including only four questions on the tip sheet.
- He adjusted the amount of social support given to students, moving from whole-class, teacher-guided instruction to more autonomous partner work.
- He encouraged guided discussion so that students could gain assistance from peers.
- He promoted collaborative decision making.
- He supported students' thinking "in the moment" by clarifying and providing hints and prompts.
- He gave students a tip sheet to scaffold thinking both on that day and in the future.

Phase 3: Organizing and Analyzing

In this phase of the unit Mr. Rodriguez and the class continue to study weather and communities during the morning literacy block and in the afternoon subject-area block. The students transition from gathering data to organizing the collected information and discovering relationships among big ideas. Mr. Rodriguez's lessons focus on the following objectives:

- Comparing and contrasting facts stored on Post-it notes and sorting them into categories.
- Attaching labels to those categories with the understanding that each label represents a big idea and that the facts within each category are supporting details.
- Discarding details that do not fit into one of the big categories (or going back to acquire more facts to beef up that category if it is important to answering the inquiry question).

- Understanding that analyzing and interpreting means putting the bits and pieces of learning together with your own thinking.
- Looking for one pattern that can tie the big ideas together.
- Using the pattern to think, talk, or write about the answer to the inquiry question.

Literacy Block

Comprehension and vocabulary development remain key instructional goals during whole-class reading. For example, Mr. Rodriguez uses an article in a children's magazine to show how the author organized the big ideas and details. Although the class has talked about text features and structures earlier in the unit, he returns to the topic to emphasize that authors group details using a few patterns—and that students can learn to do the same. He and the class also examine how authors use headings, subheadings, and visual displays, such as maps, diagrams, and charts, to organize ideas. During shared time students explore various texts on weather and communities to observe how authors organize ideas through text structures and visual displays. As they do, Mr. Rodriguez continues to provide small-group decoding and fluency instruction and meets with students, as needed, for supplemental comprehension teaching and practice. When he is not working in small groups, he confers with individuals.

> **CCSS Standards R5, 6:** Analyzing the ways texts are structured helps students to recognize importance and observe how ideas are linked together in and across informational texts in familiar ways.

Subject-Area Block

Afternoon workshop is used to apply what students learned about text features and structures in the morning. He helps students relate the knowledge they gained about texts in the literacy block to their afternoon work. In this phase, Mr. Rodriguez spends considerable time on explaining, modeling, and scaffolding how to sort the stored Post-it notes of important facts that students collected in the previous inquiry phase.

While ensuring that students practice various strategies during reading, Mr. Rodriguez develops their use of determining importance and summarizing (see Chapter 10). He works with students to further organize their labeled and sorted facts using one of three expository text structures: description, comparison–contrast, and sequencing. He scaffolds the task of finding relationships among big ideas by using corresponding graphic organizers (e.g., a Venn diagram to make comparisons). Students "try on" each of the three organizational patterns, to see which one fits the labeled categories best. We expand on the use of graphic organizers in Chapter 10.

In addition, Mr. Rodriguez explains and models analysis and interpretation. He thinks aloud to show students how he uses his knowledge along with the text's big ideas to evaluate the importance of that information as he makes meaningful connections among them. On another day, with Mr. Rodriguez's help, students decide whether it makes sense to visually represent or supplement any of their information with captioned photographs, illustrations, charts, diagrams, or maps.

Phase 4: Reflecting and Consolidating

During the week students begin to work on their final project using the information they have gathered and organized. Working on a project facilitates the integration of knowledge accumulated throughout the unit. Brody decides to make an informational picture book with PowerPoint software. Others make posters, dioramas, mobiles, or games.

The lessons in this phase, as in all phases, focus on promoting motivation, strategies use, and metacognition while building subject-area knowledge. Lessons related to knowledge development include having students see their original brainstorms so they can perceive how much they have learned. Another focus is helping students to recognize and correct any misconceptions they may have held at the outset of the inquiry. In terms of strategies lessons, the class discusses the fact that new questions arise during the inquiry process. These questions relate to learning more about their own projects, learning more about someone else's project, or learning more about weather and communities in general.

Metacognition plays a dominant role in this phase. Students evaluate everything from their use of cognitive and metacognitive strategies (e.g., facility with recognizing and solving problems) to how well they answered their inquiry questions to how well they worked with others. Motivation, given its interdependence with metacognition, is addressed as students review what they discovered about themselves as readers and learners during the unit. Being successful with the tasks in this unit engenders positive beliefs about being strategic readers and learners. And although using strategies is hard work and is time consuming, students can value this expenditure of effort because it is worthwhile.

Inquiry Phase 5: Sharing and Communicating

In Mr. Rodriguez's class, the fifth phase of the inquiry cycle ends with a culminating event scheduled on the last day. In this phase, motivation takes center stage because students not only celebrate all of their hard work but they also apply that work to meaningful activity: (1) they share their projects with others, and (2) they connect their learning to social action.

Whether children complete a PowerPoint or poster presentation, whether they participate in an individual or group project, whether they choose from a finite list of options or have free rein to demonstrate their learning, a large part of the final phase of the inquiry cycle involves communicating and celebrating students' accomplishments. In Mr. Rodriguez's class, the principal, other faculty and staff, and family members are invited to attend the displays and presentations at the end of the unit.

In addition, inquiry learning often includes applying learning to some form of social action (Harvey & Daniels, 2009; Rogovin, 2001). Mr. Rodriguez's class holds a Community Comfort Day that coincides with the students' sharing of projects. Students come to school dressed in something cuddly or cozy—but they also bring to class a contribution for a less fortunate child in the community. With winter fast approaching, they donate new or gently used clothing to help others to endure the harsh weather conditions that beset this community.

Throughout the inquiry cycle, Mr. Rodriguez transitions students toward greater independence. For example, they transfer their learning to new tasks (e.g., applying what they know about fix-up strategies to reading on the Internet, applying what they learn from mentor texts to their own work in and out of school). In the remainder of the year, Mr. Rodriguez will provide plentiful opportunities for students to extend and apply what they have learned. They will continue to activate and build knowledge, use cognitive and metacognitive strategies, and develop positive self-beliefs when engaging with new subject-area content, texts, and tasks.

LOOKING BACK, LOOKING FORWARD

In Chapter 7, we provided an overview of inquiry-based learning and discussed how to plan for such instruction. In this chapter, we demonstrated how to put these plans into action according to the GRRM-C. The overarching goal for this type of instruction is clear: to integrate the effective teaching of comprehension in the context of thematic, subject-area instruction.

Mr. Rodriguez scaffolds comprehension strategies and knowledge development. He scaffolds strategies by first explaining and modeling their use, and then by assisting the students to use strategies to construct interpretations and make evaluative judgments. He scaffolds knowledge by building some information for the students to lay a foundation for further learning, and then helping them to anchor the new knowledge to this foundation. The Post-it notes form the structure of this knowledge. Later, the students pull all of this together when creating their projects.

In Chapters 9 and 10, we shift to teaching comprehension in the last of the three literacy frameworks that we concentrate on in this text. We examine how to organize and implement effective comprehension instruction in the context of a comprehensive, published reading curriculum—the basal reading series.

APPLICATIONS AND EXPLORATIONS

1. Initially it can be hard to decide what information to include when directly explaining strategies to your students. Develop your own "starter kit" of the types of declarative, conditional, and procedural information to share with students. Or, you can obtain a sample of this information in *Teaching Strategic Processes in Reading, Second Edition* (Almasi & Fullerton, 2012).

2. Select a nonfiction book and identify one strategy that would make sense to teach with that text. Then, think through the precise information that would be important to impart to students about that strategy. Consider where you would stop to think aloud.

3. In this chapter we highlighted one flexible, research-based approach that can facilitate understanding, interpreting, critiquing, and applying content in informational texts, TSI. You can learn more about TSI by checking out the following references: R. Brown (2008); R. Brown & Coy-Ogan (1993); R. Brown et al. (1996); Pressley et al. (1992); and Reutzel et al. (2005). For comparison purposes, you might want to compare two other, more structured approaches that focus on using informational texts to support content learning in specific subject areas. Comprehensive information about these approaches can be found at the following websites: concept-oriented reading instruction (CORI; *www.cori.umd.edu*) and Seeds of Science/Roots of Reading (*www.scienceandliteracy.org*).

4. Although we did not explicitly focus on writing in this chapter, writing is a critical aspect of inquiry learning (Duke et al., 2011). Thus, you might want to consider how writing instruction could be integrated into this second-grade inquiry unit. To start you on your way, you might want to check out the article on using read-alouds of informational books in a second-grade weather unit to foster writing (Bradley & Donovan, 2010).

CHAPTER 9

Planning Comprehension Instruction in a Basal Program Framework

Ms. Fogel and her fourth-grade teammates are spending the afternoon of their staff development day planning the next 6-week unit of instruction in their basal reading program, *Journeys* (Baumann et al., 2012). They begin by surveying the selections the students will read and the skills and strategies they need to teach. The unit, the second of the year, has five major reading selections, each with a very short companion piece and leveled books for students reading below, on, and above grade level, and English language learners. The unit covers five comprehension skills, five comprehension strategies, five different authors' craft concepts, and five vocabulary skills. Figure 9.1 outlines the curriculum of this unit, titled *Do You Know What I Mean?* Ms. Fogel quips, "No! I don't know what they mean."

"Wow, that is a lot to cover," says Ms. Fogel, and her three colleagues quickly agree. The team immediately reaches consensus; they need to slim down the curriculum. They know that the weaker students will not be able to "learn" one comprehension skill and strategy a week, they doubt that their best readers need this much instruction, and the sequential focus on a strategy and skill each week is already irrelevant because the students have been predicting, asking questions, and summarizing since the first week of school. They also wonder how they will fit in the craft skills and the five vocabulary skills along with everything else they have to teach. The team also knows that they have to consult the CCSS (NGA & CCSSO, 2010), the document that was providing their curriculum guidance. The teachers are fortunate; their district does not make them follow the basal program in a lockstep fashion and they are encouraged to make professional decisions (Kersten & Pardo, 2007; Pearson, 2007).

	Lesson 1	Lesson 2	Lesson 3	Lesson 4	Lesson 5
Genre	1. Modern fairytale 2. Information	1. Information 2. Information	1. Realistic fiction	1. Realistic fiction 2. Information	1. Biography 2. Biography
Comp. Skills	Compare–contrast	Fact/opinion	Understanding character	Conclusions/generalizations	Author's purpose
Comp. Strategies	Infer/predict	Summarizing	Visualizing	Questioning	Analyze/evaluate
Author's Craft	Hyperbole	Jargon	Point of view	Repetition	Metaphor
Vocabulary Skills	Suffixes: -y, -ous	Greek, Latin roots: *phon, photo, graph, auto*	Figurative language	Antonyms	Analogies

FIGURE 9.1. Skills, strategies, and craft knowledge in one fourth-grade basal unit.

Developing reading comprehension within a basal program presents a different set of challenges than working within a literature-based or inquiry framework. In the first two frameworks the teachers and the students are constructing the curriculum—designing activities, selecting the texts, and identifying the strategies—whereas in a basal program the teacher needs to work within and modify an existing curriculum. The basal provides texts, a scope and sequence of skills and strategies, lesson plans that script the language of instruction, guided reading questions, and other instructional materials. The teacher's task is to decide what aspects of the reading program to follow, what to modify, and what to ignore.

GOALS FOR THIS CHAPTER

✓ Explore the philosophy and structure of comprehension instruction within a basal reading program.

✓ Consider how a basal program reflects the good comprehender model.

✓ Discuss how to plan a unit of instruction within a basal reading program.

✓ Discuss how to plan a weekly lesson within a basal reading program.

✓ Consider elements of effective comprehension instruction that are outside the basal reading program.

THE STRUCTURE AND PHILOSOPHY OF COMPREHENSION INSTRUCTION IN BASAL READING PROGRAMS

History of Comprehension Instruction

Comprehension instruction in basal reading programs is an amalgamation of theories and practices spanning over 100 years of evolution. In the early 1900s, comprehension instruction in basal reading programs stressed reading stories, poems, and information, with some prereading attention to vocabulary. After reading, students answered questions or gave an oral rendition of the selection. At the end of the 1920s specific comprehension skills were mentioned in basal programs (Pennell & Cusack, 1936)—sequence of ideas, organizing, evaluating, and retaining meanings. By the 1940s there was more attention to comprehension skills specifically in the workbooks that accompanied these programs.

Over the next three decades the number of comprehension skills began to expand and differentiate (Afflerbach et al., 2008), reaching a peak in the 1960s through the mid-1970s when skills management programs were in vogue (Johnson & Pearson, 1975). In these basal programs students were pretested on a large number of skills and if they did not pass teachers retaught the skill and much workbook practice ensued. The reading of basal anthology selections with page-by-page questioning continued but the balance between skills instruction and text reading shifted toward the former. Skills instruction dominated basals for the next generation until comprehension strategies entered the programs in the early 1990s.

Since the 1990s basals incorporated both skills and strategies, but it is difficult to distinguish one from another. In any given basal reading program the same mental activity, like predicting, is labeled both a skill and a strategy. In many programs one mental activity may carry more than one label. So it is common for a basal program to teach drawing conclusions, making inferences, and making generalizations, but a close study of these lessons reveals that the same mental activity is taught under several different labels (Dewitz, Jones, & Leahy, 2009). We would argue that the comprehension curriculum in most basal programs is piecemeal, overly complex, and with a confusing structure that makes little or no sense to teacher or students.

At this point we need to quickly digress to say that since 2000 basals have been labeled core reading programs. The difference is important. Basals were considered the base for reading instruction and teachers were expected to move beyond them into literature and nonfiction trade books as soon as the students were ready. A core program is considered central and important, capturing all that is necessary about learning to read. We call these basal programs throughout the book.

Comprehension Skills and Strategy Instruction

Program developers provide "explicit" comprehension skills and strategies lessons, but some publishers are more explicit than others. Basal programs should direct teachers to introduce the strategy, explain why it is important, discuss the mental process, model it, and engage students in guided practice. The reality is different. The lessons in basal programs lack explicitness and frequently fail to explain the purpose behind a strategy or discuss when it should be used. The amount of modeling and thinking aloud is limited and almost all programs put questioning ahead of guided practice (Dewitz et al., 2009). The basal programs do a weak job of following the GRRM-C because they don't consider scaffolding over the long haul.

The skills and strategies in a basal program follow a set scope and sequence. If you were to write down all of the skills and strategies in the order they appear in the program (something we suggest you do) you would be hard pressed to discern the logic of their sequence. The publishers argue that they follow a spiral curriculum with regular review, but the amount of review fails to approach the standards researchers have employed in instructional studies (Dewitz et al., 2009). All programs seem to ignore the finding that students do better when they work on multiple strategies at once helping students predict, infer, question, and summarize, instead of one or two strategies per week, the model of most basal programs (Reutzel et al., 2005).

The structure of weekly comprehension instruction in grades three through six is depicted in Figure 9.2. A weekly lesson begins with a read-aloud, vocabulary instruction, and direct teaching of skills and strategies. Just before the teachers and the students plunge into the main selection the teacher and the students preview the selection and predict what will happen. The skills and strategies are linked to the reading selection by

Prereading Instruction	During-Reading Instruction	Postreading Instruction
• Oral read-aloud • Vocabulary instruction • Skill and strategy instruction • Preview and predict • Purpose setting	• Read main selection— orally, silently, or with a partner • Pose and answer comprehension questions • Teacher models thinking • Assess skills and strategies through questioning	• Summarize • Think, compare, and make connections • Read short linking selection and pose questions • Skill and strategy instruction, practice, and review

FIGURE 9.2. The structure of comprehension instruction in a basal reading program.

the page-by-page guided reading questions. As the students read orally, silently, or with a partner (the choice is up to the teacher), the teacher stops to pose questions. Each question is labeled with the name of the comprehension skill or strategy it seeks to prompt (e.g., summarize, monitor, make inferences). Often seven or eight different skills are addressed within one lesson. Sometimes these questions help the reader develop meaning but other questions distract from the meaning by focusing on print skills, dictionary usage, or vocabulary (McKeown et al., 2009). Most programs direct the teacher to model a skill or two within the context of discussing the story, but the decision to model is not driven by any response coming from the students. After reading the text and the companion piece more skill instruction follows.

The basic prereading, during-reading, and postreading structure is repeated 30 or more times in an academic year and the lesson structure in May differs little from the lesson structure in September. Even though a basal program may have introduced *all* the major skills by midway in the school year, the lessons in the basal program maintain the same structure and employ the same instructional language until the very end. Like the movie *Groundhog Day*, these comprehension skills and strategies are taught as if the students had no prior experience with them. This instructional model does not lead to the development of expertise but to the students' continual dependency on the structure and guidance of the program as administered by the teacher.

BASAL READING PROGRAMS
AND THE GOOD COMPREHENDER MODEL

The good comprehender is motivated, knowledgeable, strategic, and metacognitive. The developers of basal reading programs, if we asked, would assert that they attend to each aspect of this model. We would counter that they fall short of the mark in several ways, because taken as a whole, the basal program is more about skill and strategy development than it is about motivation, knowledge, or metacognition (Dewitz et al., 2010).

Motivation

Consider motivation. Basal programs approach motivation in two ways. They select high-quality literature and nonfiction selections with an eye on the interest of the readings and the diversity and prominence of the authors and illustrators. Yet the reading selections within a basal program are prescribed; choice is not an option. Although 60 years ago basal programs acknowledged that reading outside the program was essential (Gray, 1952), today, from the point of view of program developers, it is not an important attribute.

The developers of basal programs will argue that the unit projects that begin an instructional unit will engage the students, that the prereading instruction will motivate the students, and that the differentiated instruction will ensure that all students succeed. All these are important aspects of motivation. Yet basal programs do little to initiate students into the wider world of children's literature, to develop an intrinsic love of books, or to build within each student a sense of efficacy. The routine nature of reading instruction in basal programs can obscure students' accomplishments if the teacher focuses too much on "getting our work done."

Teachers can build interest and motivation with a basal program by:

- Making unit projects a more central feature of reading instruction, thus giving all students a stronger purpose for reading.
- Increasing the focus on authors and illustrators so students appreciate the wider world of literature.
- Sharing interesting and exciting books and authors outside the basal.
- Creating a system where students can track their assessment results and the books they have read so they can reflect on their growth as a reader.
- Creating more opportunities for cooperative learning.
- Using the games provided in the basal program for the skill development.

Knowledge

Since skill and strategy instruction is the dominant theme in basal programs, building knowledge has taken a backseat especially in the most current versions of the programs. Basal reading programs build knowledge by constructing weekly lessons around a common idea or concept and linking all selections to it. At the beginning of each lesson the teacher's edition directs the teacher to develop knowledge through the read-aloud, the vocabulary lessons, and in some programs, through specific knowledge development lessons. Basal programs do not extend this tightly integrated approach to the construction of their 6-week units. Within a unit of instruction there are five or six main reading selections, and ideally what is learned from the first selection can provide knowledge for the next selection and so on.

When critics have studied knowledge development in basal reading programs they have noticed some strengths and weaknesses (Dewitz et al., 2010; Walsh, 2003):

- The main reading selection, its paired selection, and the leveled readers all cover the same topic and focus on the same vocabulary.
- The readings in a 5- or 6-week unit of instruction rarely stick to the same topic or theme so knowledge does not develop from one selection to another. There are few opportunities to build knowledge from one selection to another (Dewitz et al., 2010; Hirsch, 2011).
- The specific lessons geared to developing prior knowledge focus more attention on activating the knowledge students already possess than on building or growing that knowledge base, especially for concepts that are critical to understanding the selection.
- The overall goal of an instructional unit does not direct students to reflect on what they have learned or how they have grown as readers. Even though the programs often provide for unit wrap-up we suspect that these get lost in the shuffle of assessment.

Strategies

Comprehension skills and strategies are featured prominently in the basal reading programs employing a wide but shallow treatment that falls short of what the research suggests (Dewitz et al., 2009):

- Too many skills and strategies are taught in too short a time span, occasionally with the same skill taught under two or more labels.
- While basal programs provide teachers with language to explain strategies, they neglect to mention the critical motivational and metacognitive elements: "Why is this strategy important and when should I use it?" (Dewitz et al., 2009).
- Basal programs tend to push one skill and one strategy a week when the research shows that focusing on using multiple strategies flexibly yields better results (Reutzel et al., 2005; R. Brown et al., 1996).
- Basal programs tend to neglect guided practice, rarely ask students to model their thinking, or discuss how they discerned the meaning of the text (Dewitz et al., 2009).
- Basal programs do not provide as much practice with skills and strategies as would be found in the original studies that validated them.

Metacognition

Metacognition assumes a low profile in most basal reading programs, at least for the programs created since the early to mid-2000s. In all of these programs comprehension monitoring is mentioned but not vigorously developed. In the basal programs the guided reading lessons provide page-by-page discussion questions but they focus on skills and strategies. At the bottom of some pages the developers include some comprehension monitoring suggestions. The teacher can ask the students to reread if they need to clarify the text; at other times the teacher can suggest they self-correct when they are having difficulty. There is little consistency to these marginal instructional suggestions. Many basal programs boldly label teacher suggestions as "monitor and clarify," but the substance of the instruction is often nothing more than extra guided reading questions. For example, in one program monitor and clarify amounts to the literal question: "How many years can a saguaro cactus live?"

In most programs the teacher's edition guides students to make predictions and then read to confirm those predictions. This will induce students to monitor their comprehension and revise what they are thinking when the story does not develop in the predictable direction. Strangely, these instructional moves are not labeled comprehension monitoring or metacognition, a rare example of a publisher missing an opportunity to highlight a feature.

PLANNING COMPREHENSION INSTRUCTION FOR A YEAR AND FOR A UNIT

Planning for the Year

When Ms. Fogel and her colleagues sat down to plan their instruction they made some important decisions that will drive their instruction for the school year. They realized that comprehension instruction in their basal reading program is unbalanced and does not attend to knowledge, motivation, metacognition, and strategies in a manner that reflects their importance. They plan with one eye on their basal reading program and another on the CCSS (NGA & CCSSO, 2010). The decisions they make concern the texts the students will read, the skills, strategies, and craft knowledge the students need to learn, and the knowledge and motivation essential for all this to work.

Range of Texts

Ms. Fogel and her fourth-grade colleagues first consider Standard 10, Range of Reading and Level of Text Complexity (NGA & CCSSO, 2010):

> By the end of the year, read and comprehend literature, including stories, drama, and poetry at the high end of the 4–5 text-complexity band proficiently with scaffolding as needed at the high end of the range. (*Literature*)

By the end of the year, read and comprehend informational text, including history/social studies, science, and technical texts, in the grade 4–5 text-complexity band proficiently, with scaffolding as needed at the high end of the range. (*Information*)

CCSS Standard R10: The materials in a basal program alone may not satisfy the standard to read complex text, because almost all texts in a basal program are short and do not demand the construction of ideas over multiple chapters.

The fourth-grade team quickly realized that their basal reading program did not contain enough text to meet the standard for reading information, and most likely they would have to expand their students' exposure to drama and poetry. So the first step in their planning was to expand the range of texts that the students will read. They want independent reading to be a large part of their instructional program and plan to create time for it every day. Kelly and Clausen-Grace (2006) adapted the structure of sustained silent reading in a way that increased students' wide reading, metacognition, and comprehension using a framework called R5. R5 includes a process in which students read and relax, reflect and respond, and finally, rap, or talk with a partner about their reading. After participating in this process for 7 months, students improved in their reading comprehension and metacognition while also reading a wider array of genres (Kelly & Clausen-Grace, 2006). The fourth-grade teachers also plan to hold regular reading conferences so they can check on and assist students' comprehension and suggest new books and authors to each individual (Reutzel et al., 2008).

Strategies and Skills

Next, the four teachers tackle the complex comprehension curriculum in the basal program where the skills and strategies change every week. They decide to compare the CCSS against the comprehension curriculum in their basal program. Although their basal program does have a page that lists the standards addressed in each weekly lesson, they surmise that the developers of the program are generous in listing what each lesson accomplishes. They also feel that completing this exercise will force them to think about the needs of their students. In Figure 9.3 they list the genres, skills and strategies, and craft skills addressed in each weekly lesson. Next, they write in the Standards 1–9 they believe are addressed in each lesson. This reflects what the basal provides, so they can consider what they will have to add. The basal does not address all the standards.

Ms. Fogel and her team find that this analysis is useful since it identifies the standards that will be addressed by the program, as well as the

Theme Lesson	Genre	Skill	Strategy	Craft Skill	CCSS Literature	CCSS Informational
1.1	Realistic fiction	Story structure	Summarize	Flashback	1, 7	
1.2	Biography	Author's purpose	Monitor/ clarify	Point of view	1, 6, 7	
1.3	Realistic fiction	Cause–effect	Visualize	Metaphor	1, 5, 7	
1.4	Drama (realistic)	Theme	Analyze/ evaluate	Elements of drama	1, 2, 5, 7	
1.5	Tall tale	Characters	Infer/predict	Hyperbole	1, 3, 7	
2.1	Fairytale	Compare– contrast	Infer/predict	Hyperbole	1, 7	
2.2	Nonfiction	Fact/opinion	Summarize	Jargon		1, 2, 7
2.3	Realistic fiction	Characters	Visualize	Point of view	1, 6, 7	
2.4	Realistic fiction	Conclusion/ generalization	Question	Repetition	1, 7	
2.5	Biography	Author's purpose	Monitor/ clarify	Metaphor	1, 7	
3.1	Narrative nonfiction	Fact/opinion	Infer/predict	Simile	1, 7	
3.2	Historical fiction	Sequence of events	Visualize	Point of view	1, 3, 6	
3.3	Nonfiction	Cause–effect	Summarize	Metaphor		1, 2, 3
3.4	Information	Text/graphic features	Question	Imagery		1, 5, 7
3.5	Information	Main idea/ details	Monitor/ clarify	Word choice		1, 2, 3, 7

FIGURE 9.3. Aligning comprehension skill, strategy, and craft skills with the CCSS.

standards that will require some additional attention through teacher-designed activities. This analysis covers just the first half of the year, and they will need to repeat the activity after the winter break. They summarize their discoveries as follows:

- The basal program provides the opportunity to work on the details of fiction, drawing inferences, summarizing, point of view, focusing on the differences between prose, poetry, and drama, making connections, and developing a visual representation of text (e.g., graphic organizers).
- The basal program falls short in the areas of identifying theme, comparing and contrasting the treatment of similar themes and topics in various genres, and analyzing in depth setting, characters, and plot structure.
- The basal program is very limited in helping students determine word meanings from context. This skill is introduced in the third story in Theme 1 and is not mentioned again until the first story in Theme 4.
- The teachers will also need to develop their own lessons on figurative language, which is approached haphazardly in the basal program.
- Two skills, *sequence of events* and *fact and opinion*, are taught in the basal program, but do not appear to meet any of the CCSS.

CCSS Standards R1, 3: Basal programs address the basic structure of literature but teachers must supplement when working to infer theme or appreciating the power of figurative language.

The teachers decided to simplify the comprehension curriculum in the basal program, making it understandable to their students. They decided to introduce a basic set of strategies the first 2 weeks of the year that will form the core of their guided reading work and then build on to those strategies as needed. For fiction they decided to begin with *predicting, self-questioning, monitoring* or *clarifying,* and *summarizing* the strategies of RT. This will provide the focus on metacognition that many of their students need and that their basal program lacks. From that core they will explore the types of inferences that are required for reading fiction and deepen students' knowledge about the structures of fiction including the language and expressive devices that authors employ.

The core strategies for reading nonfiction will be self-questioning, monitoring or clarifying, determining importance, and summarizing. The strategy of predicting does not lend itself to nonfiction, because most readers lack the knowledge to anticipate where the author will go. The teachers plan to deepen the students' comprehension of nonfiction by helping students study and learn about the structure and features of nonfiction, and the inferences that readers must make when reading nonfiction.

CCSS Standards R1, 2: The CCSS do not tell teachers how to help students explain and infer when they read. Strategies and knowledge bring that about.

Planning a Unit

Knowledge Development

Ms. Fogel and her colleagues realize that each lesson within their basal reading program is structured to build knowledge, but the units or themes are not. The teachers brainstorm how to create units of study that have a stronger focus on building knowledge. Figure 9.4 summarizes the five sections in the first unit of study.

Ms. Fogel and her colleagues quickly realize that these five selections do not form one coherent theme, but they do divide into two coherent themes and one that does not fit. The teachers decided to pair the *Because of Winn-Dixie* (DiCamillo, 2000) segment and *How Tía Lola Came to ~~Visit~~ Stay* (Alvarez, 2002) around the theme of friendship. The *My Brother Martin* (Farris,

Genre	Title	Theme
Realistic fiction	An excerpt from *Because of Winn-Dixie* (DiCamillo, 2000)	This is a story about a young girl who has moved to a new community and is in the process of making friends with the somewhat distant librarian.
Biography	*My Brother Martin: A Sister Remembers Growing Up with the Rev. Dr. Martin Luther King Jr.* (Farris, 2005)	A recollection of Martin Luther King, Jr.'s, young life and his early encounters with discrimination and segregation.
Realistic fiction	*How Tía Lola Came to ~~Visit~~ Stay* (Alvarez, 2002)	A story about a young aunt who moved from her home in the Dominican Republic to stay with relatives in Vermont.
Realistic fiction	The Power of W.O.W.! (Hubbard, 2011)	A play about community action as a group of kids work to raise money to save the local bookmobile.
Tall tale	*Captain Stormalong* (Brimner, 2004)	A rather pointless tall tale about a 12-foot baby who grows up to be a giant sailor and has many adventures.

FIGURE 9.4. Reading genres and texts in one theme of a basal reading program.

2005) excerpt and *The Power of W.O.W.!* (Hubbard, 2011) both focus on the themes of change and community action—the second theme the students will study. *Captain Stormalong* (Brimner, 2004), the tall tale, will be held in abeyance until later in the year when the team plans to read and write folktales. Each theme will develop a set of vocabulary words and work on a common set of strategies. Let's look at the first theme that the teachers planned using the resources in the basal reading program plus additional books that bring more challenge to the students. The teachers organize their planning into eight parts as presented in Figure 9.5: Texts for read-alouds, texts for modeling and guided practice, texts for independent reading, comprehension strategies, text structure/craft skills, activities, assessments, and culminating projects.

Vocabulary Instruction

Ms. Fogel knows that her basal reading program has identified the words she should teach, but the words the program developers selected might not be the best words or enough words for her students. She realizes she must make some choices. Figure 9.6 lists the words the basal program suggests teaching and the teacher-identified words. Ms. Fogel applies the same criteria we developed in Chapter 5—some words are essential to understanding the story, some words the students already know, and some word meanings can be inferred from context as the students read. Her new list is in Figure 9.7. Ms. Fogel's new list actually allows her to attend to more vocabulary. The five words the students already know can be discussed quickly. Seven words can be discussed in the context of the reading discussion, leaving only nine and eight words, respectively, to be taught before each story. All the words can be practiced, added to the students' personal dictionaries, and used in their writing.

CCSS Standards L5, 6: It is the teacher's responsibility to select grade-appropriate and domain-specific words. The basal program suggests and the teacher decides.

Strategies

Since this is the introductory unit for the year, Ms. Fogel and her colleagues will introduce four RT strategies—*predicting, self-questioning, clarifying,* and *summarizing.* The students have been exposed to and have been using these strategies since second grade, so the initial work will focus on review rather than initial instruction. She plans an introductory lesson that will follow the guidelines in Chapter 6. The teachers will model the use of these strategies as they and their students discuss the first reading selection from the

Unit Theme/Topic	Friendships: How to make them and keep them	CCSS
Text for Reading Aloud	*The Other Side* (Woodson)	
Texts for Modeling and Guided Practice	Excerpt from *Because of Winn-Dixie* (DiCamillo) *How Tía Lola Came to ~~Visit~~ Stay* (Alvarez)	
Texts for Independent Reading	*Because of Winn-Dixie* (DiCamillo) *There's a Boy in the Girl's Bathroom* (Sachar) *Charlotte's Web* (White) *The Skin I'm In* (Flake) *Amelia Bedelia Makes a Friend* (Parish) *Happy Birthday, Ronald Morgan!* (Giff) *Corduroy* (Freeman) *Frog and Toad* (Lobel) *Just as Long as We're Together* (Blume) *The Secret Olivia Told Me* (Joy)	10
Comprehension Strategies	Predicting, self-questioning, clarifying, and summarizing	1, 2
Text Structure/Craft Skills	Story structure, simile, and metaphor	1, 2, 9
Activities	• Read and discuss the selections from the basal program. While reading, students will generate questions for discussion, identify new vocabulary words, and summarize the story. • Some students who have a weak grasp of story structure will need to review it and complete story maps. • Each student will read one to three (depending on length) books on the theme of friendship and compare the treatment of the theme between the basal program and the novels. • Students will write about friendship and share with the class what they learned from the books they are reading.	1, 2, 8
Assessments	The students will read a short story about friendship and answer open-ended and multiple-choice questions about story structure, theme, and the author's use of figurative language.	1, 2
Culminating Projects	The students will write a character sketch of a close friend explaining why they are friends, or they may compare and contrast the traits of two friends.	3

FIGURE 9.5. Planning a unit of reading instruction within a basal program.

Vocabulary from *Because of Winn-Dixie*		Vocabulary from *How Tía Lola Came to ~~Visit~~ Stay*	
Program Vocabulary	**Teacher Selected**	**Program Vocabulary**	**Teacher Selected**
consisted	selected	welcome	psychologist
positive	trembling	sensitive	annoyed
peculiar	prideful	observe	mixed feelings
novel	miss-smarty-pants	prepared	energies
talent	sighed	negative	Spanish words
advanced	pretended	include	bienvenido
property		glance	buen provecho
mention		honor	para mí
comfort		encouragement	
intends			

FIGURE 9.6. Teacher- and program-identified vocabulary words.

Source	Words Students Know	Words with Sufficient Context Support	Words to Teach
Winn-Dixie	advanced	mention	consisted
	selecting	comfort	positive (negative)
	pretended	intends	peculiar
			mood
			properly
			trembling
			prideful
			miss-smarty-pants
			sighed
Tía Lola	spoiled (unspoiled)	observe	welcome
	energy	prepared	sensitive
		glance	negative (positive)
		encouragement	include
			honor
			psychologist
			annoyed
			mixed feelings

FIGURE 9.7. Teacher-selected vocabulary words.

basal program, but they will avoid using strategies for the sake of strategies. That means they will begin a reading discussion by asking students to summarize what they have read, point out and discuss issues that were difficult to comprehend, ask students to generate their own questions, and finally predict, if necessary, what might happen next. The content is the focus not the strategies. (See Chapter 6 for a complete explanation of this discussion technique.)

> **CCSS Standards R1, 2:** The CCSS do not suggest any particular strategies but they are essential to understanding the text and making inferences.

Metacognition

Ms. Fogel tackles metacognition in three ways in this initial unit. First, she focuses on the RT strategies, predicting, clarifying, self-questioning, and summarizing that foster metacognition (Palincsar & Brown, 1984). Each of these strategies causes the students to reflect on the meaning of the passage, think about what they did not understand by stopping to clarify and question, and through summarizing engage in some self-assessment, and, if needed, take steps to rectify any confusion.

For students who lack these metacognitive insights she plans to introduce the click and clunk approach from collaborative strategic reading (CSR; Klinger et al., 2004). During small-group discussions students will be given two cards, a green one with the word *click* written on it and a red card with the word *clunk*. At designated stopping points students will indicate their understanding by playing their *click* card or lack of it by playing their *clunk* card. The *clunk* card also suggests some strategies for students to try out to repair the lack of understanding. Students might:

- Summarize what they have already learned.
- Reread the sentence with a clunk and look for key words to resolve what does not make sense.
- Reread the sentences before or after the clunk to figure out what does not make sense.
- Students might look for prefixes, suffixes, or word roots to determine the meaning of a difficult word.

Ms. Fogel plans for her students to complete a Metacognitive Log (see Figure 9.8) from the Reading Apprenticeship Program (Schoenbach, Greenleaf, Cziko, & Hurwitz, 1999). This is an activity that students complete while they are reading independently, helping them reflect on their response to reading but not the substance of the ideas. Using a Metacognitive Log the students record the date, the first page they read, the last page

Record the following at the top of each page:

Date	Book Title	Page # Started	Page # Ended	Total Pages Read	Time Spent Reading

FIGURE 9.8. Metacognitive Log.

they read, the number of pages read, and the total time spent reading. The teachers want their students to think about endurance and perseverance with the hope that each time the student reads at school or at home he or she is able to sustain the effort for a longer period of time. The second part of the log causes the students to reflect on what was going on in their mind while they were reading by responding to one of these sentence stems:

While I was reading
- I got confused when . . .
- I was distracted by . . .
- I started to think about . . .
- I got stuck when . . .
- The time went quickly because . . .
- A word/some words I didn't know were . . .
- I stopped because . . .
- I lost track of everything except . . .
- I figured out that . . .
- I first thought . . . but then I realized . . .

The students will turn in the logs once a week and the teachers plan to discuss them during their small-group time and provide written feedback.

Motivation

Ms. Fogel recognizes that motivating her students is her responsibility. While the basal program provides some motivating materials and activities, it is the use of these materials that will provide the motivation that her students need. She recognizes that many of her students do not read at home, nor do their parents. They instead are so engaged with social media that they have little time for books. So Ms. Fogel's motivational practices are built around four principles: interest, choice, success, and self-efficacy. She introduces her students to exciting books and authors, she engages them in meaningful activities where they can succeed, and she helps them reflect on and appreciate their progress as readers focusing on their accomplishments:

- Each time her students read a selection from the basal program she uses it as an opportunity to discuss other works that are available from the school library. Each reading assignment is an opportunity for an author study.
- Rather than use the read-aloud selection from the program Ms. Fogel finds books from well-published authors that her students will enjoy. She slowly builds her students' knowledge of interesting fiction and nonfiction books.
- Ms. Fogel selects and designs instructional activities with an eye on student engagement and success. She wants activities that are interesting, require effort over time, and their completion engenders a sense of satisfaction. That means she avoids workbook activities.
- Ms. Fogel confers with her students regularly to build motivation and confidence. She reviews their progress and has them reflect on their accomplishments. They look at their projects, tests scores, and assignments and decide how they are progressing as readers.

PLANNING WEEKLY COMPREHENSION ACTIVITIES

Basal reading programs are built around a standard weekly lesson that includes both whole-class and small-group activities. The typical 5-day plan (see Figure 9.9) includes the following activities:

In a typical weekly basal program lesson students read and discuss two selections, one of 1,500 to 2,000 words, plus one shorter selection of 200 to 300 words. Then later in the week the students read a leveled reader. Vocabulary is introduced at the beginning of the week and then practiced repeatedly during the week with additional vocabulary or fluency skills

	Day 1	Day 2	Day 3	Day 4	Day 5
Whole-class activities	Oral read-aloud Building background knowledge Vocabulary instruction Teaching comprehension Skills/strategies	Discuss the focus question Review vocabulary Read/discuss major basal selection Practice comprehension skills/strategies	Review focus question Teach vocabulary strategy Reread major basal selection and discuss Practice comprehension skill	Expand vocabulary Read short nonfiction selection and discuss	Discuss reading selections Review vocabulary Review comprehension skill Independent reading
Small-group activities	Vocabulary review Read and discuss the leveled reader	Vocabulary review Comprehension skill with the leveled reader	Fluency practice Responding to the leveled reader	Comprehension skills/strategies with leveled reader	Fluency practice Making connections across selections

FIGURE 9.9. A typical 5-day plan from a basal reading program.

added. Comprehension skills and strategies are introduced at the beginning of the week and practiced through teacher questioning and worksheets during the week. By the end of the week the program leaves time to assess what the students have learned.

If teachers can abandon the fixed 5-day structure, deciding that learning does not always begin on Monday to be assessed on Friday, they gain flexibility in their planning and power in their instruction. At the beginning of this chapter we proposed dividing a large, vague unit into two small, more tightly focused ones with well-defined goals. One unit covered the theme of friendship and the other social justice and community action. Let's look at how Ms. Fogel plans to teach the social justice unit covering two reading selections, *My Brother Martin* (Farris, 2005) and *The Power of W.O.W.!* (Hubbard, 2011). She realizes that these coherent small themes have the potential to build knowledge and engage students more deeply in the act of reading.

Ms. Fogel plans for the students to read the two main reading selections the first week, devoting just 2 days to each selection. The leveled readers will also be read the first week, freeing the students to read independently the second week on the topic of social justice and community action. Comprehension strategies will be introduced or reviewed the first week and then applied through small-group discussion throughout the 2 weeks the students are studying the theme. Vocabulary will be introduced the first week, but reviewed and discussed throughout the unit. Finally, graphic organizers and the unit project will be introduced early so students can work on the project for the full 2 weeks. The instructional schedule for just the first week is presented in Figure 9.10.

Ms. Fogel has moved almost all of the comprehension instruction to small-group work, where she can guide the students who need help. In addition to what the basal program requires the students will select and read three or four additional books over the 2-week unit.

READING AND RESPONDING
OUTSIDE THE BASAL READING PROGRAM

Literature Circles, Book Clubs, and Other Discussion Approaches

The discussion techniques like literature circles and book clubs can be used with the selection in a basal reading program to focus on the students' expressive or aesthetic response to their readings (Murphy et al., 2009). These techniques are well suited to basal programs because of the large

	Day 1	Day 2	Day 3	Day 4	Day 5
Whole-class activities	Introduction of unit theme, readings, and project Teach comprehension skills/strategies	Oral read-aloud #1 to model strategies Introduce vocabulary	Oral read-aloud #1 to build vocabulary Review concepts and add to the concept wall	Oral read-aloud #2 to model strategies Review progress on theme projects	Oral read-aloud #2 to build vocabulary Review vocabulary
Small-group activities	Read and discuss *My Brother Martin* Review comprehension strategies if necessary	Discuss *My Brother Martin* Review vocabulary words	Read and discuss *The Power of W.O.W.!* Fluency practice as needed	Discuss *The Power of W.O.W.!* Review vocabulary words	Discuss the leveled books and move to student-selected reading

FIGURE 9.10. Revised weekly lesson plan for social justice unit.

number of literary selections in a basal program and the need to move students beyond teacher-directed discussions. In Chapter 6 we outlined how to implement both of these student-directed discussion formats within a literature-based format; the same techniques can be used in a basal program format.

> **CCSS Standards R6, 7, 9:** Literature circles and book clubs provide a means for students to explore literature in depth and consider a range of interpretations. Discussion promotes multiple points of view.

1. Teach the students the roles for literature circles. Then assign each of these roles to your small comprehension groups. As they are reading their anthology selection or their leveled book they can complete their role sheets. Then have the students meet during their independent time to discuss what they have read. Each student completes his or her role, asking questions, sharing vocabulary, acting as a critic, and summarizing until the discussion is completed. Finally, have the students evaluate the success of their literature circle and report back to you the next time you meet with them.

2. Teach the students how to complete a response as you would for a book club. Then after the students read a selection from the basal reading program have them write a personal response summarizing the story, evaluating the plot, reflecting on the character, or discussing the main points of the author's message. Then have students from that small group meet to share their insights comparing and contrasting what they have learned.

Both of these adaptations are based on the premise that the teacher does not have to lead every student through every selection in a basal program. Indeed, the goal is to develop the students' expertise so they need the teacher less. In the next chapter we consider how to apply questioning the author and collaborative reasoning to a basal reading program.

Independent Reading

All basal reading programs acknowledge independent reading but barely. When we examined the 5-day lesson plans in several current basal programs we noted that all provided a recommendation for independent reading, but typically only 1 day a week. Some independent reading is suggested in workstation guidelines of the newest basal programs, but teachers will not find guidelines for building a classroom library or developing an extensive independent reading program. It can be argued that the developers of basal reading programs believe that the texts provided in the programs are sufficient for students to become proficient and engaged readers even though the recent research questions that sufficiency (Brenner & Hiebert, 2010; Dewitz et al., 2010).

Students who read more are better readers; they gain in fluency, vocabulary, knowledge, and comprehension (Gambrell, Marinak, Brooker, & McCrea-Andrews, 2011). Students who score in the 90th percentile on standardized reading tests spend five times as many minutes reading a day as do students at the 50th percentile and 200 times as many minutes as students at the 10th percentile (R. C. Anderson, Fielding, & Wilson, 1988). Teachers face one critical question: how to promote meaningful, engaged independent reading. The research now suggests that simply requiring a period of sustained silent reading will not achieve the desired goal because not all students are highly engaged while they are reading. Even reading management programs like the Accelerated Reader show few results unless the teacher provides considerable guidance and support (Topping, Samuels, & Paul, 2007).

> **CCSS Standard R10:** Independent reading is an ideal way to promote the reading of complex texts and match students to those texts.

Ms. Fogel and her colleagues face the task of designing an independent reading program that benefits all of their students, especially those least likely to read on their own. Their independent reading program considers the following characteristics: time, text, information, support, and engagement.

Time

Students in Ms. Fogel's class spend at least 40 minutes a day working independently or with a partner. During this time they are reading books that are tied to the unit of study and books they select from personal interest. At least 2 days a week Ms. Fogel schedules a 15-minute sustained silent reading period, so she can confer with individual students.

Text

Access to text is essential for an effective independent reading program, especially for students who have limited access to books at home. Knowing that her students have only one official day to visit the school library and often the librarian is teaching about research procedures, Ms. Fogel continually rebuilds and expands her classroom library. Her library occupies one corner of the room demarcated by two high bookcases. The additions of a carpet, beanbag pillows, and a floor lamp create a cozy space. The library is stocked with over 200 books bought with book club points, from eBay and garage sales. The books are organized by genre, topic, and color-coded for reading level. Ms. Fogel regularly rotates the books, introduces new ones, and promotes them with conviction. All students spend some of their independent time in the classroom library or reading elsewhere in the room.

Information

If you read regularly for pleasure and/or information, you know that many of your decisions about what to read are influenced by information about books. You read a new book or news article because a friend suggested it; you heard a review on National Public Radio; you read about J. K. Rowling's (2012) book, *The Casual Vacancy*. Knowledge and information are key. Ms. Fogel does everything she can to help students learn about good books and authors. She shares books with students. Students share books with each other. The class studies authors, they keep a "best-sellers" list and she regularly reads to her students. Without knowledge how do you know what to read next?

Support

Ms. Fogel knows that students will not continue to read unless they receive support and encouragement. She confers weekly with each student in the class. During these conferences, they discuss the book the student is currently reading so Ms. Fogel can informally assess comprehension and interest, providing support and encouragement as needed. She gauges the student's interests and they discuss what he or she might read next. These conferences and sharing within the classroom bring the students into the social world of reading.

Engagement

Ms. Fogel knows that it is the quality of the independent reading time and not the amount that is most critical. She ensures that her students pick books at their independent reading level and monitors their selections in the classroom and when they go to the school library. Her students complete response logs, like the Metacognitive Log (see Figure 9.8), and reading journals so they can share their thoughts with others. Most importantly, Ms. Fogel and her students are continually discussing what they read, creating a literate social environment.

LOOKING BACK, LOOKING FORWARD

A basal reading program presents a fixed format for teaching reading, which does not change as the year goes by or as the students' expertise grows. Matching a basal program against our criteria for the good comprehender we find that these programs do not address in a robust way knowledge development, metacognition, strategies use, and motivation. Teachers must therefore make decisions to augment and differentiate instruction. The basal then becomes a tool that is augmented by picture books and novels for read-alouds, a realigned set of units that build knowledge, a more vigorous focus on vocabulary, and more explicit comprehension instruction. The basal can be differentiated by adding independent reading, by employing book clubs or literature circles to build independence, and by reading texts outside the basal program. Just as these literature-based activities can be pulled into a basal program, the inquiry-based instructional ideas can be used in a basal instruction especially when the units stress reading to learn. In this chapter we stressed how to plan with a basal program. In the next chapter we move from planning to teaching.

APPLICATIONS AND EXPLORATIONS

To complete the extension and application activities you will need at least one teacher's manual from a basal reading program, preferably, two or more. Work on planning instruction as we did in this chapter. The *Essential Guide to Selecting and Using Core Reading Programs* (Dewitz et al., 2010) is a good resource for guiding your thinking about a basal reading program. We suggest the following activities:

1. Read the selections in one unit of instruction in a basal program and decide if they hang together and cover a consistent body of knowledge. If not, consider which selections can be read together to create a smaller but more cohesive unit.

2. Once you have created these small units using two or more selections from the basal reading program, then find the children's literature books for read-alouds and independent reading.

3. As we did on page 221 in Figure 9.3, make a sequential list of the comprehension skills and strategies in the program. Then align them with the CCSS or the standards used in your district.

4. Trace critical comprehension skills and strategies across one or more units of study. Decide if this is enough practice to assist your struggling readers.

CHAPTER 10

Teaching Reading Comprehension with a Basal Reading Program

Ms. Fogel is about to start teaching with her new basal reading program. She and her fourth-grade colleagues have completed their planning constructing units of instruction and consulting the CCSS (NGA & CCSSO, 2010). They will be starting the year with a small unit on friendship using two selections from the basal reading program, an excerpt from *Because of Winn-Dixie* (DiCamillo, 2000) and *How Tía Lola Came to ~~Visit~~ Stay* (Alvarez, 2002). However, planning at the unit level leaves many new questions and many decisions. Should Ms. Fogel teach the new vocabulary words following the script in the teacher's edition or devise her own instructional language? Should she ask the guiding comprehension questions as indicated in the teacher's edition or develop her own? Should she use the follow-up worksheets the program provides or develop new activities? Ms. Fogel must make many decisions as she develops her comprehension program.

Basal reading programs are not strictly scripted but come with many instructional options, some stated, some implied. In prereading instruction the teacher can embellish the program's prior knowledge instruction and expand the explanations for the new vocabulary words. When new skills are introduced he or she can put his or her stamp on the process. While students are reading the text the teacher can ask the questions provided in the teacher's edition, craft his or her own, or follow one of the research-based instructional approaches like questioning the author (QtA; Beck et al., 1997) or reciprocal teaching (RT; Palincsar & Brown, 1984). He or she has the option of using any or all of the instructional tactics that sit at the bottom of the page in his or her teacher's edition, suggestions that provide hints for working with English language learners, students who struggle with comprehension, or students who lack fluency. Finally, Ms. Fogel must decide which, if any, of the many workbook activities she will use to extend students' learning.

In this chapter we plan to guide you through many instructional decisions, and illustrate how to teach comprehension with a basal reading program. In the preceding chapter we outlined how to plan units and lessons. We now plunge into the language of instruction, the explaining, modeling, and scaffolding to help you make the best use of your basal program. In this chapter you will learn to:

GOALS FOR THIS CHAPTER

√ Manage time and students.

√ Build vocabulary and comprehension through oral read-alouds.

√ Build knowledge when activating what students already know is not sufficient.

√ Teach vocabulary, tailoring the explicitness of instruction to the needs of students and the demands of the words.

√ Improve the clarity and explicitness of comprehension strategy instruction.

√ Design a well-crafted guided reading lesson incorporating research-validated approaches such as QtA (Beck et al., 1997) and collaborative reasoning (R. C. Anderson et al., 1998).

MANAGING TIME AND STUDENTS

Basal reading programs provide instructional directions for whole-class lessons, small-group lessons, and individual work. As Ms. Fogel looks through her basal program she realizes that her teacher's edition is silent on the management of time, as are most basal programs. According to her teacher's edition, during whole-class instruction she should engage in a read-aloud, work on a comprehension skill, a comprehension strategy, a vocabulary strategy, teach vocabulary words, develop fluency, teach decoding skills, and research skills. All this cannot be accomplished during whole-class instruction so she makes some decisions, moving most of her instruction to small-group lessons and independent or partner work. Figure 10.1 shows how Ms. Fogel organizes her instructional time.

	Day 1	Day 2	Day 3	Day 4	Day 5
Whole Class (30 minutes)	• Read-aloud • Teaching vocabulary words	• Read-aloud • Knowledge development	• Read-aloud • Comprehension skill/strategy instruction	• Read-aloud • Knowledge review	• Vocabulary review
Small Group (60 minutes)— split between groups	• Small-group guided reading; focus varies depending on the students (decoding, fluency, or comp.)	• Small-group guided reading; focus varies depending on the students (decoding, fluency, or comp.)	• Small-group guided reading; focus varies depending on the students (decoding, fluency, or comp.)	• Small-group guided reading; focus varies depending on the students (decoding, fluency, or comp.)	• Small-group guided reading; focus varies depending on the students (decoding, fluency, or comp.)
Independent Activities (40 minutes +)	• Student-led discussions • Independent reading • Vocabulary practice • Fluency practice • Graphic organizers • Research and writing	• Student-led discussions • Independent reading • Vocabulary practice • Fluency practice • Graphic organizers • Research and writing	• Student-led discussions • Independent reading • Vocabulary practice • Fluency practice • Graphic organizers • Research and writing	• Student-led discussions • Independent reading • Vocabulary practice • Fluency practice • Graphic organizers • Research and writing	• Student-led discussions • Independent reading • Vocabulary practice • Fluency practice • Graphic organizers • Research and writing

FIGURE 10.1. Organizing instructional time: Whole-class, small-group, and independent activities.

Ms. Fogel uses her whole-class time to read aloud to her students building conceptual and textual knowledge, vocabulary, and their interest in books and authors. She also uses that time to teach and review specific vocabulary words, build background knowledge, and teach vocabulary and comprehension strategies. During her small-group time she works to develop comprehension through guided discussions. Some students may need to review decoding skills and others may need to work on fluency. She allocates time based on the needs of her students giving more time and attention to the struggling readers (up to 25 minutes a day) and less time to the stronger readers (Connor et al., 2007). All students have a substantial amount of independent time each day, at least 40 minutes a day, while the teacher is working with groups. Then at the end of the literacy block the students have an additional 20 minutes of independent time so that Ms. Fogel can conduct individual reading conferences.

BUILDING KNOWLEDGE AND COMPREHENSION
THROUGH READ-ALOUDS

Ms. Fogel recognizes the importance of reading aloud to her students because it builds knowledge, vocabulary, motivation, and affords her the opportunity to model the process of comprehension. To introduce the opening units on friendship and community action, she has selected the book *The Other Side* (Woodson, 2001), the story of a white girl and an African American girl who lives across the fence from her. Together they transcend the prejudice of the town to form a friendship. Ms. Fogel has paired this book with *We've Got a Job: The 1963 Birmingham Children's March* (Levinson, 2012), because focusing on two books around the same theme builds knowledge and interest (Santoro, Chard, Howard, & Baker, 2008). Students quickly realize that concepts learned in the first read-aloud will help them grasp the ideas in the second. This will also build some knowledge for the next unit on Martin Luther King, Jr. She decides not to use the read-aloud in the basal program but will return to it later since it was designed to specifically introduce the vocabulary.

Ms. Fogel approaches the read-aloud like any other comprehension task. She sets goals, deciding what she wants her students to take away from the experience. Her first read is *We've Got a Job: The 1963 Birmingham Children's March* (Levinson, 2012). She uses this book to set the scene and introduce the students to the concept of segregation and the racial issues of the early 1960s. The book is long, 170 pages, so she reads selectively from the book creating a concept map to help the students understand how life in the South was segregated and discussing the origins of discrimination against African Americans.

> **CCSS Standard R9:** Using two read-alouds allows the teacher to compare and contrast themes and topics.

Ms. Fogel then turns the students' attention to *The Other Side* (Woodson, 2001). Ms. Fogel wants the students to know that friendship requires sharing, respect, and, at times, courage especially to bridge racial divides. She also knows that a fence features prominently in the story as a symbol for the racial divide in the town. She develops her guided reading questions so that the students will come to understand the attributes of friendship and how courage may be necessary to befriend another. Since this story is set in a racially divided town the knowledge the students developed from the first read-aloud will help them understand the text and will also inform the unit on Martin Luther King, Jr. She and the students add more ideas to the concept map (see Figure 10.2).

The Other Side (Woodson, 2001) is very short and dense and requires many inferences. (You might want to go back to Chapter 5 to review

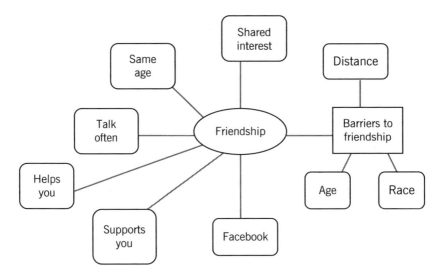

FIGURE 10.2. Concept map of friendship.

inferences.) Many of our suggestions for developing comprehension are similar to those we outlined in Chapter 6 and derive from QtA (Beck et al., 1997). The book opens with a large 2-page watercolor illustration of a rural neighborhood with a long four-rail fence that divides one house from another. Ms. Fogel begins the discussion with the lines and the questions shown in Figure 10.3.

Ms. Fogel realizes that there is considerable information and many implications in this short passage and first she wants to discover if her students have unpacked the message. Hence, the opening question: "What is

The Text	Questions
That summer the fence that stretched throughout town seemed bigger.	What is the author telling us?
We lived in a yellow house on one side of it.	Why does the fence that stretched through the town seem bigger?
White people lived on the other.	Why at the end does the author say that the fence is not safe? How might you have said it differently?
And Mama said, "Don't climb over that fence when you play."	
She said it wasn't safe.	

FIGURE 10.3. Text from *The Other Side* (Woodson, 2001) and teacher-generated questions.

the author telling us?" This allows her to look into the comprehension of her students, their thinking. She follows up by focusing on the symbolism of the fence and the conditions in the town. "Why does the fence seem bigger?" If the students do not understand, then she asks them to think about what they learned from the previous book, *We've Got a Job* (Levinson, 2012), and even points out the notes in the concept map on the board. For some students who struggle Ms. Fogel refines her questions, making them much more specific ("What does the fence separate? Why is it there?") so that the students are pushed to draw some important inferences and engage in close reading. "Why did Mama question the safety of the fence?" has many implications and many answers. When students have difficulty developing their own understanding, Ms. Fogel shares hers.

> **CCSS Standards R1, 2:** Often questioning and a close study of the text is necessary to promote deep understanding and interpretations.

When the students are done reading and discussing the story, Ms. Fogel helps them draw some conclusions about segregation and friendship and adds them to the concept map, ideas that they can apply to the other selections from the basal reading program.

BUILDING KNOWLEDGE VERSUS ACTIVATING KNOWLEDGE

All basal reading programs direct the teacher to build background knowledge before students begin to read. Once you get past the bold labels in the program, "Build Background," "Develop Background," or the smaller labels, "Assess Prior Knowledge" and "Develop Concepts," you realize that basal programs differ considerably in the knowledge that they build and the techniques that they suggest to the teachers. The clarity of the labeling does not always reflect the content to come. It is safe to say that over the past 10 years the focus on building background knowledge in basal programs has declined and the emphasis on vocabulary instruction has increased. Obviously knowledge and vocabulary are linked, but there are lessons in a basal program where the selected vocabulary does not build the conceptual knowledge that students need to understand the selection. This is the issue Ms. Fogel faces with her second unit on social justice.

> **CCSS Standard R1:** While the CCSS are mute on the role of prior knowledge it is essential to making inferences.

The social justice unit includes a biography of Martin Luther King, Jr., and a play about children raising money to save a bookmobile. The basal program, *Journeys* (Baumann et al., 2012), builds background knowledge

Vocabulary Words	Basal Program Definitions
dream	Many people have a dream of fair treatment for all. It is their goal.
injustice	Some people spend their entire lives fighting injustice or unfairness.
segregation	Laws on segregation once kept African Americans and white Americans separate.

FIGURE 10.4. Selected vocabulary words and definitions. From *Journeys* (Grade 4; Baumann et al., 2012, pp. T86–87).

through the vocabulary instruction. Ms. Fogel explains such words as *dream, injustice,* and *segregation* because often the definitions provided in the basal programs do not capture the depth of meaning students need. Consider the vocabulary words and definitions in Figure 10.4. After discussing these words, Ms. Fogel and the students read the following short paragraph from the student edition.

> Dr. Martin Luther King Jr. Do you have a *dream* that would change the whole world? Dr. Martin Luther King Jr. did. King worked for the end of *segregation* in the South in the 1950s and 1960s. He led thousands of people to fight bigotry and *injustice* against African Americans, and he *preferred* using nonviolent ways. He led *numerous* marches. He gave nourishing speeches that inspired listeners. He was sometimes jailed with supporters after *encounters* with police. (p. T89)

Ms. Fogel realizes that the background developed through the vocabulary instruction is not sufficient for the majority of her students to grasp the issues and importance of the civil rights movement; she must supplement. The read-alouds that she selected, *The Other Side* (Woodson, 2001) and *We've Got a Job* (Levinson, 2012), built some knowledge, but then she has the students view some television news reports that are available on YouTube and other websites. She then pulls all of this knowledge together by expanding the concept map the students started in the first unit. The students keep an individual copy of the concept map in their notebooks. The expanded concept map is presented in Figure 10.5.

Graphic Organizers

Graphic organizers help students build and organize knowledge. Ms. Fogel employs graphic organizers from her basal reading program and others she develops for the students. Graphic organizers are visual and spatial displays that describe the structure and content of the text. Through the use

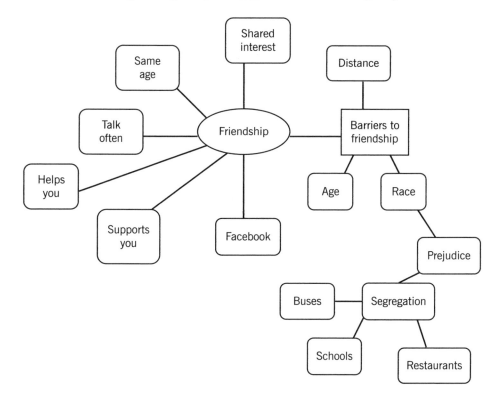

FIGURE 10.5. Concept map of friendship and its barriers.

of shapes, lines, and highlighting a graphic organizer represents the key ideas in a text and their relationship to each other. An outline is an organizer that conveys important and less important ideas through the use of Roman numerals, letters of the alphabet, and regular numerals: I, II, A, B, 1, 2, a, b. An outline lacks the impact that the visual graphic organizer conveys. A Venn diagram is a graphic organizer because it clearly displays how two concepts are alike or different. A story map is a graphic organizer (see Chapter 6) as is a character map, because both highlight important ideas and the relationship among those ideas.

The well-known chart from the K-W-L (Ogle, 1986) procedure is not a graphic organizer because it is designed to guide the reader through a process (think about what you know, ask questions, list what you learned), not to illuminate the structure or organization of ideas. Several of the charts that come with basal reading programs are similarly not graphic organizers, but illustrate a process or a strategy. Consider the following two charts in Figure 10.6.

Sample A

Text Clues	Prior Knowledge	Inferences

Sample B

Main Idea	Details

FIGURE 10.6. Typical graphic organizers from core reading programs.

In sample A, a chart to illustrate the process of making inferences, the students first write in the text clues that launched the inferential process. Next, they consider what they already know. Finally, they combine the text information with prior knowledge to formulate an inference. This process might be repeated several times in a passage but the chart does not help students understand how ideas are related. Sample B is more like a graphic organizer, but it too does not represent the structure of ideas in a text. It is actually an elaborated list with the left side showing important ideas and the right details that support them. However, this list does not capture how the several main ideas are linked together to form a concept. True graphic organizers capture the organization of ideas, as Figure 10.7 illustrates.

The problem faced by Ms. Fogel or any teacher is to select or design graphic organizers that will help students capture the structure of ideas in the text. She knows to limit her students to a few graphic organizers that capture the most common text structures: *cause–effect, problem–solution, compare–contrast, classification, process, argument–reasoning, time sequence, description,* and, for fiction, *story maps* and *character maps* (Jiang & Grabe, 2007). She also knows that the effectiveness of graphic organizers depends on students working with the same organizer for an extended period of time with proper teacher scaffolding. Ms. Fogel avoids many of the worksheets in her basal program that do little to help her students understand how ideas interrelate.

Worksheets in basal programs can be contrasted with graphic organizers in a number of ways. Many of the worksheets in a basal program ask students to reflect on what they learn by completing short-answer questions, matching items, filling in blanks or reading a new short paragraph and answering comprehension questions. These worksheets help students review the content of what they have read, but they do not teach them anything about the structure of the text or the organization of ideas. Some worksheets are better than others, and they have the following characteristics (Osborn, 1984, pp. 110–111):

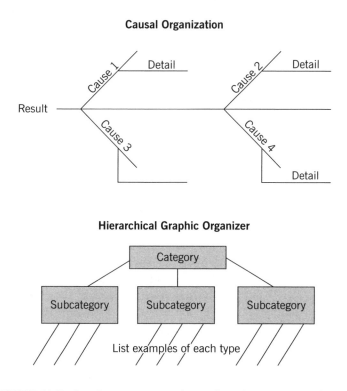

FIGURE 10.7. Graphic organizers that reflect the structure of ideas.

- The worksheet is relevant to the important tasks, strategies, or topics the students are studying.
- The worksheet should contain enough content so that there is a chance a student will review or extend his or her learning.
- The instructions to the students should be clear, unambiguous, and easy to follow without extraneous information and art.
- The vocabulary, content, and concept level of the task should be equal to that of the rest of the lesson.
- The students' responses should stress extended writing and not checking boxes, circling items, or underlining words.

Ms. Fogel follows the GRRM as she uses the graphic organizer. Initially she presents the text and the graphic organizer to the students and then models how to complete it. When the next segment of text is read she has the students begin to take over the job of completing the graphic organizer. Together she and the students fill in the top part of the organizer; then the students complete the next segment of the organizer with a partner, before sharing their results and getting feedback from the teacher. Over time the students take on more responsibility and the teacher does less. They continue to work on the same graphic organizer until Ms. Fogel believes most students can complete it without her assistance. For those students who struggle she continues to work on graphic organizers during their small-group time. Graphic organizers aid comprehension because they help students synthesize information, understand text structure, and foster meaningful independent work.

TEACHING VOCABULARY

Ms. Fogel studies the vocabulary words suggested by her basal program and decides how she needs to augment and modify the program. Words like *segregation* require more explanation than the program provides and a word like *example* less. She realizes that for some words she will need to expand beyond the instruction her program suggests and for others she will need to add in words like *waning* and *streetcar*. In her basal program, *Journeys* (Baumann et al., 2012), the vocabulary instructional guidelines are relatively complete. The program directs the teacher to:

CCSS Standards L5, 6: To meet the language/vocabulary standards a teacher will have to devote more time and attention to vocabulary than most basal programs provide.

- Pronounce the word and then have the students pronounce the word.
- Explain what the word means. "Something that is unfair is an *injustice*."
- The students discuss the words in context after Ms. Fogel reads. "Sometimes people spend their entire lives fighting *injustice* and unfairness."
- The students discuss the word with a partner. "When was the last time you experienced or saw an injustice?"
- The students then answer a question. "What is one thing you think is an injustice?"
- The class reads a paragraph about Martin Luther King, Jr., that contains many of the words.

Ms. Fogel expands the vocabulary instruction provided in the teacher's edition to ensure that the students understand the concepts that underlie the words. She wants them to distinguish between something that is *unfair* and something that is an *injustice*. It may not be fair that I can't watch another hour of TV or go out for ice cream, but these events do not constitute an injustice, so she has her students expand on the concept and discuss events that are unfair and others that are an injustice. She also insists that the students try out the word orally. She asks them to create a sentence using the word *injustice* or complete a sentence stem, "It was an injustice when. . . . "

Ms. Fogel modifies the vocabulary instruction to match the knowledge of her students and the complexity of the words (Graves, 2006). Some words on the vocabulary list require minimal instruction because they are new labels for an old concept. *Recall* being close to *retell* or *remember* is a relatively easy word to teach. Other words like *dream* are understood as a night or daytime mental event but are not understood as a goal or aspiration. Multiple meanings, synonyms, and antonyms must be addressed.

Ms. Fogel wants her students to remember and use the new vocabulary in their reading and writing, well past the typical test on Friday. She knows from the research that students need 10 to 15 meaningful encounters with a word before they truly own it and can use it (Beck et al., 2002). As she looks through her basal program she notes that in addition to the introductory lessons, the students will encounter the words when they read their main anthology selection, and when they read their leveled books. Basal programs vary in their approach to vocabulary review with some providing more stimulating activities than others. Although the program provides worksheets for vocabulary practice, Ms. Fogel believes that there is more she can do to help the students think deeply about the new vocabulary word, consider examples of the words, and develop a sense of word consciousness. Therefore, Ms. Fogel adds these vocabulary activities into her classroom routine:

- Students keep a personal dictionary where they record the new words for the week plus any other words they find during their independent reading. The words are organized alphabetically. Beside each word the student writes a definition, uses the word in a sentence, and provides a synonym and an antonym. Students are urged to use the words in their personal dictionary while writing.

- Students classify words using the simple chart below.

Words	Reason for Classification

Students take any four words from the week's list or from their personal dictionary that have something in common and record them in the left-side classification box. Students might classify a word by part of speech, number of syllables, meaning, or share a related content area. Either the student who classifies the word can provide the reason how it was classified or he or she can challenge his or her partner to do so.

- Students are challenged to think deeply about words by completing sentence stems: It was a great *injustice* when _____.

- Students think about nuances of word meanings by answering questions like: "Which is more *nourishing*, cotton candy or an apple?" "Why?" and "Why is *segregation* an *injustice*?"

Ms. Fogel expects her students to complete these vocabulary activities during their independent time, while she is working with small groups. She does provide one segment of her whole-class time for students to share the new vocabulary words they have found in their independent reading and then these words are posted on the class word wall, a means of celebrating new and interesting words (Baumann, Ware, & Edwards, 2007).

COMPREHENSION SKILL AND STRATEGY INSTRUCTION

Ms. Fogel's teacher's edition suggests that she teach a comprehension skill and strategy every week, typically on Tuesdays. In Chapter 9 we reviewed the scope and sequence of these skills and strategies so you know we do not recommend that you closely follow what the program has suggested. Instead, begin with a few strategies (predicting, questioning, making inferences, summarizing) that all students will need, and gradually add in others that focus on the genre, text structure (narrative and expository), and those that help students with the CCSS (NGA & CCSSO, 2010), evaluating and thinking critically.

Once Ms. Fogel decides which skills and strategies to teach, she turns to her basal program for instructional suggestions. There she typically finds a lesson or two that provide the instructional language for explaining the strategies and short text segments for modeling. The research on basal programs has documented that these lessons lack the explicitness that many students need or that researchers intended (Dewitz et al., 2009). The comprehension lesson in basal reading programs typically:

- Identify the strategy. They tell the students what the strategy is and what they are going to learn to do.
- The lessons are frequently weak in explaining the mental process that underlies the skill or strategy, what Duffy (2009) calls the "secret" of doing it.
- The lessons frequently do not tell the students why the skill or strategy is important. They assume that this is self-evident although the *why* adds a strong metacognitive element and some motivation.
- The lessons do not tell the student when to use a strategy. Strategies solve problems and the readers need to initiate their use.

Ms. Fogel looks over the next comprehension skill lesson in her basal program and realizes that she must make some changes. Her students are engaged in a unit on community action reading about Martin Luther King, Jr., and other civil rights activists. She wants her students to learn to summarize because this strategy will push them to decide which ideas are most important. Summarizing will also promote retention and it provides a metacognitive benefit. If you can stop and summarize while you are reading, then you are self-checking. If you can summarize what you have read, you have a sense that you understand it.

The basal program Ms. Fogel uses provides some guidelines for teaching summarizing but a review of the lessons suggests that she will need to augment what the program offers. For example, the basal program states that a summary is a brief statement of the most important ideas. Summarizing helps readers understand because they must decide what are the most important ideas. The lesson goes on to point out that the main idea might be stated in a topic sentence but often the main idea is implied from the details. During the modeling phase of the lesson, the manual encourages the teacher to examine the first sentence to see if it contains the main idea. If it is not stated, then the teacher's edition encourages the teacher to infer one and explain the process to his or her students. It is up to the teacher to develop a clear explanation. The basal program is correct, summarizing and determining importance are part and parcel of the same strategy.

Ms. Fogel knows that her basal program is on the right track (some programs are much less explicit) but she knows she can make this lesson even more engaging and explicit. The format for Ms. Fogel's lesson follows the same three-part process we introduced in Chapters 6 and 8: (1) *define the strategy* and *discuss why it is important,* (2) *discover the process,* and (3) *determine when to use the strategy.* After this three-part introduction Ms. Fogel will continue with the GRRM.

CCSS Standards R1, 2, 3: Strategies are a necessary component of reading instruction because they capture the mental procedures that some students need to make inferences or generate summaries.

The literature on summarizing is positive and complex. Many researchers have successfully designed studies that have helped students learn to summarize. Some researchers have taught students explicit rules for constructing a summary consisting of (1) deleting unimportant and redundant information, (2) grouping details into a larger category (apples, bananas, peaches = fruit), (3) looking for topic sentences (main idea statements), (4) constructing them when none occur, and (5) then merging what remains into a summary (A. L. Brown, Day, & Jones, 1983). Other researchers have focused on developing an understanding of the text structure and using it to identify big ideas (Armbruster et al., 1987; Taylor & Beach, 1984). In each text segment, signaled by a heading or subheading, the reader looks for the explicit main idea statement or infers them from details. The reader constructs a one-sentence summary for each section and eventually these are merged into an overall summary.

Because Ms. Fogel's students will be reading biographies she decided to focus on text structure as the route to summarizing. She wants her students to understand how different periods of an individual's life, childhood, education, and young adult years affect their goals, as seen in Figure 10.8.

After this introductory lesson Ms. Fogel and her students continue to read and summarize. Occasionally they refer back to the chart "How to Find Important Ideas," especially when one of them has difficulty understanding and relating what has been read.

Define the Strategy Why is summarizing important?	Ms. Fogel starts with the problem because strategies are used to solve problems, thus defining the importance of the strategy. "We are studying the civil rights era and we will be reading many biographies and other informational books." She asks, "Do you think you can remember everything you read?" Only one brave student claims he can; the rest of the class acknowledges that it is very hard to remember everything. Ms. Fogel then explains that today we will learn to summarize because in the process of constructing a summary we will need to focus on the most important ideas. Ms. Fogel then explains that a summary is a brief retelling of the most important ideas in a story, biography, or informational book (Duffy, 2009). The key is to find just the important ideas and then restate them in your own words. Summaries may be oral or written and during our study of the civil rights era I will be calling on you to do both.
Discover the Process	Ms. Fogel then asks her students to list the important parts of any person's life. The students respond that it is important to know where people were born, how they were raised, did they get a good education, what kinds of jobs they had. The students acknowledge that all of these events might determine what they became and what they did with their life. Ms. Fogel explains that a biography is typically organized around each element or stage in a person's life. We are going to determine what was important and then summarize it. She then introduces the following graphic organizer:

EXAMINING A BIOGRAPHY

The subject _____

What were his or her major accomplishments?	

	What were the important events in this person's life?	Why were these events so important?
Childhood		
Education		
Adulthood		
Death		
What can we learn from this person's life?		

(continued)

FIGURE 10.8. Introducing the strategy of summarizing.

Ms. Fogel then has the students read the first part of the biography of Martin Luther King, Jr., and together they set out to discover the most important ideas and then formulate a summary.

We were born in the same room, my brother Martin and I. I was an early baby, born sooner than expected. Mother Dear and Daddy placed me in the chifforobe drawer that stood in the corner of their upstairs bedroom. I got a crib a few days afterward. A year and a half later, Martin spent his first night in that hand-me-down crib in the very same room.

The house where we were born belonged to Mother Dear's parent, our grandparent, the Reverend and Mrs. A. D. Williams. We lived there with them and our Aunt Ida, our grandmother's sister. . . .

And although Daddy, who was an important minister and Mother Dear, who was known far and wide as a musician, often had work that took them away from home, our grandmother was always there to take care of us. I remember days sitting at their feet, as she and Aunt Ida filled us with grand memories of their childhood and read to us about all the wonderful places in the world. (Farris, 2005)

Ms. Fogel starts the discussion by modeling and explaining, "Let's think about what we know about Martin Luther King's life. He worked to end discrimination and segregation against African Americans. He was also a minister, as were his father and grandfather. That suggests that his family was an early influence on what he became and what he did. So we will start to make a chart detailing our rules for how to find important ideas. The chart will be our guide whenever we need to find important ideas and summarize them." (Note that Ms. Fogel is keeping two charts, one that captures the life of Martin Luther King and the other the process and procedures of the strategy.)

How to find important ideas:
- Think about what you know.

Ms. Fogel then writes the following on the "Examining a Biography" graphic organizer: *Martin Luther King came from a family of ministers and teachers.* On the other side of the chart she writes: *This inspired him to help others.*

The instruction continues in this vein, section by section; each time the students and the teacher discover a new principle of determining importance it is added to the chart. Inevitably they consider other texts because other informational writing provides clues to importance that biographies do not— headings, subheadings, and bold print. After considering several texts the list now looks like this:

How to find important ideas:
- Think about what you know.
- Examine the headings, subheadings, and bold print.
- Look for topic sentences.
- If you can't find a topic sentence construct one.

(continued)

FIGURE 10.8. *(continued)*

	After Ms. Fogel and the students have completed the "Examining a Biography" graphic organizer, she begins to link the ideas together to construct a written summary on a larger piece of chart paper. Later, especially during guided reading discussion, she or one of the students will summarize orally, illustrating that summaries do not always need to be written down.
Discuss When to Summarize	In the last step of the lesson Ms. Fogel discusses when to summarize and reiterates the why. She points out that there are two times when it is important to summarize: "First, we should consider stopping and summarizing while we read. This helps the reader maintain a firm handle on the meaning of the passage. We know if we can summarize what we read and the summary makes sense, then we have grasped the gist of the passage. So from now on when we are reading and discussing a passage I am going to ask one or two of you to summarize what we have read. "It is also useful to summarize when we have finished reading. That helps us pull together what we have read. When we are reading a biography we will keep our notes on the graphic organizer, and then write them as one well-developed summary. We can use the notes and the summary to create an oral report, a written report, or another project."

FIGURE 10.8. *(continued)*

GUIDED READING LESSONS

Ms. Fogel meets regularly with her students in small groups to guide the development of their comprehension, assess their capabilities, and provide the necessary support when she detects problems. In Chapters 6 and 8 we presented our guidelines for effective teacher-guided small-group discussions. We are going to reiterate a bit of what we already wrote and then make some suggestions about using small-group guided instruction in a basal program successfully. As you know, a basal program includes narrative texts, poetry, and informational texts, so much of what we presented in previous chapters still applies. Yet, a basal program comes complete with page-by-page guided reading questions and suggestions for teacher modeling. Most of what basals direct teachers to do is ask questions with questioning constituting 75% of teacher actions (Dewitz et al., 2009).

Planning Guided Reading

Planning guided reading with a basal reading program needs to start with the same kind of thinking and planning as does any guided reading lesson. We recommend you read each selection twice by yourself, first just to enjoy and understand it, next to look for the problems your students might face

(Kucan et al., 2011). Do not faithfully rely on the script provided by the program.

> **CCSS Standards R1, 2, 3, 4:** A close reading of the text, spurred on by teacher-guided discussion, is necessary to help students focus on the explicit meaning or to draw inferences.

• *Consider what big ideas and understandings you want your students to construct with the passage.* Most basal programs imply that the main purpose of reading instruction is the development of skills and strategies. Some programs focus on important or essential questions; not all do. If your program does not lead you and your students to consider big ideas, make that a priority.

• *What vocabulary words do your students need to know?* As we discussed in Chapter 5 you will need to make some decisions, adding words or ignoring the suggestions of the program developers depending on the needs of your students.

• *What knowledge do your students need to know prior to reading?* Most likely you will need to build more knowledge than what your teacher's edition suggests.

• *What text-processing and text structure problems are your students likely to encounter?*

   ◆ Complex pronoun–noun relationships.
   ◆ Complex sentences obscuring cause–effect and other relationships.
   ◆ Ideas or sentences that must be linked one to another.
   ◆ Inferences required for understanding the text.

We do not believe that such thinking goes into the development of comprehension questions in the basal reading programs and each company seems to take a different approach to guided reading. In some programs the questions are skill and strategy driven and the developers repeatedly pose questions around specific skills and strategies. If the lesson focuses on problem solution, inferences, and dictionary skills, you will find the bulk of the questions targeted on those skills. In other programs, or units within a program, the questions are more content driven and the developer does seek to focus on the plot or developing ideas in nonfiction.

All basal programs disrupt, at times, the focus on content and meaning of the passage and ask teachers to pose questions about vocabulary words, vocabulary skills, author's craft, and genre. It would be better if these issues were addressed in a second reading of the passage where the students could delve deeper into the author's language. All basal programs provide mini-lessons that direct teachers to model a strategy and think aloud. Use these mini-lessons with discretion, employing them only when necessary. Finally, all basal programs provide the teacher with much less guidance for reading and discussing the small leveled books than the main anthology selections. For these texts you will need to develop your own guided reading lesson. To our general suggestions above we would add the following about guided reading in basal programs:

- Read all of the questions through and decide if they focus on the same ideas that you want to emphasize.
- Do the questions anticipate the problems your students will have?
- Look closely at questions that focus on vocabulary words, vocabulary strategies, or the author's craft. If these questions do not directly help the students to grasp the content of the passage, ask them after the selection has been discussed.
- Examine the suggestions to model and think aloud. Use these only if you feel that they will benefit your students.
- Don't be afraid to add your own questions or to turn the questioning over to the students.

MOVING DISCUSSION INTO THE BASAL READING PROGRAM

Our primary focus in this last section is to move beyond the teacher-guided lesson we outlined above into discussions that promote higher-order thinking. National assessments of reading achievement document that 67% of our students can read above a basic level, meaning they can grasp the meaning of a passage, make simple inferences, and relate a text to their own lives (National Center for Education Statistics, 2011). However, less than 34% were able to read at a proficient level, make judgments, examine a text critically, and explain their judgments. So to move students beyond the basic level to one that is required for college and career work demands different instructional approaches. We will consider how two types of discussion might be used with basal program text to develop higher-order thinking skills.

A discussion is a process, led by a teacher or a student, where students make public their positions, arguments, and feelings about issues in a text, consider the position of other students, and then attempt to reconcile conflicting views (Wilkinson & Son, 2011). It is through this process that the students reach a higher level of understanding, especially reconciling opposing views. The social context of discussion is critical to the development of higher-order thinking. According to Wertsch, Del Rio, and Alvarez (1995) when students interact with others what they learn and are able to do is typically beyond the ability of any individual in that group. Accordingly, L. W. Anderson and Krathwohl (2001) suggest that "thinkers must hear several voices within their own head representing different perspectives on the issues. The ability and disposition to take more than one perspective arise from participating in discussions with others who hold different perspectives" (p. 2).

CCSS Standards R6, 7: These discussion techniques help students consider alternative points of view, various themes, and learn how to think critically.

If discussion is a social interaction designed to help students develop new insights and new ways of thinking, few of the suggestions or questions in a teacher's edition of a basal program would spur this kind of thinking. Close to 50% of the questions in a basal program have their answers right in the text; there is little to discuss or debate. Twenty-five percent of the questions demand some inferential thinking, and another 11% of the suggestions in the manual are really prompts for the teacher to supply information through think-alouds. Only 4% of the questions lead students to evaluate or think critically about what has been read. One program, *Storytown* (Beck, Farr, & Strickland, 2009), does come with a supplemental manual that helps teachers apply QtA (Beck et al., 1997), an approach designed to help the students develop a more critical stance toward the text.

Classroom discussions can take on three different approaches or stances, focusing on different ways of thinking (Murphy et al., 2009) and all seem effective in promoting higher-level thinking. Collaborative reasoning (R. C. Anderson et al., 1998) helps students adopt a critical analytic stance to the text. Instructional conversations (Goldenberg, 1993) and QtA (Beck et al., 1997) helps students acquire information from the text, what we called in Chapter 1, an efferent stance. Finally, literature circles and books clubs, which we discussed in Chapter 6, help students take an aesthetic or expressive stance focusing on personal response and judgments.

Since we already discussed literature circles and book clubs previously we now take a closer look at how two techniques can be applied within a basal program. QtA (Beck et al., 1997) is designed to help students read a text closely and think critically about the author's ideas and arguments. Collaborative reasoning is designed to promote critical thinking and it too can be applied to the selections in a basal reading program.

Questioning the Author

The QtA technique (Beck et al., 1997) influenced our thinking when we designed the teacher-guided suggestions we presented in Chapters 6, 8, and this chapter. However, QtA involves more than we outlined and it is designed to lead students to take a distinct perspective on a text. The teacher begins the discussion by stating that the author is fallible and our failure to understand is sometimes his or her fault. So a good reader questions the author trying to get at his or her intent, craft, organization, and ideas. Students read a selection of text and then the discussion begins with queries such as these. They are called queries because the intent is to drive thinking, not assess what the students have learned.

- What is the author trying to tell you?
- Why is the author telling you that?
- How does this connect with what the author told us before?
- Does the author say it clearly?
- How could the author have said things more clearly?

The opening query is designed to elicit what the students learned from the passage and the following queries are designed to clarify misunderstandings, repair them, and then consider the author's intent. The teacher keeps the discussion moving and helps the students understand the text. Because the teacher understands the text and its pitfalls he or she works not to explain the text but to help the students find a way through it. To keep the discussion focused the teacher employs specific actions:

1. *Marking.* The teacher marks and notes the key ideas that the students bring forth. This is not just praise, "Oh, John, what a great comment," but an acknowledgment that an idea is critical to understanding the text. The teacher might repeat or rephrase what the student said to highlight its importance.

2. *Turning back.* This is the act of turning the students' attention back to the text to find support and evidence for their position or to elaborate on a position. This encourages students to make connections between their interpretations and the evidence in the text. You want the students to grapple with the meaning, not affirm or reject what they said. Another sense of turning back is to guide students to consider what another has said. Dealing with other points of view is the essence of developing higher-order thinking.

3. *Revoicing.* Revoicing is the act of saying, "in other words." A student has made a comment that you recognize as important, but he or she

expresses it very poorly. By rephrasing it you accomplish two things: You validate what the student has said, in effect praising the insight, and model for him or her another way to express the thought.

4. *Modeling.* During modeling the teacher makes public how he or she thinks during a particularly difficult part of the text. The teacher should not model the easy stuff, like making a prediction, but the parts of text processing where it is difficult to reach an understanding or make an interpretation. We believe that the modeling suggestions in most basal programs border on the obvious.

5. *Annotating.* This is the act of supplying information that the text lacks and the students cannot supply themselves.

6. *Recapping. Summarizing* is another word for *recapping*, pulling everything together. It is interesting to note that the approach of QtA begins with a summary, What is the author telling us?, and ends with a summary.

Both the queries and the teacher moves are critical to the quality of the discussion. The six actions listed above are at the heart of the discussion and move students to consider others' ideas, assemble insight, and arrive at new understandings. As a discussion technique QtA is primarily efferent and it helps the students learn from the text, but the technique also promotes students' ability to engage in critical/analytic thinking (Chinn et al., 2001).

Collaborative Reasoning

In the process of collaborative reasoning (Chinn et al., 2001) the teacher states a central question and the students take a position presenting evidence and reasons for supporting their argument. Consider the biography of Martin Luther King, Jr. You might begin the collaborative reasoning process with the following question: "As a boy, Martin Luther King, Jr., and his brother and sister played with the white children across the street. One day the white children's parents told them that they were no longer welcome to play. If you were Martin Luther King, Jr.'s parents, what would you do and why?" To answer this question the student would need to take a position and then argue from the information in the story providing evidence and reasons. In collaborative reasoning:

- Begin the discussion with a question or questions that force students to take a position. The students need to take a critical/analytic stance.
- *Prompt* students and ask for their position, a reason, evidence, or evaluation. As students get better you will need to prompt less.

- Ask for *clarification* and help them become more precise in their arguments.
- *Challenge* the students with new ideas they have not thought up. These challenges come only after the students have exhausted one line of argument.
- *Encourage* the students by acknowledging and praising their efforts. Make your praise very specific and include words like *reasons, evidence, position,* and *opinion* in your statements.
- *Sum up* what the students have said and encourage the students to do so.
- *Foster independence* because you want students to talk to each other. Three moves promote independence (Dillon, 1988): (1) don't say anything, just wait and see if the students will talk; (2) simply restate what another student has said, but do not ask another question; and (3) attach names to ideas: "What do you think of Erica's ideas?"

We have presented two discussion techniques. One, QtA, is focused on helping students understand the ideas in the text and dealing with the problems that most authors create. It does include some elements of critical analysis. The other technique, collaborative reasoning, is designed to foster higher-level thinking by helping students think analytically and foster reasoned argument. Both have been shown to improve reading comprehension (Wilkinson & Son, 2011), but whether they are more effective than a focus on comprehension strategies as presented in RT (Palincsar & Brown, 1984) and TSI (see Chapter 8; R. Brown et al., 1996) is unknown. Discussion is the new kid on the block but it shares much in common with the best strategy instruction. All of these approaches are built around important and interesting texts. Students work with a teacher and other students to construct an understanding while they read. The teacher is the guide and the expert.

LOOKING BACK, LOOKING FORWARD

To teach comprehension well you have to step outside the confines of the basal reading program. Those steps will take you to new texts and new instructional ideas. You will need to move your students to novels, nonfiction trade books, and the Internet. You will need to build more background knowledge and vocabulary than your program suggests using explanations that are clearer and more robust. You may need to add additional graphic organizers so that your students understand the structure of the texts and the organization of ideas. Your explanations of comprehension strategy must become crisper and more engaging. Students do not relish learning strategies for the sake of strategies. Finally, you will need to change your discussion patterns to help your students achieve higher levels of thinking.

APPLICATIONS AND EXPLORATIONS

As in the previous chapter you will need a teacher's edition from a basal reader to complete these activities. The book *Making the Most of Your Basal Reading Program* (Dewitz & Wolskee, 2012) is a good resource for guiding your thinking about how to plan lessons with a basal program. We suggest that you read two or three complete lessons from a basal program and then try out these activities. When you are done you will have gone through the planning necessary for effective instruction.

1. Examine how the words in the vocabulary lesson are explained. How can you improve on these explanations?

2. What prior knowledge do your students need to understand the selection? How can you develop that knowledge?

3. Read a comprehension skill or strategy lesson from a basal reading program and compare it to the lesson on page 251. In what ways can you make the lesson in the basal reading program more explicit and engaging?

4. Study the page-by-page guided reading questions from one selection. Categorize these questions using a questioning strategy such as question–answer–relationship (QAR; Raphael, 1986). Once you understand the questions in your program, write some of your own that will produce greater levels of thought.

5. Take one or more selections and plan one or more questions that cause the students to take a critical stance.

CHAPTER 11

Conclusion

What We Hope You Have Learned

Reading comprehension is a complex phenomenon and its complexity was realized over 100 years ago when Edmund Burk Huey (1908/2009) wrote the following:

> And so to completely analyze what we do when we read would almost be the acme of a psychologist's achievement, for it would be to describe very many of the most intricate workings of the human mind, as well as to unravel the tangled story of the most remarkable specific performance that civilization has learned in all its history. (p. 4)

In writing this book, our first goal was to lay out the complexity of reading comprehension, because for a decade or more educators had narrowed down the teaching of reading comprehension to a select number of "magic" or essential strategies leaving the impression that teaching those strategies was the core of comprehension instruction. This belief coincided with the standards movement as most states defined a relatively small set of skills and strategies—finding the main idea, summarizing, making inferences, and determining the author's purpose—as the core of their state curriculum. The focus on skills and strategies drove out a consideration of other equally important aspects of reading comprehension, namely using and building knowledge, motivation, and metacognition.

Test developers are adept at assessing students' ability to apply individual skills and strategies, and the tests they create reinforce the idea that comprehension is a series of skills and strategies. It is a vicious circle with the tests driving the curriculum and the curriculum driving the tests. Assessing motivation or metacognition is more difficult and has been avoided in almost all state assessments. Although these attributes of comprehension are absent from most formal assessments, they should be continually on your radar while teaching and observing your students.

Our second goal was to persuade you that theories and models of reading are very practical (Pearson & Johnson, 1978). We began our book with the presentation of several models of reading comprehension, because the elements of these models have significant implications for instruction. The construction–integration model teaches us that readers rely on knowledge to both construct their initial understanding of the text and then to complete what the author only implied. While prior knowledge was a hot topic in the 1980s strategies then became our focus. The constructively responsive and engaged reader models told us that the good reader is metacognitive, employs strategies as needed, monitors the construction of understanding, and is motivated. The sociocultural model directs us to the importance of social interaction and discussion in the development of students' thinking and comprehension. The transactional model emphasizes that readers adopt different stances in response to reading texts based on their purpose for reading.

By describing these models of comprehension, we took you deeper into the comprehension process and especially in Chapters 3 and 6 exposed you to the number of connections that are essential for a reader to construct meaning. This construction process is worth your and your students' attention. As you listen to children discuss what they read note their ability to make small but important connections between ideas within the text. We hope you learned that comprehension happens because of these many small connections and because of the effective use of a few broad strategies.

Our third goal was to convince you that context and content are vital to the teaching of reading comprehension. We organized our book around three frameworks—literature, inquiry–information, and basal reading programs—because each of these contexts presents different challenges to the teacher and the reader. In a very real sense we view all reading as content reading. Without content there is nothing to comprehend. Within each of these frameworks, instruction is organized differently. The thematic or genre units of literary study are quite different from an inquiry unit about weather. Well-crafted units of study are very important because they provide the motivation students need to build the knowledge that is essential for comprehension to occur. On a cursory level it appears that the same strategies and approaches are used in each framework, but the knowledge base for making an inference about a character's traits is quite different from the one for making an inference about what causes weather patterns. Finding the main ideas of an informational text is different from identifying the theme while reading a piece of fiction. We hope our focus on frameworks made this clear and suggested that comprehension is not a monolithic enterprise, but rather a process that must be adapted to the text, the learning tasks, and your individual students.

Our third framework, basal reading programs, became a major focus because these structured programs, which are so prevalent in U.S. schools, present different challenges to teaching comprehension. In the literature and inquiry framework teachers build their own curriculum; in the basal reading program framework, teachers negotiate with an existing framework. You must decide if the basal program provides all that students need in terms of knowledge development, strategy instruction, and motivation. When using a core program you can modify the scope and sequence of instruction, supplement the instructional units, improve the explicitness of instruction, and modify the scope and build greater and more connected knowledge than the program suggests.

The fourth goal of our book was to showcase the relationship between our multifaceted approach to developing comprehension and the CCSS. The CCSS do not prescribe any particular method or sequence of instruction for teaching the standards. In Chapters 6–10 we illustrated the links between our instructional ideas, some comprehension approaches, and the standards. We specifically avoided a prescribed approach to teaching the standards, so you did not find explicit lessons for teaching students to compare the theme in one novel with another, or to relate the illustrations in a book to its text. What you did find were instructional approaches and guidelines that support the CCSS in building vocabulary, examining a text closely, understanding a text's structure, and making comparisons with other texts.

In one important way we departed from the CCSS. We would not be pleased if all the experiences students had with print and digital text were focused solely on close intense reading looking for details, finding examples, making inferences, citing the text carefully, and providing evidence to support views. Not all reading is close reading. Some books should be relished. If we sacrifice enjoyment we undermine motivation.

WHAT YOU DID NOT LEARN

Our book is not a complete study of reading comprehension instruction because its teaching is an evolving field. While the broad outlines of effective instruction can be spelled out, there is still much to learn. We can safely say that there are several issues that require much further study.

How best to conduct a comprehension discussion remains an open question. If you read Chapters 3, 6, and 8 closely, we stress the importance of letting the content of the passage be the focus of the discussion. The teacher should guide the students by focusing on the critical concepts, linking important ideas together, and making the inferences necessary to understand the passage. The students use strategies—questioning, inferring, summarizing, visualizing—but they remain in the background of the discussion.

We suspect that an important aspect of comprehension is making connections between ideas in a text or the construction process that is at the heart of the construction–integration model. Making these small connections is critical to comprehension, but we do not yet know how to focus on these connections during a discussion especially for children who do not make these connections naturally.

Throughout the book we showcased several approaches to discussion— transactional strategies instruction, literature circles, collaborative reasoning, and questioning the author. We presented these approaches because all are valuable techniques, but we can't say which is better. Each takes a different stance toward the text. Questioning the author takes a more critical and efferent approach to a text, literature circles are focused on aesthetic or expressive response to a text, and transactional strategies instruction is more interpretative but also efferent and aesthetic. We can't say which approach leads to greater growth in comprehension because none have been compared to another.

In each of our instructional chapters we stressed the importance of vocabulary instruction. We provided guidelines for selecting and teaching vocabulary words. Despite our advice it is still an open question which words should be taught. Many would like a definitive list of vocabulary words and some feel that lists of academic vocabulary words like those of Marzano (2004) or Coxhead (2000) should suffice. We still believe the selection of vocabulary words comes down to teacher judgment but we lack the research to guide that judgment.

We devoted one full chapter to assessment, but left with unanswered questions. We believe that the most valuable assessment data for guiding instruction comes from the informal observations that teachers make day to day. Yet many teachers, especially those of you who work in public schools that require high-stakes assessment, regularly give your students more formal assessments, benchmarks, or interim assessments. We don't fully understand the impact of these assessments, but we suspect they have the effect of raising anxiety and narrowing the focus of instruction to a select number of skills and strategies at the expense of our broader focus on knowledge, metacognition, and motivation.

There is still so much to learn about comprehension instruction. We don't know yet how things will evolve in this era of the CCSS and high-stakes testing. Helping students make sophisticated interpretation required by the CCSS will take study and experimentation. We also need research that tackles unanswered and unresolved issues like the ones we raised above. Finally, we hope that comprehension instruction will continue to focus on content and context, moving away from isolated skills and strategy instruction.

We want you to take away one clear message. The teaching of reading comprehension is still as much an art as a science, and research has provided us with a reliable profile of what good readers do. So no matter whether someone reads literature to gain insight into the human condition or reads informational text to learn something new, good readers will always need to be knowledgeable, strategic metacognitive, and motivated. And if we can teach these components in every classroom, we can be assured that students will become stronger readers who embrace all kinds of texts to accomplish important goals and celebrate the joys of reading.

References

Afflerbach, P. (2007). *Understanding and using reading assessment*. Newark, DE: International Reading Association.

Afflerbach, P., & Cho, B. (2009). Identifying and describing constructively responsive comprehension strategies in new and traditional forms of reading. In S. Israel & G. Duffy (Eds.), *Handbook of reading comprehension research* (pp. 69–90). Mahwah, NJ: Erlbaum.

Afflerbach, P., Pearson, P. D., & Paris, S. G. (2008). Clarifying differences between reading skills and reading strategies. *The Reading Teacher, 61*(5), 364–373.

Alexander, P., Kulikowich, J., & Jetton, T. (1994). The role of subject-matter knowledge and interest in the processing of linear and nonlinear text. *Review of Educational Research, 64*(2), 201–252.

Alexander, P. A. (2003). Profiling the developing reader: The interplay of knowledge, interest and strategic processing. In C. M. Fairbanks, J. Worthy, B. Maloch, J. V. Hoffman, & D. L. Schallert (Eds.), *The 52nd yearbook of the National Reading Conference* (pp. 47–65). Oak Creek, WI: National Reading Conference.

Alexander, P. A. (2005). The path to competence: A lifetime developmental perspective on reading. *Journal of Literacy Research, 37*(4), 413–436.

Alexander, P. A., & Jetton, T. L. (2000). Learning from text: A multidimensional and developmental perspective. In M. L. Kamil, P. B. Mosenthal, P. D. Pearson, & R. Barr (Eds.), *Handbook of reading research* (Vol. 3, pp. 285–310). Mahwah, NJ: Erlbaum.

Almasi, J. F. (1995). The nature of fourth graders' sociocognitive conflicts in peer-led and teacher-led discussions of literature. *Reading Research Quarterly, 30*(3), 314–347.

Almasi, J. F., & Fullerton, S. K. (2012). *Teaching strategic processes in reading* (2nd ed.). New York: Guilford Press.

Anderson, L. W., & Krathwohl, D. R. (2001). *A taxonomy for learning, teaching and assessing*. New York: Longman.

Anderson, R. C., Chinn, C., Waggoner, M., & Nguyen, K. (1998). Intellectually stimulating story discussions. In J. Osborn & F. Lehr (Eds.), *Literacy for all: Issues in teaching and learning* (Vol. 1, pp. 170–186). New York: Guilford Press.

Anderson, R. C., Fielding, L. G., & Wilson, P. T. (1988). Growth in reading and how children spend their time outside of school. *Reading Research Quarterly, 23,* 285–303.

Anderson, R. C., & Freebody, P. (1981). Vocabulary knowledge. In J. Guthrie (Ed.), *Comprehension and teaching: Research reviews* (pp. 77–117). Newark, DE: International Reading Association.

Anderson, R. C., & Pearson, P. D. (1984). A schema-theoretic view of basic processes in reading comprehension. In P. D. Pearson, R. Barr, M. L. Kamil, & P. Mosenthal (Eds.), *Handbook of reading research* (Vol. 1, pp. 255–291). New York: Longman.

Anderson, T. H., & Armbruster, B. B. (1984). Content area textbooks. In. R. C. Anderson, J. Osborn & R. J. Tierney (Eds.), *Learning to read in American schools: Basal readers and content texts* (pp. 193–226). Hillsdale, NJ: Erlbaum.

Anderson, V. (1992). A teacher development project in transactional strategy instruction for teachers of severely reading-disabled adolescents. *Teaching and Teacher Education, 8,* 391–403.

Armbruster, B. B., Anderson, T. H., & Ostertag, J. (1987). Does text structure/summarization instruction facilitate learning from expository text? *Reading Research Quarterly, 22*(1), 331–346.

Atwell, N. (1998). *In the middle: New understandings about writing, reading, and learning.* Portsmouth, NH: Heinemann.

Baer, J., Baldi, S., Ayotte, K., & Green, P. (2007). *The reading literacy of U.S. fourth-grade students in an international context: Results from the 2001 and 2006 Progress in International Reading Literacy Study* (PIRLS; NCES 2008-017). National Center for Education Statistics.

Baker, L. (2002). Metacognition in comprehension instruction. In C. C. Block & M. Pressley (Eds.), *Comprehension instruction: Research-based best practices* (pp. 77–95). New York: Guilford Press.

Baker, L., & Wigfield, A. (1999). Dimensions of children's motivation for reading and their relations to reading activity and reading achievement. *Reading Research Quarterly, 34*(4), 452–477.

Bakhtin, M. (1981). *The dialogic imagination* (C. Emerson & M. Holquist, Trans.). Austin: University of Texas Press.

Baumann, J. F. (1984). The effectiveness of a direct instruction paradigm for teaching main idea comprehension. *Reading Research Quarterly, 20*(1), 93–111.

Baumann, J. F., Chard, D. J., Cooper, J. D., et al. (2012). *Journeys.* Boston: Houghton Mifflin Harcourt.

Baumann, J. F., & Graves, M. F. (2010). What is academic vocabulary? *Journal of Adolescent and Adult Literacy, 54*(1), 4–12.

Baumann, J. F., Ware, D., & Edwards, E. C. (2007). "Bumping into spicy, tasty words that catch your tongue": A formative experiment on vocabulary instruction. *The Reading Teacher, 61*(2), 108–122.

Bazerman, C. (1985). Physicists reading physics schema-laden purposes and purpose-laden schema. *Written Communication, 2*(1), 3–23.

Beach, R., & Marshall, J. (1991). *Teaching literature in the secondary school.* Orlando, FL: Harcourt Brace Jovanovich.

Beck, I. L., Farr, R. & Strickland, D. (2009). *Storytown*. Boston, MA: Houghton Mifflin Harcourt.

Beck, I. L., & McKeown, M. G. (1981). Developing questions that promote comprehension: The story map. *Language Arts, 58*(8), 913–918.

Beck, I. L., McKeown, M. G., Hamilton, R. L., & Kucan, L. (1997). *Questioning the author*. Newark, DE: International Reading Association.

Beck, I. L., McKeown, M. G., & Kucan, L. (2002). *Bringing words to life: Robust vocabulary instruction*. New York: Guilford Press.

Beck, I. L., McKeown, M. G., Sinatra, G. M., & Loxterman, J. A. (1991). Revising social studies text from a text-processing perspective: Evidence of improved comprehensibility. *Reading Research Quarterly, 26*(3), 251–276.

Bereiter, C., & Bird, M. (1985). Use of thinking aloud in identification and teaching of reading comprehension strategies. *Cognition and instruction, 2*(2), 131–156.

Betts, E. A. (1946). *Foundations of reading instruction*. New York: American Book Company.

Black, P., & Wiliam, D. (1998). Assessment and classroom learning. *Assessment in Education, 5*(1), 7–14.

Block, C. C., Gambrell, L. B., & Pressley, M. (2002). *Improving comprehension instruction: Rethinking research, theory, and classroom practice*. San Francisco: Jossey-Bass.

Block, C. C., Parris, S. R., Reed, K. L., Whiteley, C. S., & Cleveland, M. D. (2009). Instructional approaches that significantly increase reading comprehension. *Journal of Educational Psychology, 101*(2), 262–284.

Bloom, B. S. (1956). *Taxonomy of educational objectives: Handbook I. The cognitive domain*. New York: David McKay.

Bradley, L. G., & Donovan, C. A. (2010). Information book read-alouds as models for second-grade authors. *The Reading Teacher, 64*(4), 246–260.

Bråten, I., & Samuelstuen, M. S. (2004). Does the influence of reading purpose on reports of strategic text processing depend on students' topic knowledge? *Journal of Educational Psychology, 96*(2), 324–336.

Brenner, D., & Hiebert, E. H. (2010). If I follow the teachers' editions, isn't that enough? Analyzing reading volume in six core reading programs. *The Elementary School Journal, 110*(3), 347–363.

Brown, A. L., & Day, J. D. (1983). The macrorules for summarizing text: The development of expertise. *Journal of Verbal Learning and Verbal Behavior, 22*(1), 1–14.

Brown, A. L., Day, J. D., & Jones, R. S. (1983). The development of plans for summarizing texts. *Child Development, 54*, 968–979.

Brown, A. L., & Smiley, S. S. (1977). Rating the importance of structural units of prose passages: A problem of metacognitive development. *Child Development, 48*, 1–8.

Brown, R. (2002). Straddling two worlds: Self-directed comprehension instruction for middle schoolers. In C. C. Block & M. Pressley (Eds.), *Comprehension instruction: Research-based best practices* (pp. 337–350). New York: Guilford Press.

Brown, R. (2008). The road not yet taken: A transactional strategies approach to comprehension instruction. *The Reading Teacher, 61*(7), 538–547.

Brown, R., & Coy-Ogan (1993). The evolution of transactional strategies instruction in one teacher's classroom. *The Elementary School Journal, 94*, 221–233.

Brown, S., & Kappes, L. (2012). Implementing the common core state standards: A primer on "close reading of text" Aspen Institute. Retrieved, January 3, 2013, from *www.aspendrl.org/portal/browse/DocumentDetail?documentId=1396&download*

Brown, R., Pressley, M., Van Meter, P., & Schuder, T. (1996). A quasi-experimental validation of transactional strategies instruction with low-achieving second-grade readers. *Journal of Educational Psychology, 88*(1), 18–37.

Brown, S., & Kappes, L. (2012). *Implementing the common core state standards: A primer on "close reading of text."* Washington, DC: Aspen Institute.

Bruner, J. (1986). *Actual minds, possible worlds.* Cambridge, MA: Harvard University Press.

Burns, K. (Producer & Director). (1990). *The Civil War* [Television documentary]. New York: Public Broadcasting Service.

Caccamise, D., Snyder, L., & Kintsch, E. (2008). Constructivist theory and the situation model: Relevance to future assessment of reading comprehension. In C. C. Block, S. R. Parris, & P. Afflerbach (Eds.), *Comprehension instruction: Research-based best practices* (2nd ed., pp. 80–97). New York: Guilford Press.

Cain, K., Oakhill, J. V., Barnes, M. A., & Bryant, P. E. (2001). Comprehension skill, inference-making ability, and their relation to knowledge. *Memory and Cognition, 29*(6), 850–859.

Caine, R. (2008). How neuroscience informs our teaching of elementary students. In C. C. Block, S. R. Parris, & P. Afflerbach (Eds.), *Comprehension instruction: Research-based best practices* (2nd ed., pp. 127–141). New York: Guilford Press.

Calkins, L. (1994). *The art of teaching writing* (new ed.). Portsmouth, NH: Heinemann.

Cartwright, K. B. (2009). The role of cognitive flexibility in reading comprehension: Past, present, and future. In S. E. Israel & G. Duffy (Eds.), *Handbook of research on reading comprehension* (pp. 115–139). New York: Routledge.

Cartwright, K. B. (2010). *Word callers: Small-group and one-to-one interventions for children who "read" but don't comprehend.* Portsmouth, NH: Heinemann.

Cervetti, G. N., & Barber, J. (2009). Text in hands-on science. In E. H. Hiebert & M. Sailors (Eds.), *Finding the right texts: What works for beginning and struggling readers* (pp. 89–108). New York: Guilford Press.

Chambliss, M., & Calfee, R. C. (1998). *Textbooks for learning: Nurturing children's minds.* Oxford: Blackwell.

Chen, G. (2011, January 21). History gone awry: Mistakes in Virginia's public school textbooks. *Public School Review.* Retrieved from *www.publicschoolreview.com/articles/292.*

Chinn, C. A., Anderson, R. C., & Waggoner, M. A. (2001). Patterns of discourse in two kinds of literature discussion. *Reading Research Quarterly, 36*(4), 378–411.

Coiro, J. (2003). Exploring literacy on the Internet: Reading comprehension on the Internet: Expanding our understanding of reading comprehension to encompass new literacies. *The Reading Teacher, 56*(5), 458–464.

Coiro, J. (2011). Talking about reading as thinking: Modeling the hidden complexities of online reading comprehension. *Theory Into Practice, 50*(2), 107–115.

Coiro, J., & Dobler, E. (2007). Exploring the online reading comprehension strategies used by sixth-grade skilled readers to search for and locate information on the Internet. *Reading Research Quarterly, 42*(2), 214–257.

Collins, B. (1988). Introduction to poetry. *The apple that astonished Paris: Poems.* Fayetteville: University of Arkansas.

Collins, C. (1991). Reading instruction that increases thinking abilities. *Journal of Reading, 34*(7), 510–516.

Connor, C. M., Jakobsons, L. J., Crowe, E. C., & Meadows, J. G. (2009). Instruction, student engagement, and reading skill growth in Reading First classrooms. *Elementary School Journal, 109*(3), 221–250.

Connor, C. M., Morrison, F. J., & Underwood, P. S. (2007). A second chance in second grade: The independent and cumulative impact of first- and second-grade reading instruction and students' letter–word reading skill growth. *Scientific Studies of Reading, 11*(3), 199–233.

Cope, B., & Kalantzis, M. (2000). Multiliteracies: The beginning of an idea. In B. Cope & M. Kalantzis (Eds.), *Multiliteracies: Literacy learning and the design of social futures* (pp. 3–8). London: Routledge.

Coxhead, A. (2000). *Academic word list.* Retrieved June 2, 2012, from *www.uefap.com/vocab/select/awl.htm.*

Daniels, H. (1996). *Literature circles.* York, ME: Stenhouse.

Davey, B. (1983). Think aloud: Modeling the cognitive processes of reading comprehension. *Journal of Reading, 27,* 44–47.

Davidson, J. W., & Stoff, M. B. (2011). *The American nation.* New York: Pearson.

Davis, B. H., Resta, V., Davis, L. L., & Comacho, A. (2001). Novice teachers learn about literature circles through collaborative action research. *Journal of Reading Education, 26*(3), 1–6.

Davis, F. B. (1944). Fundamental factors of comprehension in reading. *Psychometrika, 9,* 185–197.

Dewitz, P., Carr, E. J., & Patberg, J. P. (1987). Effects of inference training on comprehension and comprehension monitoring. *Reading Research Quarterly, 22*(1), 99–121.

Dewitz, P., & Dewitz, P. K. (2003). They can read the words, but they can't understand: Refining comprehension assessment. *The Reading Teacher, 56*(5), 422–435.

Dewitz, P., Jones, J., & Leahy, S. (2009). Comprehension strategy instruction in core reading programs. *Reading Research Quarterly, 44*(2), 102–126.

Dewitz, P., Leahy, S. B., Jones, J., & Sullivan, P. M. (2010). *The essential guide to selecting and using core reading programs.* Newark, DE: International Reading Association.

Dewitz, P., & Wolskee, J. (2012). *Making the most of your core reading program.* Portsmouth, NH: Heinemann.

Dillon, J. T. (1988). *Questioning and teaching: A manual of practice.* New York: Teachers College Press.

Duffy, G. G. (2009). *Explaining reading: A resource for teaching concepts, skills, and strategies* (2nd ed.). New York: Guilford Press.

Duffy, G. G., Roehler, L. R., Meloth, M. S., Vavrus, L. G., Book, C., Putnam, J., et al. (1986). The relationship between explicit verbal explanations during reading skill instruction and student awareness and achievement: A study of reading teacher effects. *Reading Research Quarterly, 21*(3), 237–252.

Duke, N. K. (2000). 3.6 minutes per day: The scarcity of informational texts in first grade. *Reading Research Quarterly, 35*(2), 202–224.

Duke, N. K., & Bennett-Armistead, V. S. (2003). *Reading and writing informational text in the primary grades.* New York: Scholastic Teaching Resources.

Duke, N. K., & Pearson, P. D. (2002). Effective practices for developing reading comprehension. In A. E. Farstrup & S. J. Samuels (Eds.), *What research has to say about reading instruction* (3rd ed., pp. 205–243). Newark, DE: International Reading Association.

Duke, N. K., Pearson, P. D., Strachan, S. L., & Billman, A. K. (2011). Essential elements of fostering and teaching reading comprehension. In S. J. Samuels & A. E. Farstrup

(Eds.), *What research has to say about reading instruction* (4th ed., pp. 51–93). Newark, DE: International Reading Association.

Durkin, D. (1978–1979). What classroom observations reveal about reading comprehension instruction. *Reading Research Quarterly, 14*(4), 481–533.

Eccles, J. S., & Wigfield, A. (2002). Motivational beliefs, values, and goals. *Annual Review of Psychology, 53*(1), 109–132.

Education Market Research. (2010). *Elementary reading market: Teaching methods, textbooks/materials used and needed, and market size.* Rockaway Park, NY: Author.

Eeds, M., & Wells, G. (1989). Grand conversations: An exploration of meaning construction in literature study groups. *Research in the Teaching of English, 23*(1), 4–29.

Fisher, D., & Frey, N. (2012). Close reading in elementary schools. *The Reading Teacher, 66*(3), 179–188.

Fitzgerald, J., & Spiegel, D. L. (1983). Enhancing children's reading comprehension through instructions in narrative structure. *Journal of Reading Behavior, 15*(2), 1–17.

Flavell, J. H. (1976). Metacognitive aspects of problem solving. In L. B. Resnick (Ed.), *The nature of intelligence* (pp. 231–235). Hillsdale, NJ: Erlbaum.

Fountas, I. C., & Pinnell, G. S. (2009). *Leveled book list, K–8.* Portsmouth, NH: Heinemann.

Frayer, D., Frederick, W. C., & Klausmeier, H. J. (1969). *A schema for testing the level of cognitive mastery.* Madison, WI: Wisconsin Center for Education Research.

Freire, P. (1985). *The politics of education: Culture, power, and liberation* (D. Macedo, Trans.). South Hadley, MA: Bergin & Garvey.

Fry, E. (1977). Fry's readability graph: Clarification, validity, and extension to level 17. *Journal of Reading, 21,* 242–252.

Fry, E. (2002). Readability versus leveling. *The Reading Teacher, 56*(3), 286–291.

Gallagher, S. (2000). Philosophical conceptions of the self: Implications for cognitive science. *Trends in Cognitive Science, 4*(1), 14–21.

Gambrell, L. B., Marinak, B. A., Brooker, H. R., & McCrea-Andrews, H. J. (2011). The importance of independent reading. In S. J. Samuels & A. E. Farstrup (Eds.), *What research has to say about reading instruction* (4th ed., pp.143–158). Newark, DE: International Reading Association.

Gambrell, L. B., Palmer, B. M., Codling, R. M., & Mazzoni, S. A. (1996). Assessing motivation to read. *The Reading Teacher, 50*(1), 518–533.

Gersten, R., Fuchs, L. S., Williams, J. P., & Baker, S. (2001). Teaching reading comprehension strategies to students with learning disabilities: A review of research. *Review of Educational Research, 71*(2), 279–320.

Goldenberg, C. (1993). Instructional conversations: Promoting comprehension through discussion. *The Reading Teacher, 46*(4), 316–324.

Goldenberg, C., & Patthey-Chavez, G. (1995). Discourse processes in instructional conversations: Interactions between teacher and transition readers. *Discourse Processes, 19*(1), 57–73.

Goldman S., & Rakestraw, J. (2000). Structural aspects of constructing meaning from text. In M. Kamil, P. Mosenthal, P. D. Pearson, & R. Barr (Eds.), *Handbook of reading research* (Vol. 3, pp. 311–335). Hillsdale, NJ: Erlbaum.

Gordon, C. J., & Pearson, P. D. (1983). *The effects of instruction in metacomprehension and inferencing on children's comprehension abilities* (Tech. Rep. No. 277). Urbana: University of Illinois, Center for the Study of Reading.

Goren, P. (2010). Interim assessments as a strategy for improvement: Easier said than done. *Peabody Journal of Education, 85,* 125–129.

Graesser, A. C., León, J. A., & Otero, J. (2002). Introduction to the psychology of science text comprehension. In J. Otero, J. A. Léon, & A. C. Graesser (Eds.), *The psychology of science text comprehension* (pp. 1–15). Mahwah, NJ: Erlbaum.

Graesser, A. C., McNamara, D. S., & Louwerse, M. M. (2003). What do readers need to learn in order to process coherent relations in narrative and expository text. In A. B. Sweet & C. E. Snow (Eds.), *Rethinking reading comprehension* (pp. 82–88). New York: Guilford Press.

Graves, M. F. (2006). *The vocabulary book.* New York: Teachers College Press.

Graves, M. F., & Graves, B. (2003). *Scaffolding reading experiences: Designs for student success* (2nd ed.). Norwood, MA: Christopher-Gordon.

Graves, M. F., & Watts, S. M. (2002). The place of word consciousness in a research-based vocabulary program. In S. J. Samuels & A. E. Farstrup (Eds.), *What research has to say about reading comprehension* (3rd ed., pp. 140–165). Newark, DE: International Reading Association.

Gray, W. S. (Ed.). (1952). *Improving reading in all curriculum areas* (No. 76). Chicago: University of Chicago Press.

Guthrie, J. T. (2001, March). Contexts for engagement and motivation in reading. *Reading Online, 4*(8). Available at *www.readingonline.org/articles/art_index.asp?HREF=/articles/handbook/guthrie/index.html.*

Guthrie, J. T. (2002). Preparing students for high-stakes test taking in reading. In A. E. Farstrup & S. J. Samuels (Eds.), *What research has to say about reading instruction* (3rd ed., pp. 370–391). Newark, DE: International Reading Association.

Guthrie, J. T., McGough, K., Bennett, L., & Rice, M. E. (1996). Concept-oriented reading instruction: An integrated curriculum to develop motivations and strategies for reading. In L. Baker, P. Afflerbach, & D. Reinking (Eds.), *Developing engaged readers in school and home communities* (pp. 165–190). Hillsdale, NJ: Erlbaum.

Guthrie, J. T., McRae, A., & Klauda, S. L. (2007). Contributions of concept-oriented reading instruction to knowledge about interventions for motivations in reading. *Educational Psychologist, 42*(4), 237–250.

Guthrie, J. T., & Wigfield, A. (2000). Engagement and motivation in reading. In M. L. Kamil, P. B. Mosenthal, P. D. Pearson, & R. Barr (Eds.), *Handbook of reading research* (Vol. 3, pp. 403–422). New York: Erlbaum.

Guthrie, J. T., Wigfield, A., & Perencevich, K. C. (Eds.). (2004). *Motivating reading comprehension: Concept-oriented reading instruction.* Mahwah, NJ: Erlbaum.

Hacker, D., & Tenant, A. (2002). Implementing reciprocal teaching in the classroom: Overcoming obstacles and making modifications. *Journal of Educational Psychology, 94*(4), 699–718.

Hansen, J. (1981). The effect of inference training and practice on young children's reading comprehension. *Reading Research Quarterly, 16*(1), 391–417.

Hartocollis, A. (2012, April 20). When pineapple races hare, students lose, critics of standardized tests say. *New York Times.* Retrieved from *www.nytimes.com/2012/04/21/nyregion/standardized-testing-is-blamed-for-question-about-a-sleeveless-pineapple.html?pagewanted=all&_r=0.*

Harvey, S., & Daniels, H. (2009). *Comprehension & collaboration.* Portsmouth, NH: Heinemann.

Harvey, S., & Goudvis, A. (2007). *Strategies that work.* Portland, ME: Stenhouse.

Heath, S. B. (1983). *Ways with words: Language, life, and work in communities and class-rooms.* New York: Cambridge University Press.

Hiebert, E. F. (2012). Text complexity multi-index. Retrieved from *http://textproject.org/professional-development/text-matters/the-text-complexity-multi-index/January 12, 2013.*

Hirsch, E. D. (2011). Beyond comprehension: We have yet to adopt a common core curriculum that builds knowledge grade by grade—but we need to. *American Educator, 34*(4), 30–36.

Hoffman, J. (2009). In search of the "simple view" of reading. In S. E. Israel & G. G. Duffy (Eds.), *Handbook of research on reading comprehension* (pp. 54–65). New York: Routledge.

Hoover, W. A., & Gough, P. B. (1990). The simple view of reading. *Reading and Writing, 2*(2), 127–160.

Hornof, M. (2008). Reading tests as a genre study. *The Reading Teacher, 62*(1), 69–72.

Hruby, G. G. (2009). Grounding reading comprehension theory in the neuroscience literatures. In S. Israel & G. Duffy (Eds.), *Handbook of research on reading comprehension* (pp. 189–223). New York: Routledge.

Huey, E. B. (1908/2009). *The psychology and pedagogy of reading.* Newark, DE: International Reading Association.

Israel, S. E., & Duffy, G. G. (2009). *Handbook of research on reading comprehension.* London: Routledge.

Ivey, G., & Broaddus, K. (2000). Tailoring the fit: Reading instruction and middle school readers. *The Reading Teacher, 54*(1), 68–78.

Jiang, X., & Grabe, W. (2007). Graphic organizers in reading instruction: Research findings and issues. *Reading in a Foreign Language, 19*(1), 34–55.

Johnson, D. D., & Pearson, P. D. (1975). Skills management systems: A critique. *The Reading Teacher, 28*(5), 757–764.

Juel, C., Hebard, H., Haubner, J. P., & Moran, M. (2010). Thinking like a scientist. *Reading, 67*(6), 12–17.

Kelly, M., & Clausen-Grace, N. (2006). R⁵: The sustained silent reading makeover that transforms readers. *The Reading Teacher, 60*(2), 148–157.

Kersten, J., & Pardo, L. (2007). Finessing and hybridizing: Innovative literacy practices in Reading First classrooms. *The Reading Teacher, 61*(2), 146–154.

Kintsch, W. (1998). *Comprehension: A paradigm for cognition.* Cambridge, UK: Cambridge University Press.

Kintsch, W. (2004). The construction–integration model of text comprehension and its implications for instruction. In R. Ruddell & N. Unrau (Eds.), *Theoretical models and processes of reading* (5th ed., pp. 1270–1328). Newark, DE: International Reading Association.

Kintsch, W., & Kintsch, E. (2005). Comprehension. In S. G. Paris & S. A. Stahl (Eds.), *Current issues in reading comprehension and assessment* (pp. 71–92). Mahwah, NJ: Erlbaum.

Kletzien, S. B. (2009). Paraphrasing: An effective comprehension strategy. *The Reading Teacher, 63*(1), 73–77.

Klingner, J. K., & Vaughn, S. (1999). Promoting reading comprehension, content learning and English acquisition through collaborative strategic reading. *The Reading Teacher, 52*(7), 738–747.

Klingner, J. K., Vaughn, S., Arguelles, M. E., Hughes, M. T., & Leftwich, S. A. (2004).

Collaborative strategic reading "real-world" lessons from classroom teachers. *Remedial and Special Education, 25*(5), 291–302.

Klingner, J. K., Vaughn, S., & Schumm, J. S. (1998). Collaborative strategic reading during social studies in heterogeneous fourth-grade classrooms. *Elementary School Journal, 99*(1), 3–22.

Krystal, A. (2012, May 28). Easy writers. *New Yorker*, pp. 81–83.

Kucan, L., Hapgood, S., & Palincsar, A. S. (2011). Teachers' specialized knowledge for supporting student comprehension in text-based discussions. *Elementary School Journal, 112*(1), 61–82.

Kuhn, M. (2004). Helping students become accurate, expressive readers: Fluency instruction for small groups. *The Reading Teacher, 58*(4), 338–344.

Labaree, D. F. (2010). *Someone has to fail: The zero-sum game of public schooling.* Cambridge, MA: Harvard University Press.

Langer, J. A. (1981). From theory to practice: A prereading plan. *Journal of Reading, 25*(2), 152–156.

Lee, C. D., & Spratley, A. (2010). *Reading in the disciplines: The challenges of adolescent literacy.* New York: Carnegie Corporation.

Leslie, L., & Caldwell, J. S. (2010). *Qualitative reading inventory–5.* Boston: Pearson.

Leu, D. J., Coiro, J., Castek, J., Hartman, D. K., Henry, L. A., & Reinking, D. (2008). Research on instruction and assessment in the new literacies of online reading comprehension. In C. C. Block, S. Parris, & P. Afflerbach (Eds.), *Comprehension instruction: Research-based best practices* (pp. 321–345). New York: Guilford Press.

Leu, D. J., Jr., Leu, D. D., and Coiro, J. (2004). *Teaching with the Internet: Lessons from the classroom* (4th ed.). Norwood, MA: Christopher-Gordon.

Leu, D. J., McVerry, J. G., O'Byrne, W. I., Kiili, C., Zawilinski, L., Everett-Cacopardo, H., et al. (2011). The new literacies of online reading comprehension: Expanding the literacy and learning curriculum. *Journal of Adolescent and Adult Literacy, 55*(1), 514.

Luke, A. (1995). Text and discourse in education: An introduction to critical discourse analysis. *Review of Research in Education, 21*, 3–48.

Luke, A. (2004). On the material consequences of literacy. *Language and Education, 18*(4), 331–335.

MacGinitie, W. H., MacGinitie, R. K., Maria, K., & Dryer, L. (2000). *Gates–MacGinitie reading test* (4th ed.). Itasca, IL: Riverside.

Madden, K. (2013). *Remembering Ed Koch.* Retrieved March 13, 2013, from *cityroom.blogs.NYtimes.com/2013/02/01/remembering-ed-koch.*

Manning, M., Lewis, M., & Lewis, M. (2010). Sustained silent reading: An update of the research. In E. H. Hiebert & D. R. Reutzel (Eds.), *Revisiting silent reading: New directions for teachers and researchers* (pp. 112–128). Newark, DE: International Reading Association.

Mar, R. A., & Oatley, K. (2008). The function of fiction is the abstraction and simulation of social experience. *Perspectives on Psychological Science, 3*(3), 173–192.

Marzano, R. J. (2004). *Building background knowledge for academic achievement: Research on what works in schools.* Alexandria, VA: Association for Supervision and Curriculum Development.

McKenna, M. C., & Stahl, K. A. D. (2009). *Assessment for reading instruction.* New York: Guilford Press.

McKeown, M. G., Beck, I. L., & Blake, R. G. K. (2009). Rethinking reading comprehension instruction: A comparison of instruction for strategic and content approaches. *Reading Research Quarterly, 44*(3), 218–256.

McMahon, S., & Raphael, T. (1997). *The book club connection: Literacy learning and classroom talk.* New York: Teachers College Press.

McNamara, D. S., Kintsch, E., Butler-Songer, N., & Kintsch, W. (1996). Are good texts always better?: Interactions of text coherence, background knowledge, and levels of understanding in learning from text. *Cognition and Instruction, 14*(1), 1–43.

Meyer, B. J. F., Brandt, D. M., & Bluth, G. J. (1980). Use of top-level structure in text: Key for reading comprehension of ninth-grade students. *Reading Research Quarterly, 16*(1), 72–103.

Moje, E. B., Stockdill, D., Kim, K., & Kim, H. (2011). The role of text in disciplinary learning. In M. L. Kamil, P. D. Pearson, E. B. Moje, & P. P. Afflerbach (Eds.), *Handbook of reading research* (Vol. 4, pp. 453–486). New York: Routledge.

Mokhtari, K., & Reichard, C. A. (2002). Assessing students' metacognitive awareness of reading strategies. *Journal of Educational Psychology, 94*(2), 249–261.

Moll, L. C., Amanti, C., Neff, D., & Gonzalez, N. (1992). Funds of knowledge for teaching: Using a qualitative approach to connect homes and classrooms. *Theory Into Practice, 31*(2), 132–141.

Moore, D. W., & Readence, J. E. (1984). A quantitative and qualitative review of graphic organizer research. *Journal of Educational Research, 78*(1), 11–17.

Moss, B. (1991). Children's nonfiction trade books: A complement to content area texts. *The Reading Teacher, 45*(1), 26–32.

Moss, B. (2004). Teaching expository text structures through information trade book retellings. *The Reading Teacher, 57*(8), 710–718.

Murphy, P. K., Wilkinson, I. G., Soter, A. O., Hennessey, M. N., & Alexander, J. F. (2009). Examining the effects of classroom discussions on students' high-level comprehension of text: A meta-analysis. *Journal of Educational Psychology, 101*(3), 740–746.

Musca, T. (Producer), & Menendez, R. (Director). (1988). *Stand and deliver* [motion picture]. United States: Warner Brothers.

NAEEP. (2011). *Reading 2011, National Assessment of Educational Progress at Grades 4 and 8.* Washington, DC: National Center for Educational Statistics, U.S. Department of Education.

National Center for Education Statistics. (2011). *The nation's report card: Reading 2011* (NCES 2012-457). Washington, DC: National Center for Education Statistics.

National Center on Education and the Economy. (1998). *New standards performance standards.* Retrieved February 3, 2013, from *www.ncee.org/publications/archived-publications/new-standards-2.*

National Governors Association & Council of Chief State School Officers. (2010). *Common Core State Standards for English Language Arts & Literacy in History/Social Studies, Science, and Technical Subjects.* Washington, DC: Author.

Neuman, S. B. (1990). Assessing children's inferencing strategies. In J. Zutell & S. McCormick (Eds.), *Literacy theory and research: Analysis from multiple paradigms 39th yearbook* (pp. 267–274). Oak Creek, WI: National Reading Conference.

No Child Left Behind (NCLB) Act of 2001, Pub. L. No. 107-110, § 115, Stat. 1425 (2002).

Oakhill, J. (1984). Inferential and memory skills in children's comprehension of stories. *British Journal of Educational Psychology, 54*(1), 31–39.

Oakhill, J., & Cain, K. (2007). Issues of causality in children's reading comprehension.

D. S. McNamara (Ed.), *Reading comprehension strategies: Theories, interventions, and technologies* (pp. 47–71). Hillsdale, NJ: Erlbaum.

Oakhill, J., & Yuill, N. (1986). Pronoun resolution in skilled and less-skilled comprehenders: Effects of memory and inferential complexity. *Language and Speech, 7(1),* 25–37.

Ogle, D. M. (1986). K-W-L: A teaching model that develops active reading of expository text. *The Reading Teacher, 39*(6), 564–570.

Osborn, J. (1984). The purposes, uses, and contents of workbooks and some guidelines for publishers. In R. C. Anderson, J. Osborn, & R. J. Tierney (Eds.), *Learning to read in American schools* (pp. 45–112). Hillsdale, NJ: Erlbaum.

Palincsar, A. S., & Brown, A. L. (1984). Reciprocal teaching of comprehension fostering and comprehension monitoring activities. *Cognition and Instruction, 1*(2), 117–175.

Palincsar, A. S., & Schutz, K. M. (2011). Reconnecting strategy instruction with its theoretical roots. *Theory Into Practice, 50*(2), 85–92.

Pappas, C. C. (2006). The information book genre: Its role in integrated science literacy research and practice. *Reading Research Quarterly, 41*(2), 226–250.

Paris, S. G. (2005). Reinterpreting the development of reading skills. *Reading Research Quarterly, 40*(2), 184–202.

Pearson, P. D. (2007). An endangered species act for literacy education. *Journal of Literacy Research, 39*(2), 145–162.

Pearson, P. D. (2009). The roots of reading comprehension instruction. In S. E. Israel & G. G. Duffy (Eds.), *Handbook of research on reading comprehension* (pp. 3–31). London: Routledge.

Pearson, P. D. (2011, April). *The tortured history of reading comprehension assessment: Are there lessons from the past? Is there hope for the future? Will we ever get it right?* Paper presented at the annual meeting of the American Educational Research Association, New Orleans.

Pearson, P. D., & Gallagher, M. C. (1983). The instruction of reading comprehension. *Contemporary Educational Psychology, 8*(3), 317–344.

Pearson, P. D., & Hamm, D. N. (2005). The assessment of reading comprehension: A review of practices: past, present, and future. In S. G. Paris & S. A. Stahl (Eds.), *Children's reading comprehension and assessment* (pp. 13–69). Mahwah, NJ: Erlbaum.

Pearson, P. D., & Johnson, D. (1978). *Teaching reading comprehension.* New York: Holt, Rinehart & Winston.

Pennell, M. A., & Cusack, A. M. (1936). *The children's own readers.* Boston: Ginn.

Piaget, J. (1928). *The child's conception of the world.* London: Routledge & Kegan Paul.

Pressley, M., & Afflerbach, P. (1995). *Verbal protocols of reading.* Hillsdale, NJ: Erlbaum.

Pressley, M., Borkowski, J. G., & Schneider, W. (1989). Good information processing: What it is and how education can promote it. *International Journal of Educational Research, 13*(8), 857–867.

Pressley, M., Duke, N. K., Gaskins, I. W., Fingeret, L., Halladay, J., Hilden, K., et al. (2009). Working with struggling readers: Why we must get beyond the Simple View of Reading and visions of how it might be done. In T. B. Gutkin & C. R. Reynolds (Eds.), *The handbook of school psychology* (4th ed., pp. 522–546). Hoboken, NJ: Wiley.

Pressley, M., Gaskins, I. W., Schuder, T., Bergman, J., Almasi, L., & Brown, R. (1992). Beyond direct explanation: Transactional instruction of reading comprehension strategies. *Elementary School Journal, 92*(5), 511–534.

Race to the Top Act of 2011, H.R. 1532, 112th Congress. (2011).

Ramis, H., & Albert, T. (Producers) & Ramis, H. (Director). (1993). *Groundhog day* [motion picture]. United States: Columbia Pictures.

Raphael, T. E. (1986). Teaching question answer relationships, revisited. *The Reading Teacher,* 516–522.

Ravitch, D. (1989). The revival of history: A response. *The Social Studies, 80*(3), 89–91.

Ray, K. W. (2002). *What you know by heart: How to develop curriculum for your writing workshop.* Portsmouth, NH: Heinemann.

Renkl, A., Mandl, H., & Gruber, H. (1996). Inert knowledge: Analyses and remedies. *Educational Psychologist, 31*(2), 115–121.

Resnick, L. B. (1987). The 1987 presidential address: Learning in school and out. *Educational Researcher, 16*(9), 13–54.

Reutzel, D., Jones, C. D., Fawson, P. C., & Smith, J. A. (2008). Scaffolded silent reading: A complement to guided repeated oral reading that works! *The Reading Teacher, 62*(3), 194–207.

Reutzel, R. D., Smith, J. A., & Fawson, P. C. (2005). An evaluation of two approaches for teaching reading comprehension strategies in the primary years using science information texts. *Early Childhood Research Quarterly, 20*(3), 276–305.

Ricketts, J., Nation, K., & Bishop, D. V. M. (2007). Vocabulary is important for some, but not all reading skills. *Scientific Studies of Reading, 11*(3), 235–257.

Rogovin, P. (2001). *The research workshop: Bringing the world into your classroom.* Portsmouth, NH: Heinemann.

Romance, M. R., & Vitale, H. R. (2001). Implementing an in-depth expanded science model in elementary schools: Multi-year findings, research issues, and policy implication. *International Journal of Science Education, 23*(4), 373–404.

Rosenblatt, L. (1937). *Literature as exploration.* New York: Appleton Century Croft.

Rosenblatt, L. (1978). *The reader, the text, the poem.* Carbondale: Southern Illinois University.

Rosenshine, B., & Meister, C. (1994). Reciprocal teaching: A review of the research. *Review of Educational Research, 64*(4), 479–530.

Rosenshine, B., Meister, C., & Chapman, S. (1996). Teaching students to generate questions: A review of the intervention studies. *Review of Educational Research, 66*(2), 181–221.

Santoro, L. E., Chard, D., Howard, L., & Baker, S. K. (2008). Making the *very* most of classroom read-alouds to promote comprehension and vocabulary. *The Reading Teacher, 61*(5), 396–408.

Saul, E. W., & Dieckman, D. (2005). Choosing and using information trade books. *Reading Research Quarterly, 40*(4), 502–513.

Schoenbach, R., Greenleaf, C., Cziko, C., & Hurwitz, L. (1999). *Reading for understanding: A guide to improving reading in middle and high school classrooms.* San Francisco: Jossey-Bass.

Schwanenflugel, P. J., Meisinger, E. B., Wisenbaker, J. M., Kuhn, M. R., Strauss, G. P., & Morris, R. D. (2006). Becoming a fluent and automatic reader in the early elementary school years. *Reading Research Quarterly, 41*(4), 496–522.

Shanahan, C. (2009). Disciplinary comprehension. In S. E. Israel & G. G. Duffy (Eds.), *Handbook of research on reading comprehension* (pp. 240–260). New York: Routledge.

Shanahan, C., Shanahan, T., & Misischia, C. (2011). Analysis of expert readers in three disciplines: History, mathematics, and chemistry. *Journal of Literacy Research, 43*(4), 393–429.

Shanahan, T., & Shanahan, C. (2008). Teaching disciplinary literacy to adolescents: Rethinking content-area literacy. *Harvard Educational Review, 78*(1), 40–59.

Share, D. L. (1995). Phonological recoding and self-teaching: "Sine qua non" of reading acquisition. *Cognition, 55*(2), 151–218.

Shepard, L. A. (2010). What the marketplace has brought us: Item-by-item teaching with little instructional insight. *Peabody Journal of Education, 85*(2), 246–257.

Short, K. G., & Pierce, K. M. (Eds.). (1990). *Talking about books: Creating literate communities.* Portsmouth, NH: Heinemann.

Sieff, K. (2010, October 20). Virginia 4th-grade textbook criticized over claims on black Confederate soldiers. *The Washington Post.* Retrieved from *www.washingtonpost. com/wpdyn/content/article/2010/10/19/AR2010101907974.html.*

Singer, H., & Donlan, D. (1982). Active comprehension: Problem-solving schema with question generation for comprehension of complex short stories. *Reading Research Quarterly,* 166–186.

Snow, C. (2002). *Reading for understanding: Toward an R&D program in reading comprehension.* Santa Monica, CA: RAND Corporation.

Stahl, S. A., & Heubach, K. M. (2005). Fluency-oriented reading instruction. *Journal of Literacy Research, 37*(1), 25–60.

Stahl, S. A., & Nagy, W. E. (2006). *Teaching word meanings.* Mahwah, NJ: Erlbaum.

Stanovich, K. E. (1986). Matthew effects in reading: Some consequences of individual differences in the acquisition of literacy. *Reading Research Quarterly, 21*(4), 360–407.

Stein, N. L., & Glenn, C. G. (1979). An analysis of story comprehension in elementary school children. In R. Freedle (Ed.), *New directions in discourse processing* (pp. 61–83). Norwood, NJ: Ablex.

Sternberg, R. J., & Powell, J. S. (1983). Comprehending verbal comprehension. *American Psychologist, 38*(8), 878–887.

Taylor, B. M., & Beach, R. W. (1984). The effects of text structure instruction on middle-grade students' comprehension and production of expository text. *Reading Research Quarterly, 19*(2), 134–146.

Taylor, B. M., Pearson, P. D., Clark, K., & Walpole, S. (2000). Effective schools and accomplished teachers: Lessons about primary-grade reading instruction in low-income schools. *Elementary School Journal, 101*(2), 121–165.

Tierney, R. J., & Cunningham, I. W. (1984). Research on teaching reading comprehension. In P. D. Pearson, R. Barr, M. L. Kamil, & P. Mosenthal (Eds.), *Handbook of reading research* (pp. 609–656). New York: Longman.

Topping, K. J., Samuels, J., & Paul, T. (2007). Does practice make perfect?: Independent reading quantity, quality and student achievement. *Learning and Instruction, 17*(3), 253–264.

Townsend, D., Filippini, A., Collins, P., & Biancarosa, G. (2012). Evidence for the importance of academic word knowledge for the academic achievement of diverse middle school students. *Elementary School Journal, 113*(3), 497–519.

Tracey, D., & Morrow, L. M. (2012). *Lenses on reading: An introduction to theories and models* (2nd ed.). New York: Guilford Press.

Valencia, S. W., Pearson, P. D., & Wixson, K. K. (2011). *Assessing and tracking progress in reading comprehension: The search for keystone elements in college and career readiness.* Princeton, NJ: Educational Testing Service, Center for K–12 Assessment and Performance Management.

van den Broek, P., & Kremer, K. (2000). The mind in action: What it means to comprehend during reading. In B. M. Taylor, M. F. Graves, & P. van den Broek (Eds.), *Reading for meaning: Fostering comprehension in the middle grades* (pp. 1–31). Newark, DE: International Reading Association.

Vygotsky, L. S. (1978). *Mind in society: The development of higher psychological processes.* Cambridge, MA: Harvard University Press.

Walsh, K. (2003). Basal readers: The lost opportunity to build the knowledge that propels comprehension. *American Educator, 27*(1), 24–27.

Wertsch, J. V., Del Rio, P., & Alvarez, A. (Eds.). (1995). *Sociocultural studies of mind.* New York: Cambridge University Press.

Wilkinson, I. A. G., & Son, E. H. (2011). A dialogic turn in research on learning and teaching to comprehend. In M. L. Kamil, P. D. Pearson, E. B. Moje, & P. P. Afflerbach (Eds.), *Handbook of reading research* (Vol. 4, pp. 359–387). New York: Routledge.

Williams, J. P. (2008). Explicit instruction can help primary students learn to comprehend expository text. In C. C. Block, S. R. Parris, & P. Afflerbach (Eds.), *Comprehension processes: Research-based best practices* (2nd ed.). New York: Guilford Press.

Williams, J. P., Lauer, K. D., Hall, K. M., Lord, K. M., Gugga, S. S., Bak, S. J., et al. (2002). Teaching elementary school students to identify story themes. *Journal of Educational Psychology, 94*(2), 235–248.

Williams, J. P., Stafford, K. B., Lauer, K. D., Hall, K. M., & Pollini, S. (2009). Embedding reading comprehension training in content-area instruction. *Journal of Educational Psychology, 10*(1), 1–20.

Willingham, D. T. (2006). The usefulness of brief instruction in reading comprehension strategies. *American Educator, 30*(4), 39–45.

Wineburg, S. S. (1991a). Historical problem solving: A study of the cognitive processes used in the evaluation of documentary and pictorial evidence. *Journal of Educational Psychology, 83*(1), 73–87.

Wineburg, S. S. (1991b). On the reading of historical texts: Notes on the breach between school and academy. *American Educational Research Journal, 28*(3), 495–519.

Wood, D., Bruner, J. S., & Ross, G. (1976). The role of tutoring in problem solving. *Journal of Child Psychology and Psychiatry, 17*(2), 89–100.

Wren, S. (2006). *The simple view of reading: R+DxC.* Retrieved from *www.balancedreading. com/simple.html.*

Yuill, N., & Oakhill, J. (1991). *Children's problems in text comprehension: An experimental investigation.* New York: Cambridge University Press.

CHILDREN'S BOOK REFERENCES

Alvarez, J. (2002). *How Tía Lola came to ~~visit~~ stay.* New York: Yearling.

Asimov, I. (2005). *The fun they had.* In I. L. Beck, R. C. Farr, & D. S. Strickland (Eds.), *Trophies: Distant voyages* (pp. 584–592.) Chicago: Harcourt.

Bancroft, H., & Van Gelder, R. G. (1997). *Animals in winter.* New York: HarperCollins.

Barrett, J. (1978). *Cloudy with a chance of meatballs.* New York: Aladdin Paperbacks.

Berger, M., & Berger, G. (1993). *How's the weather?: A look at weather and how it changes.* Nashville, TN: Ideals Children's Books.

Blume, J. (1984). *Freckle juice.* New York: Simon & Schuster.

Blume, J. (2011). *Just as long as we're together.* New York: Delacorte.

Bradbury, R. (1950a). *The Martian chronicles*. New York: Doubleday.

Bradbury, R. (1950b). There will come soft rains. From *The Martian Chronicles*. New York: Bantam Books.

Branley, F. M. (1985). *Flash, crash, rumble, and roll*. New York: Thomas & Crowell Junior Books.

Brett, J. (2003). *Town mouse, country mouse*. Toronto: Penguin Books.

Brimner, D. (2004). *Captain stormalong*. Minneapolis, MN: Compass Point Books.

Burton, V. L. (1978). *The little house*. New York: Houghton Mifflin.

Cleary, B. (1984). *Ramona forever*. New York: Avon Books.

Collins, S. (2010). *The hunger games*. New York: Scholastic.

Creech, S. (2000). *The wanderer*. New York: HarperTrophy.

Cronin, D., & Lewin, B. (2000). *Click, clack, moo: Cows that type*. New York: Antheneum Books.

Curley, J. (2011). *Tornado!: A meteorologist and her prediction*. Lawrence Hall of Science: University of California. Available from *http://lawrencehallofscience.stores.yahoo. net/tomeandherpr.html*.

Curtis, C. P. (1999). *Bud, not Buddy*. New York: Delacorte Press.

Dahl, R. (1988). *Matilda*. New York: Puffin.

dePaola, T. (1988). *The mysterious giant of Barletta*. New York: Sandpiper Books.

DiCamillo, K. (2000). *Because of Winn-Dixie*. New York: Candlewick.

DeWitt, L., & Croll, C. (1991). *What will the weather be?* New York: HarperCollins.

Esbensen, B. J. (1994). *Baby whales drink milk*. New York: HaperCollins.

Farris, C. K. (2005). *My brother Martin: A sister remembers growing up with the Rev. Dr. Martin Luther King Jr*. New York: Aladdin Books.

Flake, S. (1998). *The skin I'm in*. New York: Hyperion.

Freeman, D. (2011). *Corduroy*. New York: Viking.

Geisert, B., & Geisert, A. (1998). *Prairie town*. New York: Houghton Mifflin.

Geisert, B., & Geisert, A. (1999). *River town*. New York: Houghton Mifflin.

Geisert, B., & Geisert, A. (2000). *Mountain town*. New York: Houghton Mifflin.

Geisert, B., & Geisert, A. (2001). *Desert town*. New York: Houghton Mifflin.

Gibbons, G. (1992). *Weather words and what they mean*. New York: Holiday House.

Gibbons, G. (1993). *From seed to plant*. New York: Holiday House.

Gibbons, G. (1996). *The reasons for seasons*. New York: Holiday House.

Giff, P. R. (1988). *Happy birthday, Ronald Morgan!* New York: Puffin.

Giff, P. R. (2002). *Pictures of Hollis Woods*. New York: Yearling.

Hakim, J. (2003). *A history of US*. New York: Oxford University Press.

Henderson, K., & Howard, P. (1996). *A year in the city*. Cambridge, MA: Candlewick Press.

Hesse, K. (1999). *Out of the dust*. New York: Scholastic.

Hopping, L. J. (1999). *Wild weather: Blizzards!* New York: Scholastic.

Hubbard, K. (2011). The power of W.O.W.! In J. E. Baumann, D. J. Chard, et al. (Eds.), *Journeys*. Boston: Houghton Mifflin Harcourt.

Joy, N. (2007). *The secret Oliva told me*. New York: Just Us Books.

Kalman, B. (2000). *What is a community?: From A to Z*. New York: Crabtree.

Kellogg, S. (2004). *The mysterious tadpole*. New York: Puffin.

Kinney, J. (2002). *Diary of a wimpy kid*. New York: Amulet.

Konigsburg, E. L. (1996). *The view from Saturday*. New York: Aladdin Books.

Kurlansky, M., & Schindler, S. D. (2006). *The story of salt*. New York: G. P. Putnam's Sons.

Levinson, C. (2012). *We've got a job: The 1963 Birmingham children's march*. Atlanta, GA: Peachtree Publishers.

Lightning chasers. (2013, March). *Scholastic News/Weekly Reader, 69*(6).

Lima, C. W., & Lima, J. A. (2006). *A to zoo: Subject access to children's picture books*. New York: Bowker.

Lionni, L. (1973). *Frederick*. Boston, MA: Knopf.

Lobel, A. (1994). *Frog and toad*. New York: HarperCollins.

Martin, J. B. (1999). *Snowflake Bentley*. New York: Scholastic.

McCully, E. A. (1992). *Mirette on the high wire*. New York: Putnam & Grosset.

McPhail, D. M. (1988). *The bear's toothache*. Boston: Little, Brown Books for Young.

Parish, P. (2011). *Amelia Bedelia makes a friend*. New York: Greenwillow.

Paulsen, G. (1987). *Hatchet*. New York: Simon & Schuster.

Paulsen, G. (1989). *The voyage of the frog*. New York: Bantam Doubleday.

Pilkey, D. (1995). *Dogzilla*. New York: Sandpiper.

Polacco, P. (1994). *Pink and say*. New York: Philomel Books.

Rockwell, A. (2008). *Clouds*. New York: HarperCollins.

Rockwell, A., & Halsey, M. (2004). *Four seasons make a year*. New York: Bloomsbury: Walker.

Rodda, E. (2004). *Rowan of rin*. New York: Greenwillow.

Rowling, J. K. (1999). *Harry Potter and the sorcerer's stone*. New York: Scholastic.

Rowling, J. K. (2012). *The casual vacancy*. Boston, MA: Little Brown.

Rylant, C. (1988). *Every living thing*. New York: Simon & Schuster.

Sachar, L. (1987). *There's a boy in the girls' bathroom*. Boston: Knopf.

Sachar, L. (1998). *Holes*. Boston: Farrar, Straus and Giroux.

Sharmat, M. W. (2002). *Nate the great*. New York: Delacorte.

Steig, W. (1969). *Sylvester and the magic pebble*. New York: Simon & Schuster.

Steig, W. (1986). *Brave Irene*. New York: Farrar, Straus & Giroux.

Sterling, K. (2008a). *Living in rural communities*. Minneapolis, MN: Lerner.

Sterling, K. (2008b). *Living in suburban communities*. Minneapolis, MN: Lerner.

Sterling, K. (2008c). *Living in urban communities*. Minneapolis, MN: Lerner.

Time-Life Books (1989). *Wind and weather*. Alexandria, VA: Time-Life.

Tisdale, S. (1920). There will come soft rains. In *Flame and shadow*. New York: Macmillan.

Viorst, J. (1972). *Alexander and the horrible, no good, very bad day*. New York: Macmillan.

Weber, B. (1975). *Ira sleeps over*. New York: Sandpiper.

White, E. B. (2002). *Charlotte's web*. New York: HarperCollins.

Woodson, J. (2001). *The other side*. New York: Putnam.

Index